Developing cognitive abilities

Teaching children to think

ROBERT E. VALETT, Ed.D.

Professor, School of Education,
California State University,
Fresno, California

THE C. V. MOSBY COMPANY

Saint Louis   1978

Cover photograph by Christopher Perkins

Printed in the United States of America

Distributed in Great Britain by Henry Kimpton, London

The C. V. Mosby Company
11830 Westline Industrial Drive, St. Louis, Missouri 63141

Library of Congress Cataloging in Publication Data

Valett, Robert E   1927-
   Developing cognitive abilities.

   Bibliography: p.
   Includes index.
   1.   Reasoning (Child psychology).   2.   Learning
disabilities.   I.   Title.
LB1117.V28   371.9′2   77-9912
ISBN 0-8016-5213-8

GW/CB/CB   9   8   7   6   5   4   3   2   1

To think is to live.
CICERO

*There is an art of reading, as well as
an art of thinking.*
D'ISRAELI

Preface

The purpose of this book is to help teachers and psychoeducational therapists develop the cognitive abilities of learning-handicapped children. Of special concern are the development of sound thinking skills and the remediation of conceptual deficits that may interfere with academic achievement.

A basic premise of this book is that all special educators should give priority to the evaluation of fundamental thinking, processing, and problem-solving dysfunctions. Diagnostic-prescriptive teachers should work in close collaboration with regular educators and administrators to help design developmental programs in normal school environments that will prevent learning and related cognitive disorders.

It is hoped that this book may serve to bridge the gap between theory and practice that too often exists in education. In this regard the book should be of value to students in education, psychology, language and communicative disorders, and the related helping professions. This is a limited work in that it emphasizes primary and elementary approaches; for a broader coverage and in-depth consideration of cited studies the reader is encouraged to go directly to the references and other related sources.

I am indebted to many teachers, students, and children who through the years have enabled me to clarify my own thinking about the development and remediation of cognitive disabilities; unfortunately, the list is far too extensive to include here.

My appreciation is also extended in advance to all those persons who may be stimulated to engage in work that furthers the cognitive development of children. If this book is helpful in enabling some child to think and learn more effectively, my primary objective will have been reached.

Robert E. Valett

Contents

Developing
cognitive abilities
Teaching children to think

Photo by Michael Hayman, Image, Inc., Nashville, Tennessee.

CHAPTER 1

Why Johnny doesn't think

and therefore can't read and learn

Millions of children and adults suffer from some kind of learning disability. Many of these disabilities are most evident in the great difficulty persons have in thinking about and solving the daily problems that confront them. In school and other academic learning situations, these appear as reading, writing, arithmetic, and related errors and problems.

The incidence of cognitive learning disabilities such as these is very high. Reliable estimates of the incidence of reading disabilities in the school population alone range from 20% to 40% (Goldberg and Schiffman, 1972, p. 14). Government sources report that between 8,000,000 and 20,000,000 pupils may have serious reading problems (*Research Conference Report*, 1967). Statistical studies also show that 25% of our population have IQs below 90 and that approximately 16% of the children in this group have been recognized as slow learners who have distinctive thinking and cognitive disabilities and who require some sort of special or remedial education (Jensen, 1972). In addition, other studies show that the prevalence of specific language-learning disabilities in schoolchildren with normal or higher intelligence is between 7% and 8% (Myklebust and Boshes, 1969). Many other studies report that the number of hyperkinetic children with minimal brain dysfunction and associated learning disabilities can be conservatively estimated as 3% of the school population (*Report of the Conference*, 1971).

When added together, these figures make rather impressive statistics as to the prevalence of thinking and learning problems in our society. But these figures are even more meaningful when placed in a practical context of personal family or classroom experience. Almost all experienced teachers can readily testify to the existence in their classes of a considerable number of children who have not profited from the ordinary curriculum and are obviously in need of special help and accommodation. Most families have also had at least one serious encounter with these problems as experienced by their children or relatives. In fact, the problem is so widespread that several states have finally

1

begun to recognize the need and have even started to provide additional financial support for this kind of special or supplementary education. California, for instance, officially recognizes and provides for up to 2% of the school population as having special educational handicaps and learning disabilities; however, this is just a token recognition of, and provision for, the vast numbers of children in need who remain on waiting lists for some kind of special help.

Although there is no typical portrait of these children, the following case history of Johnny is one that is commonly presented by concerned teachers and parents.

Johnny is a 10-year-old boy in the third grade (who was retained a year in the second grade). Most of his work is still on the second grade level although his tests show him to be of normal intelligence. He has a long history of reading and language problems. His writing and spelling are poor, and he continues to make reversals, inversions, and omissions. He displays illogical reasoning in the way he approaches his work. Johnny is very slow and lethargic in school, has poor posture, complains of headaches and fatigue, and is obviously unhappy in the classroom. An extensive physical examination disclosed normal health and developmental patterns. Johnny's parents are warm and supporting and are increasingly frustrated about his learning difficulties and what to do about them.

Considerable research has been done to help determine the major personal traits of children with these kinds of learning difficulties. One government report summarizes the major characteristics as follows (Hallahan and Cruickshank, 1973, p. 46).

1. Restricted and limited knowledge
2. Concrete thought processes
3. Poor reflective and introspective thinking
4. Reading failure
5. Short-term planning
6. Poor imagery

To this list we might add "limited attention and concentration" which often result in poor listening habits and subsequent confusion in learning. Poor attention is also reflected in a lack of muscular inhibition and limited self-control, which further interferes with the learning process and increases the chance of failure in school.

To prevent or remedy such problems, it is important to consider some of the etiological factors involved. If the causes can be identified, it is often possible to do something about them. Five major causes will be briefly discussed here: genetic determinants, disease, family determinants, social-cultural indifference, and inappropriate education. Since this book is primarily concerned with cognitive development programs within the schools, emphasis will be given to specifying what inappropriate education consists of and what might possibly be done about it.

GENETIC DETERMINANTS

The human biological system is programmed by 46 chromosomes, which contain several thousand gene pairs. Each gene pair is subject to variation as a result of mutation or abnormal recombination, translocation, and distribution. Since cellular action is largely under genetic control, aberrations in a single gene can impair proper chemical reactions and negatively affect total biological functioning—including learning.

A number of genetic aberrations have been identified and acknowledged as the primary determinants in certain kinds of cognitive and perceptual disturbances. The common element in such abnormalities is biochemical dysfunction, which affects behavior through sensory and perceptual distortion and poor psychoneurological integration. Some of the more commonly recognized genetic disorders include Down's syndrome, sickle-cell anemia, epilepsy, and schizophrenia (Kallman, 1959). A considerable number of studies point out the negative effect of genetic disorders on learning. Bernard Rimland (1974) has reported that since 1954 approximately 16 inherited diseases have been discovered that have behavioral components and nevertheless can be treated in part through biochemical and orthomolecular therapy. Extensive research has confirmed the contribution of genetic factors to the etiology of schizophrenia and similar dysfunctions such as early childhood autism and schizoid behaviors (Heston, 1973); most of these abnormalities are characterized by perceptual distortion, confused thought patterns, and associated emotional disturbance.

The work of Critchley (1964) and others on developmental dyslexia has also shown that biochemical and chromosomal aberrations produce abnormal visual responses and are usually present in family members of certain children with chronic severe reading problems. Many other investigations have reached similar conclusions. Although it appears that a relatively small percentage of cognitive disorders have demonstrable genetic causes, genetic factors must be recognized as significant.

Obviously, genetic treatment and intervention programs are largely beyond the scope of the educator—but not entirely. The public needs to be continually educated about the current findings in this field. So do parents of cognitively disabled children. Genetic counseling and orthomolecular medicine are frequently needed. In addition, nutritional and dietary treatment programs appear to be other promising forms of intervention and amelioration that require health education.

DISEASE

The diseases and traumatic insults to the human nervous system that result in cognitive disorders and learning problems are almost too numerous to mention. Therefore we will only be concerned here with a few representative ones that have distinctive educational implications.

The human brain is most vulnerable during the first year of life. Most neurological growth and learning occur in the first 5 years of life, although critical sensory integration and brain development continue until approximately 8 years of age. Myelination of nerve fibers is dependent on adequate protein and related nutritional substances during these critical periods of growth. Prolonged protein-calorie malnutrition results in toxemia, mental retardation, apathy, and a number of associated learning disabilities. Cravioto (1972) and his colleagues have summarized the extensive evidence on the effect of nutrient deprivation and learning.

Although malnutrition may be the most prevalent form of disease resulting in cognitive learning disorders, there are many others that are of significant concern as well. Birth defects of the brain caused by anoxia or unusual cranial pressures (especially among boys, who have larger heads) are commonly recognized by the medical profession. So, too, is the ingestion of toxic substances of all kinds by young children, which may damage psychoneurological integration and functioning. Viral infections of brain tissue can have similar long-lasting effects but may not always be as easily determined or apparent. Highly unusual traumatic events such as overt brain damage caused by automobile and other accidents may result in a loss of previously acquired cognitive skills such as language and reading.

Of increasing concern to educators are the ecological traumas that may be somewhat controlled within the school environment itself. For example, the evidence that artificial food colors and additives adversely affect attention and behavior (Feingold, 1975) has caused some educational administrators to provide more natural and nutritional foods in school vending machines, snacks, and cafeteria menus. Recent actions by the Food and Drug Administration in banning many food dyes (for example, red dye No. 4, found in candy such as jelly beans and licorice) because of possible carcinogenic effects have also been noted by teachers and parents alike ("FDA Bans," 1976).

Another ecological example is the recent research finding of the Environmental Health and Light Institute that standard cool-white fluorescent light tubes emit harmful radiation and produce hyperkinetic and inattentive behavior in children (Ott, 1976). Changing to full-spectrum fluorescent tubes with lead foil shields can produce more natural daylight and eliminate the adverse behavioral reactions.

Special educators should be more conscious of environmental poisons and pollutions, distractions, and other similar factors that may be traumatic enough to actually produce or to exacerbate disease processes. Much needs to be done in this regard to educate boards of education, parents, school architects, school dietitions, and other persons responsible for designing and changing school learning situations and classroom environments.

FAMILY DETERMINANTS

It has long been known that the family structure is an important factor in how well a child learns and behaves. The child's first human interactions are with parents and siblings, and his thinking and behavior are quickly shaped and conditioned within that context. But it has not been until fairly recent times that the important dynamics of family interactions have been understood.

One early study by Baldwin, Kalhorn, and Breese (1945) disclosed some highly relevant and significant findings on the importance of discipline in the home. It was found that the IQs of 4- to 7-year-old children tended to increase with time if parental discipline consisted of responsive and realistic interactions and explanations. Conversely, mental ability tended to fall if parental discipline consisted of nonchalant unresponsiveness and unrealistic demands for obedience. Later, the importance of this finding was to be underscored by Coleman's monumental study of 600,000 school children. Coleman found that the single most important contribution to the child's intellectual development (as measured by standardized intelligence and achievement tests) was family background, including the parent's education and the presence and use in the home of reading and other learning materials (Bronfenbrenner, 1974).

Perhaps the most important single (and immediately relevant) study conducted to date is directed by Heber and known as the Milwaukee project. This is an ongoing longitudinal research project, now in its tenth year, focusing on the intellectual development of children of retarded mothers living in slum neighborhoods. The remarkable findings show that when poor and deprived mothers are provided with remedial education, vocational training, and useful child care skills, they can then learn to help their children improve their own abilities and achievement. Special education was provided to children in this project at birth, the mothers were involved in the teaching of specific language and cognitive skills. Mental ability and achievement scores increased steadily over those of control groups and have held up through the years. At 9 years of age, the children in this program have an average IQ of 121, which is 20 points higher than the average of the control group (Trotter, 1976).

Many other studies show the effect of social and family disorganization on children's mental growth and performance. It is difficult if not impossible for children to learn to think, to question, and to develop functional cognitive operations without parental interest and support. Parents broken by poverty, unemployment, ignorance, and disease are ill equipped to help their children. For example, data show that as unemployment and economic deprivation increase, so, too, do human stress, mental illness, alcoholism, and suicide rates (Rice, 1975).

The message is increasingly clear that we must do everything possible to strengthen family life and to provide sound parent-child interactions if we are concerned with improving thinking and cognitive performance in children. Early stimulation, interaction, verbalization, and discipline are essential prerequisites for the child's success in school learning and cognitive growth.

SOCIAL-CULTURAL INDIFFERENCE

As strange as it may seem, a major reason that children do not think or learn to read is that society (and authority figures within that society) does not want them to develop these abilities or, even worse, is indifferent toward what happens to them. Discrimination, suppression, hostility, apathy, and negative attitudes of all kinds still abound in many parts of our country, including the homes and schools in which children with cognitive difficulties live out their daily lives.

Free public schools were not established until rather late in this country. Even then, almost all minority and exceptional children were excluded. The poor, the deprived, and the handicapped of all kinds were the last to be granted educational rights and advantages. In some places these children were systematically singled out and discriminated against because it was believed that they should be "kept in their place" or that they were not capable of thinking or learning. Even today, this gross neglect continues, as recently evidenced by a House of Representatives committee report that disclosed that millions of needy children (including 770,000 retarded and learning disabled) are not receiving treatment even though federal funds have been allocated for that purpose; the committee reported that deliberate misuse and mismanagement of funds were coupled with reluctance to implement the necessary programs. Such crass neglect "needlessly condemns" these children to a crippled or retarded existence (Rennert, 1976).

Unfortunately, much of this negativism is also seen in local communities and homes. In some families, the child's place is still to be seen but not heard. In others, any form of active questioning and overt thinking is actually frowned on to the point of punishment. Even teachers have been known to demonstrate such negative and detrimental attitudes toward some children; these attitudes have retarded their continued achievement and total school performance (Rosenthal and Jacobson, 1968).

Other parents and professional persons have even believed that a child's mental ability was fixed at birth and that little or nothing could be done to help him grow and learn. The retarded, the slow learning, and children with specific cognitive disorders have often been condemned to an educational limbo because of such attitudes. When these attitudes are further generalized to include educational policy makers such as school board members and administrators, little can be done. Without priority support and investment in cognitive development programs of all kinds, by both parents and educators, Johnny will not learn to think or read or do many other things he is capable of doing.

INAPPROPRIATE EDUCATION

It is reasonable to assume that schools should provide children with an education that will enable them to solve real life problems. To solve any kind of problem, the person must first be able to think about it and consider alternative solutions. There are, of course, many different ways of thinking, the most commonly recognized being imaginative thinking, convergent thinking, and divergent thinking. Specific problem solving usually requires considerable convergent thinking in that such basic mental operations as associative memory, discrimination, and computation are brought into focus and use.

Most higher order thinking of this kind is of an abstract nature. The pupil must mentally respond to the stimuli presented by quickly sorting out the various associations and finally integrating them in a way that enables him or her to perceive meaningful relationships. These relationships must then be conceptualized and understood in such a way that they can be expressed in symbolic forms such as words, formulas, and music.

A good elementary school education should provide children with much practice in the development of these critical thinking skills. It takes trained teachers, good school organization, and much systematic instruction for children to learn to think. Considerable time and effort and years of growth and development are required before most children develop their mental operations to the level of abstract-symbolic reasoning. The essential prerequisites for acquiring higher order thinking and problem-solving abilities are fairly well known and are reflected in most primary school curricula. The child must first be taught to look and listen carefully and to attend to what is happening in that learning situation. Then he learns to discriminate and match objects and symbols presented in that environment. Gradually, he begins to compare, contrast, sort, and classify. Next, the pupil is taught to synthesize and integrate the data and information acquired. Finally, the child learns to reflect on the implications of his newly acquired knowledge and stores it for future use and association in the continual development of more difficult mental concepts and operations.

This kind of thinking is not automatic; it is shaped by numerous cultural experiences and by the nature of the educational process itself. Undoubtedly, many schools do a fairly good job in imparting these skills to their pupils, but some school systems provide poor or inadequate education in this respect. And most schools are grossly inadequate in their meager attempts to provide learning-disabled children of all kinds with appropriate developmental and remedial cognitive education.

We know, for instance, that children can be taught to improve their thinking and reasoning skills. Cognitive deficits can also be remedied through appropriate forms of supplemental and corrective special education. Even the most fundamental thinking skill deficits such as inattention and perceptual-motor control can be ameliorated. The extensive work of Hagen and Kail (1975) on the role of attention in perceptual and cognitive development concludes that direct training of this basic and critical skill does have beneficial results on higher order learning. Other similar studies further demonstrate that certain instructional strategies can improve self-control, mental ability, and school performance of impulsive children (Hallahan and Cruickshank, 1973, p. 244).

There is no longer any doubt that environmental complexity and specific training affect brain chemistry and total mental development (Krech, Rosenzweig, and Bennett, 1969). Highly specific sensory-motor and perceptual training improves neurological functioning and integration and total human performance; visual form and space perception skills appear to be those sensory-perceptual skills most directly related to cognitive development (Ayres, 1973). Recent research by Ornstein (1973) has also shown that the integration of left brain functions (verbal, symbolic, and abstract abilities) and right brain functions (spatial orientation, depth perception, gestalt organization) results from a proper total education that improves human functioning. A host of other studies such as those of Fretz, Johnson, and Johnson (1969), Painter (1966), Sabatino and Streissgrith (1972), and Morrison and Pothier (1972) have helped to demonstrate the relevance of developmental and prescriptive sensory and perceptual training to higher order cognitive functioning in children.

Most school districts now have some provision for the early screening and identification of children with suspected learning disabilities. This screening often begins with a concerned teacher completing a pupil referral form such as the one on pp. 9 and 10. By briefly rating, describing, and giving examples of the learning problem, it is usually possible to pinpoint significant areas of concern and to obtain some form of consultative or administrative aid in helping the child to learn more effectively.

The fact remains, however, that even when such skill deficits have been clearly identified and diagnosed in learning-disabled children, the appropriate education has still not been provided. Instead, these children have continued to be placed in the regular curriculum and learning groups without due consideration given to their developmental level or to their lack of the necessary entry skills required for success in that situation. Through this kind of neglect and improper treatment, the educational system actually exacerbates and compounds whatever learning or cognitive disability may exist.

In other school settings inadequate time and effort are devoted to correcting or remedying even the most apparent conceptual problems that children may present. Instead of devoting available time to direct remediation of an obvious cognitive deficit the teacher may focus on extraneous objectives and activities and seldom work on the priority concern. Without adequate time, attention, and proper practice these children will never learn to think properly or develop the skills they need for successful learning. It must also be acknowledged that some children do suffer only from poor teaching, in that improper teaching models, methods, and strategies may actually interfere with or prevent proper learning.

PUPIL REFERRAL FORM
Basic referral data for pupils with suspected learning or behavioral disabilities

Pupil's name _____ Birthdate _____

Referring teacher _____ School _____

Rate this pupil by placing a circle around the appropriate number to the right of each learning ability area listed below. Use this code:
1. No apparent learning problems or disabilities
2. Very few learning problems
3. Several learning problems
4. Many learning problems
5. Very many learning problems and possible disabilities

Write a brief description of a school or classroom example of each problem area.

Gross motor development (large muscle activities, physical health, strength, flexibility)   1 2 3 4 5

EXAMPLES:

Sensory-motor integration (attention, concentration, balance, organization, dexterity)   1 2 3 4 5

EXAMPLES:

Perceptual-motor skills (auditory, visual, visual-motor performance)   1 2 3 4 5

EXAMPLES:

Language development (speaking, reading, writing, spelling)   1 2 3 4 5

EXAMPLES:

Conceptual skills (reasoning, thinking, comprehending, computing, problem solving)   1 2 3 4 5

EXAMPLES:

Continued.

PUPIL REFERRAL FORM—cont'd
Basic referral data for pupils with suspected
learning or behavioral disabilities

Social/personal skills (cooperation, friendship, responsibility,   1 2 3 4 5
self-control, maturity)

EXAMPLES:

_____

Estimated reading grade placement and comments:

Summary of available achievement test results:

What are your priority learning objectives for this pupil at this time?

How do you suggest this pupil might best be helped to learn?

Other comments:

Signature of referring teacher _____

Date of referral _____

Some of the most important causes of cognitive disability in children are summarized in the checklist on p. 11. This checklist has been found to be of value as part of an initial evaluation of a pupil with critical thinking and learning problems. By completing the checklist on these children, teachers and consultants can begin to consider what might be given priority attention in the development of a remedial plan to help each child.

PRESCRIPTIVE IMPLICATIONS

In this chapter we have seen that schools have a high proportion of children who experience significant learning problems. Many of these pupils have spe-

SOME CAUSES OF COGNITIVE DISABILITIES

Pupil's name _____ Age _____ School/class _____

Does this child:	Yes	?	No
1. Have a developmental history indicating possible hereditary or genetic defects?			
2. Show history or evidence of significant nutritional or bio-chemical disorders?			
3. Suffer from ecological distress (pollution, contamination, distractors, noise)?			
4. Have a history of disease or central nervous system damage?			
5. Come from a poverty-level family with a history of chronic unemployment?			
6. Have a preschool history of inadequate stimulation and instructional interaction with parents or other adults?			
7. Lack the necessary specific readiness or prerequisite skills required by current curricular demands?			
8. Have undiagnosed and untreated learning difficulties or disabilities?			
9. Have a school history that may indicate poor teaching or inadequate instruction?			
10. Currently require intensive individualized prescriptive teaching that he or she is not yet receiving?			

Comments:

Circle the two most important causative factors above and briefly state what might be done about them.

cific cognitive defects that interfere with their performance and achievement in reading and other academic subjects.

We have also reviewed some of the major factors that produce these learning deficits in children. Most of the determinants mentioned (genetic determinants, disease, family determinants, and social-cultural indifference) are beyond immediate control or intervention by educators. However, the last one—inappropriate education—is almost fully within the realm of educators and educational policy makers, and it is this one with which this book is primarily concerned.

But even inappropriate education is far too broad a topic to consider in any depth in a single textbook. The emphasis in this book is on prescriptive cognitive education and therapy. Our focus will be on what interested teachers and special educators can do within their classrooms and learning centers to help improve the acquisition of thinking and cognitive skills in children.

The first part of this book presents the results of major studies on how children have been taught to think. Models of cognitive abilities and related instructional programs are presented next. The relationship of prerequisite skills to the reading process is discussed and followed by several prescriptive case studies. In order that teachers may clearly understand the nature of specific cognitive skills, these are enumerated and illustrated with examples in the Critical Thinking Skills Survey, which can actually be used for evaluation purposes by those concerned. The book then concludes with a consideration of teaching strategies and some broader implications of what is involved in the right of every person to learn and develop in accord with his or her own potential.

DISCUSSION QUESTIONS AND ACTIVITIES

1. Visit a regular classroom and ask a teacher to estimate the proportion of children with learning disabilities in his or her class. How many of these children are estimated to have specific thinking or cognitive problems?
2. What might "concrete thought processes" consist of?
3. How might the school lunch and snack vending machine program at your school be made more nutritionally sound?
4. List several of the poor environmental factors in a school that might adversely affect pupil learning and achievement.
5. What is the unemployment rate in your community? To what extent has this affected the schools (and the children within them)?
6. To what extent does your community provide prescriptive remedial education for children with learning disabilities?
7. Complete the checklist of causes of cognitive disabilities for a selected child. Discuss the results and implications with a fellow student or teacher.
8. How do you think teachers might best be helped to improve their educational program for teaching thinking and cognitive skills?

CHAPTER 2

Learning to think

In this book we are concerned with how public education eventually was recognized as an essential element in the pursuit of life, liberty, and happiness itself. Gradually, the idea that education was worthwhile for *all* persons became an acceptable one. Then the contributions of such pioneers as Itard, Montessori, and Binet forced us to acknowledge the possibility that even inferior mentalities might be able to grow and develop through appropriate special education. But what is the actual evidence that such a radical proposition might be true? And how is mental growth to be determined? Finally, just what is the nature of the educational process that may result in such important changes in human mentality? In this chapter we will begin with the second question and then consider data relating to the first question; educational processes and procedures will be discussed in detail in the other parts of this book.

MENTAL GROWTH

As we have seen, one of the commonly accepted goals of education is to "develop the mind." The mind is the totality of such mental processes as thinking, feeling, willing, perceiving, and intuiting. These integrated processes comprise the unique human psyche and intellect. It is believed that through the refinement and development of these varied processes we improve our individual personalities and our capabilities for adaptation and survival.

Our purpose here is to acknowledge that "thinking" is a very important mental process, although it is only one of many. Thinking processes usually involve the integration and understanding of specific perceptual relations and the ability to manipulate and judge these abstractions for speculation and eventual problem solving.

Traditionally, education has focused on the teaching and development of subject matter competence rather than on thinking processes themselves. For instance, the study of history, chemistry, or music obviously involves somewhat different kinds or ways of thinking and performing. But all academic subjects, as well as the so-called nonacademic ones, require certain psychological "sets" and attitudes that center energy and attention. The set is in reality a personal willingness to invest one's energy in learning to follow the particular thinking processes required in understanding a given subject or skill. As a result of such a personal involvement, the learner gradually begins to "think appropriately" and thereby increases his skill achievement or performance. In this way, mental growth occurs through the cumulation of many different ways of thinking that have been acquired from the discipline of education and relevant experience.

Mental growth can be measured in several different ways. Perhaps the best approach is to actually measure progress in the specific skill or abilities of concern. If we are primarily interested in determining growth and achievement in such thinking skills as particular mathematical operations, piano proficiency, or artistic design, we had better measure them directly in some depth and over a period of time. This form of evaluation is most always the preferable one for use by regular teachers and special educators alike, since it lends itself most directly to meaningful curricular development and remediation.

However, when children are experiencing difficulty in thinking and problem solving it is also necessary to conduct a survey of their overall thinking processes. Such a survey should consist of samples of the more important mental operations to determine what processes and problem-solving skills the child is having most difficulty with.

Most mental tests are general ones in that they consist of a selection of several different kinds of thinking skills. Usually, these subtests include listening and following directions, solving puzzles of various kinds, reading, judging, figuring, comparing and relating things, drawing, evaluating problems, synthesizing data, and hypothesizing. All of these skills are gradually acquired and refined through maturational experience and education. And all of them are constantly used in thinking about or "dealing with" the more regular subject matter presented in the normal school curricula.

Various kinds of mental "intelligence" tests have been designed to sample the child's current functional level of thinking. Tests such as the Stanford-Binet, the Weschler Intelligence Scale for Children, the Comprehensive Tests of Basic Skills, and numerous others actually consist of a multitude of subtests that merely sample the thinking skills mentioned above. By comparing the individual pupil's performance with hundreds or even thousands of other children of the same chronological age, it is possible to determine the overall rate of mental growth and functioning as well as the probable areas of strength and difficulty.

The intelligence quotient, or IQ, score is nothing more than an index of functional skills sampled at that given time. It is usually derived by dividing the earned mental age score by the person's chronological age and then multiplying by 100. Therefore if a child passes many skills expected of children beyond his or her age, the IQ will be over 100. Conversely, a slow-learning pupil or one with specific skill disabilities may fail many of the problems and expectancies of his age group, and his IQ score will then fall below 100. In reality, then, the

IQ is a current index of functional skills acquired and learned to that point in time.

When used by itself the IQ score is merely an indication of total mental growth. If a child scores below expectation, it signals the need for a careful look at the subtests to help determine the kinds of problems he or she may be having. The subtests may then suggest more specific diagnostic tests that might be administered for the purpose of helping the child through developmental or remedial education. Then if an appropriate prescriptive education program is developed that uses the child's strengths while focusing on his or her deficiencies, total mental growth and improvement in thinking skills become a distinct possibility.

In a review of relevant studies, Anastasi (a widely recognized authority on mental testing) has concluded that emphasis should be given to measuring specific skills rather than using single IQs or other broad developmental indices. She recommends that

> training in sensorimotor functions should not be expected to improve verbal skills; training in the development of object permanence should be assessed by a test of object permanence, and so forth. In addition, *the content of the intervention program should be tailored to fit the needs of the individual child with reference to the development attained in specific skills* (emphasis mine).*

Actually, both survey tests of critical thinking skills and more in-depth assessments of selected high-priority skills are required. Both have their place in special education; they complement one another. When they are used together with other forms of evaluation, such as careful clinical observation and anecdotal recording, both general mental growth and specific skill achievement can be determined.

A growing body of evidence indicates that mental ability and thinking skills of all kinds can be improved through the appropriate kind of special education. In the following sections, we will examine some of the more provocative studies in this regard. Most of those reported have followed traditional research designs with proper control groups and statistical analysis of general mental ability scores to determine the significance of whatever progress was made. Several major studies, however, have been largely clinical in nature, and these are so indicated.

These studies are discussed on three levels: the preschool years, the elementary school years, and the secondary and adult levels. First, bibliographic references are cited. Then a brief summary of the major findings is presented. Interested readers are encouraged to go directly to the original sources for more detailed information. It should also be remembered that those studies cited are merely illustrative of *successful* attempts to improve mental ability and thinking

---

*From Anastasi, A. *Psychological testing* (4th ed.). New York: Macmillan Publishing Co., Inc., 1976, p. 336.

skills through education; the literature abounds in studies reporting failure in this endeavor, but these are not germane to our primary concerns.

PRESCHOOL YEARS

Most of the research on the effects of education on mental growth has been done with preschool nursery-aged children. Siegel (1968) of the Merrill-Palmer Institute has objectively commented that "the growing body of learning studies have demonstrated the modifiability of cognitive growth during the nursery school period."

Rice, R. Premature infants respond to sensory stimulation. *APA Monitor,* 1975, 6(11), 8-9.

In this recent study, 30 premature infants (37 weeks or less in gestational age) were randomly placed in experimental and control groups. The groups did not differ in sex, racial distribution, or birth variables. All of the infants in both groups had been born in a large city-county hospital to mothers of low socioeconomic status.

The experimental group was provided with sensory stimulation consisting of stroking and massaging of the entire body, rocking, and cuddling. The treatment was initiated by public health nurses and then continued by the mothers for 15-minute periods, four times a day, for 30 days. Mothers were trained to time their treatments and to maintain observation notes and charts.

At 4 months of age, when treatment had ended, all children were reassessed by a pediatrician, a psychologist, and a pediatric nurse. Significant statistical differences in favor of the experimental group included the development of more mature neurophysiological reflex responses, weight gains with increases in enzymatic and endocrine function, and gains in total mental function as measured by the Bayley Scales of Infant Development. In addition, subjective results indicated that the group who received sensory stimulation had become more adaptive and aggressive and that the mother-infant relationship was enhanced and nurtured.

Fowler, W. Cognitive learning in infancy and early childhood. *Psychological Bulletin,* 1962, 59, 115-152.

This is a major compilation of the early research. A number of significant studies are reported. One such study was done by Wellman with 267 children in seven nursery groups; mean gains of 14.5 points on the Merrill-Palmer scale were significant over the control subjects. Gains were attributed to the nature of the preschool program, which included pegboard tasks, picture puzzles, and block building, and which correlated closely with the criterion test.

Skeels, H. M. Adult status of children with contrasting early life experience. *Child Development Monographs, 31*(3), 1969.

This is a 30-year follow-up study of infants of retarded mothers. At the age of 2 years, 13 children whose average IQ was below 70 were placed in a special intervention program with much environmental stimulation by surrogate mothers. During an 18-month experimental period the mean IQ increased 28 points while the mean IQ of the control group dropped 26 points. Thirty years later, all 13 children in the experimental group were living normal and productive lives. By contrast, all persons in the control group were either dead, having suffered from significant mental or physical disabilities, or still institutionalized.

Dawe, H. C. A study of the effect of an educational program upon the language development and related mental functions in young children. Unpublished doctoral dissertation, University of Iowa, 1940.

A 50-hour intensive instructional period emphasizing verbal and informational experiences for children in an orphanage produced an average IQ gain of 14 points for the experimental group over the control group.

Bereiter, C., and Engelmann, S. *Teaching disadvantaged children in the preschool.* Englewood Cliffs, N.J.: Prentice-Hall, Inc., 1966.

In this classic study an educational program was developed to help children develop facility in basic patterns of reasoning, such as "if-then" and "either-or" concepts. Much emphasis was placed on the children performing conceptual operations of comparing, combining, and translating information in highly structured lessons. Each concept was presented in 15-minute sessions daily with children rotating through several such concept-training sessions. In four different replications of the program, IQ gains averaged 15 points for participating children.

Klaus, R. S., and Gray, S. W. The early training project for disadvantaged children. A report after five years. *Monographs of the Society for Research in Child Development, 33*(4), 1968.

Nineteen 3-year-old black children were provided intensive training in verbal interaction, perceptual discrimination, concept formation, number ability, and language. Training sessions were held 4 hours a day, with five children in a group, over three 10-week summer sessions. During the winter months, weekly home visits were made by special teachers who taught the participating mothers how to continue the program with their children. At the end of the 3-year experiment, the experimental group averaged a 9-point IQ increase over the matched control group. At the end of the regular fourth grade of school attendance, retesting showed that the experimental group had maintained the 9-point increase over the controls.

Karnes, M. B., Hodgins, A. S., Stoneburner, R. L., Studley, W. M., and Tesks, J. A. Effects of a highly structured program of language development on intellectual functioning and psycholinguistic development of culturally disadvantaged three-year olds. *Journal of Special Education*, 1968, 2, 405-412.

Preschool children given intensive 20-minute learning sessions in mathematical concepts, reading readiness, language fluency, etc. showed an average 8-point gain in Binet IQ over counterparts placed in traditional or Montessori preschool programs.

Blank, M., and Solomon, F. A tutorial language program to develop abstract thinking in socially disadvantaged preschool children. *Child Development*, 1968, *39*, 379-389.

A training program consisting of activities to teach sequential organized thinking, the comprehension of events, and the ability to structure behavior in choosing alternatives was devised for disadvantaged children. The program consisted of individual tutoring in 15- to 20-minute daily sessions, 5 days per week, spread over several months. Average gain on Binet IQ test was 14.5 points. A second group tutored in the same way, but only 3 days a week, gained an average of 7 points.

Siebert, H. *Investigation of specific variables involved in preschool education of the educationally vulnerable child.* Doctoral dissertation, Wayne State University, Department of Special Education, 1975.

In one of the more recent studies of preschool children, Siebert found that "educationally vulnerable" children in a developmental-prescriptive program made significant gains over controls. The Valett Developmental Survey of Basic Learning Abilities was given to 119 prekindergarten children, and the 40 children with the lowest scores were then divided into equal experimental and control groups. The experimental group was provided with a special program for 2½ hours per day, 2 days per week, for 16 weeks to develop the following basic skills: motor integration and physical development, tactile awareness, visual-motor integration, visual discrimination, auditory discrimination, conceptual (number) development, language development, and verbal expression. With special training using carefully selected developmental learning materials, the high-risk experimental children made real gains in total development; the greatest gains were made in the language development and verbal expression areas (almost four times that of the control group). The most successful part of the program was judged to be parent participation and involvement. The entire program has now been expanded on a district-wide basis in the L'Anse Creuse schools in Mt. Clemens, Michigan. An excellent 36-minute documentary film describing this successful program is available.*

Bloom, B. S. Letter to the editor. *Harvard Educational Review*, 1969, *39,* 419-421.
In this brief but highly significant report, Bloom presented data on the effects of the Israeli kibbutz preschool education program. Children of European origin who are brought up in their own homes have average IQs of 105. Children who are raised in the kibbutz nursery program have an average IQ of 115 if they continue in the 22-hour-per-day program for 4 years. Although children from mid-Eastern Jewish families have an average IQ of 85 when brought up in individual homes, identical children brought up in the kibbutz also have an average IQ of 115. Clearly, the kibbutz educational program has a profoundly positive effect on the mental development of disadvantaged Jewish children.

Heber, R., Garber, H., Harrington, S., Hoffman, C., and Falender, C. *Rehabilitation of families at risk for mental retardation. Progress report.* Madison: University of Wisconsin, Rehabilitation Research and Training Center in Mental Retardation, 1972.
This is by far the most significant study of its kind to date; as it is a longitudinal study, periodic reports will be issued in the future. The project concerns the children of 40 retarded mothers. Special educators began developmental instruction with the children when they reached the age of 3 months. Individual teaching sessions were held with each child and its mother until the child reached 2 years of age. Then children were tutored in small groups to the age of 5 or 6 when they entered regular public schools. A 4-day-per-week training session consisted of 20-minute periods structured to cover sensory, perceptual, and language skills.
At the time of this report the experimental mean IQ score was 124 and the control group mean IQ score was 94. Tentative results indicate that the benefits of mental growth and skill development are directly related to the amount and kind of training presented. Because of its great importance, the preschool program is outlined here.

I. Preschool language program
   A. Comprehension
   B. Vocabulary acquisition
   C. Communication
   D. Critical thinking
      1. Open ended questions

---

*Greensquares to Kindergarten (16 mm, color and sound), Peach Enterprises, Inc., 4649 Gerald, Warren, Mich. 48092.

      2. Sentence completion
      3. Pretending games
      4. Guessing games
      5. Describing games
      6. Predicting outcomes

II. Preschool reading program
  A. Reading readiness activities
      1. Visual skills (discrimination, memory, visual-motor activities, spatial relations)
      2. Auditory skills (discrimination and memory of sounds, and sounds in words)
      3. Symbolic representation—alphabet recognition (visual discrimination of letters, formal letter naming, recognition, analysis)
  B. Formal reading program
      1. Language experience approach (experience reading charts, building word banks)
      2. Phonics program (rhyming activities and games, initial consonant sounds, blends, digraphs, letter substitution and word families)

III. Math and problem-solving program
  A. Perception
      1. Kinesthetic discrimination
      2. Auditory discrimination
      3. Tactile discrimination
      4. Olfactory discrimination
      5. Gustatory discrimination
      6. Visual discrimination
  B. Concept evaluation
      1. Same/different
      2. Size
      3. Quantity (weight, volume, sets, etc.)
      4. Number
      5. Size and shape
      6. Shape
      7. Contrasting opposite conditions
      8. Position in space
      9. Function
    10. Color
  C. Organization
      1. Association (functional matching and memory)
      2. Classification (grouping, arranging, dividing, sorting, labeling)
      3. Correspondence (pair matching, identity and conservation games, comparisons)
      4. Seriation (sequencing, causality and time ordering, ordering by property such as length, height, surface, pitch, tempo, pressure, texture, size, arranging patterns)
  D. Reasoning
      1. Analysis (describing, listing, identifying, dividing into parts, critique making)
      2. Synthesis (integrating parts, anticipating visual sequences, completing complex patterns, creating sentence and story completions, playing with riddles and puzzles)

This detailed progress report contains the program rationale and statistical analysis of all findings. In addition, an extensive appendix presents numerous lesson plans used in both the infancy and preschool programs, which will undoubtedly be used as models for future cognitive development programs.

Modified lesson example: Pattern seriation
Look at this bead string.

Now take your beads and make a string using the same beads but *reversing* their order.
- What bead will you put on first?
- What bead goes on last?
- What bead will be in the middle?
- Now complete your string and then tell me what bead is to the left of the square.
- What bead is to the right of the triangle?

ELEMENTARY SCHOOL YEARS

Any mental growth that occurs between 5 and 12 years of age is certainly affected by the nature of the child's elementary school experience. For a number of years, Bloom (1964) studied the changes in human characteristics and mental abilities from birth through early adulthood; he concluded that most (about half) of the child's thinking skills and mental abilities are developed by age 5 years, which supports the idea of the primary importance of the first 5 years of life and early home-preschool training. But Bloom also discovered that the most significant period of mental growth during the school years occurred between 5 and 8 years of age. In kindergarten and the first and second grade, emphasis should be placed on the development of critical thinking skills and abilities and on the identification and beginning remediation of any learning disabilities that may have been discovered.

Research also indicates the need for a very careful curricular match with the developmental stage and mental structures of the child. That is, we must be sure that the child has developed adequate thinking skills, psychoneurological processes, and mental operations that are required by the nature of the general school curriculum. The work of Inhelder and Piaget (1959) on the growth of logical thinking during these childhood years consists of a great number of clinical experiments with children. One finding from these studies is that the mind is not a "tabula rosa," subject merely to educational imprinting through formal schooling:

> If the social milieu is really to influence individual brains, they have to be in a state of readiness to assimilate its contributions, so we come back to the need for some degree of maturation of individual cerebral mechanisms. . . . When knowledge acquired through special schooling does not correspond to the

mental structures indispensible to the assimilation of such knowledge this is immediately recognized through qualitative questioning and evaluation.*

Throughout these early formative years at least, continued mental growth is dependent on the proper balance of maturation and educational experience. Although desirable mental growth cannot be rushed by special education, it can be *stimulated* and enhanced. And whenever the psychoneurologically mature child lacks adequate thinking skills it is probably caused by a lack of proper and intensive educational experience. It is at this point that prescriptive cognitive therapy and developmental education become essential to stimulate the child's move to the next growth stage. The following studies show the effect of such training during the elementary school years.

Itard, J. *The wild boy of Aveyron.* New York: Appleton-Century-Crofts, 1962.
This is by far the most detailed study of clinical teaching that has been recognized as a classic in the professional literature. In the year 1795, a 10-year-old "wild boy" was discovered in a French forest. Jean Itard, a physician by training, took the boy into his home, named him Victor, and began prescriptive teaching that extended over a 5-year period. At the beginning of his special education, Victor was described as a savage who undoubtedly was developmentally retarded; he was without language and lacked appropriate thinking skills and abilities. Consequently, Itard selected a series of cognitive objectives for Victor that included "extending the range of Victor's ideas and enabling him to employ the simplest mental operations." In his diary Itard maintained detailed records of his prescriptive teaching and carefully noted his observations of mental growth and development in the boy. Although Victor was 10 years of age when instruction started—and therefore past the most formative years of childhood—he was still able to make remarkable progress in his acquisition of mental operations. At the conclusion of this intensive experiment Itard felt frustrated by the slow rate of growth, but he did report several specific gains and concluded that sensory training contributed powerfully to the development of Victor's intellectual faculties and that the boy did come ". . . to know the symbols of thought by naming objects, their qualities, and their actions."

Casey, M., Davidson, H., and Harter, D. Three studies on the effect of training in similar and identical material upon Stanford-Binet test scores. *Twenty-seventh yearbook of the National Society for the Study of Education: Nature and nurture, Part I.* Chicago: University of Chicago Press, 1928.
This volume contains descriptions of several experiments concerning the effect of education on mental growth. Several studies with elementary schoolchildren show changes in IQ test scores as the result of intensive prescriptive tutoring. Casey et al found that when experimental groups are trained with identical material used in the Binet tests, immediate IQ changes took place. However, such scores declined with the passage of time. It was concluded that periodic retraining and continued drill and practice on specific thinking skills are required if performance levels are to be maintained over time.

---

*From Inhelder, B., and Piaget, J. *The growth of logical thinking from childhood to adolescence.* New York: Basic Book, Inc., 1959, p. 338.

Gallagher, J. J. Productive thinking in children. In *Review of child development research* (Vol. 1). New York: Russell Sage Foundation, 1964.

This report reviews the effects of various special training programs that have attempted to improve cognitive abilities in children. Included are studies that demonstrate that educable retarded children in special education classes who are provided with specific instruction in divergent thinking skills such as verbal fluency, flexibility, and originality do make significant gains over control groups of retarded children maintained in regular classes without such instruction. Gallagher recommended the development of other similar programs for stimulating specific cognitive abilities in retarded children as the most feasible approach to training the mind.

Sapir, S. The prevention of learning disability through deficit centered classroom training (Project of U.S. Office of Education, Division of Handicapped Children and Youth, Columbia University, Teachers College). Paper presented at the annual convention of the Council for Exceptional Children, March 1967.

This paper described an experimental project concerned with determining the effect of a deficit-centered training curriculum with first grade children by measuring the child's developmental growth and academic achievement before and after the intervention program. Deficits were determined by psychological testing and then interpreted directly to the teacher who conducted prescriptive instruction. Emphasis was placed on structure, slow pacing, verbal mediation, and much overlearning of skills. The experimental group gained a mean of 10 points on the Wechsler Intelligence Scale for Children, which was a significant gain over the control group. Specific subtest skills in which the most improvement was shown were object assembly, picture arrangement, similarities, and comprehension.

Vernon, P. E. Symposium on the effects of coaching and practice on intelligence tests. *British Journal of Educational Psychology,* 1954, *24,* 5-8.

A number of different experiments were conducted in English schools to determine just how much IQ scores could be raised by special training programs. Most of these projects involved direct coaching by special tutors who focused directly on test items and concepts failed. A symposium of educational psychologists determined that the average gain reported was approximately 11 points. However, some individuals showed much greater improvement, indicating that coaching and practice was not only worthwhile but highly desirable in their cases.

Jensen, A. R. *Genetics and education.* New York: Harper & Row, Inc., 1972, pp. 179-192.

This book contains a review of research on various educational attempts to increase IQ and concludes that emphasis should be placed on preparing persons to develop specific skills and abilities required for life functions and job-related tasks. The magnitude of IQ and scholastic achievement gains "resulting from enrichment and cognitive stimulation programs authentically range between about 5 and 20 points for IQ's." Greater gains are possible in academic achievement when instructional techniques are intensive and highly focused. It is recommended that educators would probably do better to concern themselves with teaching highly specific skills of recognized importance.

Scarr, S., and Weinberg, R. IQ test performance of black children adopted by white families. *American Psychologist,* 1976, *31,* 726-739.

This is an important recent study on the effects of environmental variables on the functional intelligence of black children. Some of the goals of this study were to determine how well black children reared in white families performed in school and how accurately IQ performance could be predicted from the characteristics of their adoptive homes.

More than 130 black adopted children were included in this study, which involved demographic analysis, public welfare reports, school achievement tests, and individually administered intelligence tests. The overwhelming majority of black children were placed in their adoptive white families during the first year of life. The IQ scores of the adopted children at placement were not as high as those of either the adoptive parents or their biological children.

Children who were adopted earlier in life, who had spent more years in their adoptive homes, and who had "better quality placement" were found to have developed higher IQ scores, with the mean score being 106. The significant increase in these scores was 16 points above the average of 90 achieved by black children reared in their own homes in the north central region of the United States.

This study concluded that the better than average learning environments in the adopted homes were a massive intervention at a critical period, which resulted in significant cognitive development for the adopted children. Some of the positive environmental characteristics affecting positive intellectual growth included the amount and quality of parent-child interaction, parental attitudes and practices, employment, economic security, and cultural values of adoptive parents.

Levi, A. Treatment of a disorder of perception and concept formation in a case of school failure. *Journal of Consulting Psychology,* 1965, *29,* 289-295.

This is an outstanding clinical study that has been widely quoted in the literature. Levi worked with an 11-year-old sixth grade boy with specific learning disabilities. Initial psychological testing produced a WISC total IQ of 88 and a 6th percentile rating on the Raven Progressive Matrices. Treatment goals centered on teaching categorization and perceptual scanning techniques. Of special interest is the use of the Columbia Mental Maturity Scale, which was used to actually teach object characteristics and differences and to help the child acquire "categories." Much verbal mediation and discussion were used to be sure the child had acquired each categorical skill before moving on to another task. The posttest full scale IQ score on the WISC was 101; the greatest gains were made on the similarities and coding subtests. The Raven Progressive Matrices posttest score was at the 38th percentile, confirming that the concepts learned and the relations between conceptual elements had been generalized over a 1-year training period.

Valett, R. A developmental task approach to early childhood education. In *Programming learning disabilities,* Belmont, Calif.: Fearon Publishers, Inc., 1969, pp. 99-109.

This case study report describes a prescriptive program for special education of a 7-year-old exceptional child with a full scale WISC IQ of 83 and a Leiter International Performance Scale IQ of 100. A detailed task analysis of the Valett Developmental Survey of Basic Learning Abilities is presented to show how such a criterion instrument can be used to supplement IQ tests in determining goals and objectives for prescriptive teaching. Changes in IQ scores can best be effected when other evaluation devices are used to extend item analysis and to program learning deficits.

SECONDARY AND ADULT LEVELS

The evidence that we have examined so far indicates that the most rapid growth of mental abilities occurs in the preschool and elementary school years. However, thinking skills do continue to develop through adolescence and the adult years as well. Most studies have shown that specialized skills and mental functions continue to improve with use and practice to at least middle age. Some of the more representative research using specialized tests of mental aptitude as criterion measures is presented here.

Bloom, B., and Broder, L. *Problem-solving processes of college students.* Chicago: University of Chicago Press, 1950.

As an educational psychologist, Bloom was interested in the possibility of improving the performance of low-scoring college students applying for admission to programs in the University of Chicago and other institutions. Traditional tutorial training sessions were held over at least 10 to 12 different time periods. It was found that improvement on low aptitude scores was proportional to the amount of time spent in relevant tutorial instruction. Of most importance, however, was the process used. Training that emphasized "thinking aloud," or verbalization of the various problem-solving steps used, was essential for real success. It was suggested that remedial training should focus on thinking-out-loud in future problem-solving situations if the proper thinking skills were to be maintained.

Marron, J. E. *Special test preparation, its effect on College Board scores and the relationship of effected scores to subsequent college performance.* West Point, N.Y.: Office of the Director of Admissions and Registrar, U.S. Military Academy, November 1, 1965.

In this unusual study a total of 714 West Point applicants with low scores on the Scholastic Aptitude Test (SAT) were provided with special training. The students were sent to 10 different special preparatory programs located in schools throughout the country. Intensive remedial training was carried on for one semester. Training focused on the specifics of verbal reasoning, reading comprehension, and mathematical concepts. At the end of the study it was found that scores on the verbal aptitude part of the SAT increased an average of 57 points and scores on the mathematical aptitude increased an average of 79 points. The gains were significant and allowed participants to meet admission standards.

Sheils, M., Monroe, S., Camp, H., and Ma, C. Minority report card. *Newsweek,* July 12, 1976, pp. 74-75.

This was a special report on various attempts throughout the nation to help minority students gain admission to professional schools. Since 1969 the federally funded Council on Legal Education Opportunity has provided 6-week training programs on law school campuses across the country to "help students develop the verbal and reasoning skills" required on admissions tests. In each special training program four law-school professors and several upperclassmen served as faculty. In other special law-tutoring programs held between 1971 and 1973, a total of 300 minority students were trained to pass the bar examination successfully; 276 of them passed on their first try!

Whimbey, A. *Intelligence can be taught.* New York: E. P. Dutton & Co., Inc., 1975, pp. 62-67.

This book contains a detailed report of individual prescriptive tutoring with a graduate student who had failed the Graduate Record Examination (GRE) and the Law School Admission Test. Training took place for 2 hours per day, 4 days per week, over a 4-month period and centered on reading and thinking aloud, reasoning, and reading comprehension problems. Highly significant gains occurred; the student's GRE score improved more than 140 points. It was recommended that an even more effective training procedure would have been to have the subject read written protocols or models of the teacher's thinking processes (or of a peer model's thinking processes) of the particular problem-solving steps involved. Some of the actual steps and lessons used with the subject were reported by the same author in a popular article entitled "You Can Learn to Raise Your IQ Score" in *Psychology Today,* Volume 9, January 1976.

CONCLUSIONS AND IMPLICATIONS

In this chapter a number of varied research studies have been summarized; they show that persons can learn to improve their thinking skills and abilities. What can be concluded from these reports, and what are the implications for educational practice? These may be briefly summarized as follows:

1. The essence of thinking is to be found in the process of collecting and distinguishing sensory data and in putting such information into proper relation with the environment (Montessori, 1964). Recently, the Board of Scientific Affairs of the American Psychological Association has published a report emphasizing the importance of acquired skills, knowledge, learning sets, and generalization tendencies that are available at any one period of time (Cleary et al., 1975).

2. Evidence clearly indicates that thinking skills and the mental abilities of Americans have increased slowly but steadily since such measurements have been devised. Most investigators agree that this improvement is mainly a result of increases in average education and environmental changes (Block and Dworkin, 1976). The level of mental functioning can also be raised for individuals and particular subgroups with appropriate training (Cleary et al., 1975, p. 23).

3. Cognitive skills and thinking processes have different growth patterns and require proper timing and sequencing for optimum development (Covington, 1968; Tuddenham, 1965).

4. Problem-solving strategies can be taught to persons. Strategies that present clear models and require verbal mediation, labeling, and systematic verbalization are most effective (Stern, 1967; Jensen, 1966).

5. Gains in IQ scores can be obtained from training exercises appropriate to each mental skill or ability such as verbal, numerical, or spatial-visualization skills; recognizing classes; seeing relationships; understanding systems of knowledge; and making transformations and drawing implications from data (Guilford, 1967).

6. Improvement in thinking skills can be measured using traditional intelligence test scores, but more meaningful and significant instructional gains are noted from subtest profiles (Bennett, 1976) or from the use of specific formative and summative criterion instruments (Bloom, Hastings, and Madams, 1971).

Finally, we can conclude that persons learn to think in many different ways and that the development or remediation of deficits in specific thinking skills is best done through highly individualized and prescriptive instruction over a long period of time. How well children learn to think is directly proportional to the specificity of the instructional program and the time and effort involved. Diagnostic-prescriptive therapy and special education can make a significant difference in the life of the learning-handicapped child.

DISCUSSION QUESTIONS AND ACTIVITIES

1. Define "skill" and list several different kinds.
2. What are some of the limitations of a single IQ score?
3. How can "growth or improvement" in thinking skills and abilities be determined?
4. Why have most "mental growth studies" been done on preschool and primary-aged children?
5. Research and report on the current status of Heber's project (the Milwaukee project).
6. What are some of the financial implications for education of Bloom's study of changes in human characteristics from birth through early adulthood?
7. What might have been a limiting factor in Itard's success with Victor?
8. Critique Levi's use of the Columbia Mental Maturity Scale as a tool for prescriptive teaching.
9. To what extent do you think high school students should be trained and prepared to pass college entrance or other similar examinations?

CHAPTER 3

Models of cognitive abilities

There are many different kinds of thinking. People acquire different styles of thinking and problem solving through distinctive cultural experience and education. The quality and style of thinking are also dependent on the basic genetic and biological integrity of the human organism. Once we begin to conceptualize the cognitive process itself, it then becomes possible to specify some of the critical thinking and intellectual skills involved. With operational definitions and task analysis, we can even select priority skills for educational development.

For example, if we encounter a child with a severe expressive language problem who is suffering in part from undeveloped auditory decoding and sequencing skills, we can begin to proceed meaningfully with educational remediation. In such a case the first step might be to attempt to measure the extent of the hypothesized psycholinguistic deficiency, which involves distinctive operational approaches.

In this way conceptual models of cognitive skills and abilities finally produce some pragmatic formulation and application. The application most often begins with some kind of theoretical taxonomy that classifies the various skills or abilities so that they can be evaluated, measured, and then used objectively in curriculum planning or special education.

CONCEPTUALIZATION

Like all mental and intellectual products, models of cognitive abilities originate in the minds of persons who have been thinking and reflecting on them. Such models are nothing more than organizational schemata for integrating related theoretical classes and abstractions. Invariably, these models arise out of the unique experiences and training of the person formulating them. They are therefore born from the empirical methods of observation and practice, as well as from the results of scientific experimentation.

An illustration of this process is seen in the history of the Stanford-Binet tests. When Alfred Binet was called on to devise a means to differentiate slow- from fast-learning schoolchildren, he began by pondering the situational demands. As a result of his training and experience he postulated that school learning required such skills as attention, memory, initiative, judgment, adaptation, autocriticism, comprehension, common sense, and imagination (among others). This became the basic model from which he proceeded to select and devise concrete test items that might logically measure such skills.

Binet's model was created from the integration of clinical and laboratory experience, and its use demanded careful qualitative observation and interpretation. Later, it was more refined, became a highly standardized instrument, and was seldom used as a criterion source of tasks for mental orthopedics or prescriptive cognitive education.

In this chapter we will consider several major models of cognitive abilities and how they have been used in remedial and special education. These models have been divided into two major divisions according to their conceptual base. The first group will be considered developmental task taxonomies because they have been largely created from the observation and organization of maturational and clinical data; the common element in these models is the specification of operationally defined behavioral tasks that should be developed at certain stages or times in the life of the child. The second group is described as psychometric approaches because the common element is standardization and comparison of individual skill performance with statistically derived normal distributions of the test population.

The developmental task taxonomies and the psychometric approaches have both contributed much to our present knowledge of cognitive functioning. Both of them must be considered and should be used in the planning of any special education program for learning-disabled children. Only a few of the major models will be outlined and briefly described in this chapter. For real understanding and in-depth application of any model, the reader must consult the major references cited. However, the outlines that follow should be sufficient as an introduction to the kinds of cognitive models that have been devised and that are currently being used as the theoretical bases for many educational programs and practices.

DEVELOPMENTAL TASK TAXONOMIES

The four models presented here are those of Piaget, Bloom, Valett, and Boehm. Piaget's is a well-known maturational–developmental stage model of cognitive operations. Bloom and his colleagues were among the first to formulate an organized theoretical taxonomy of educational objectives in the cognitive domain of learning. Valett has created a developmental taxonomy of basic learning abilities that includes psycholinguistic and conceptual skills. Boehm's model of specific verbal concepts is included because it illustrates how one kind of cognitive operation (verbal conceptualization) can be operationally classified and defined for educational purposes.

Developmental stages of Piaget

Piaget has described the growth and development of cognitive abilities in several major life stages (Inhelder and Piaget, 1958). The process begins at birth with the development of sensory-motor skills, proceeds through preoperational thought and concrete thinking stages, and culminates in the appearance of formal mental operations at approximately 11 years of age. With maturation and experience these cognitive structures appear naturally in the life of the child, and each stage of development results in the ability to do more complex thinking and problem solving.

In the outline shown below, some of the specific cognitive operations developing at each stage are listed and examples are given. Most children begin

---

THE PIAGET MODEL

Formal operations (perceptual reorganization): 11 to 15 years

- Hypothetical-deductive logic
$$\begin{matrix} A \to X \\ B \to X \end{matrix} \quad A + B = X?$$
- Propositional thinking (mammals feed on milk; whales are mammals)
- Reversibility ($10 \times 5 = ?$; $50 \div 5 = ?$)
- Symbolic functioning (area = length $\times$ width)

Concrete operations: 7 to 11 years

- Groupings of logical relationships (ducks, birds, animals)
- Arithmetic groups and measurement (sets, etc.)
- Simple classification (color, shape)

Preoperational thought: 2 to 7 years

- Intuitional abstractions (animistic thinking), 5 to 7 years
- Simple irreversible representations (water level problems), 4 to 5½ years
- Beginning representations (egocentric interpretations), 2 to 4 years

Sensory-motor stages (beginning of time, causality, space, object permanence, play assimilation, imitation): birth to 2 years

- Invention of new means through mental combinations (pushes doll carriage away from wall), 18 months
- Discovery of new means through active experimentation (moves pillows to obtain covered watch), 12 to 18 months
- Coordination of schemata and first intentional behaviors (places mother's hand on music box), 8 to 12 months
- Motor recognition and procedures for making interesting sights last (shakes head when moving object stops), 4 to 8 months
- First acquired adaptations and sensory-motor responses (grasps toys when presented), 1 to 4 months
- Use of reflexes (sucking and assimilation), birth to 1 month

---

school with preoperational thought levels that are largely intuitive in nature. Gradually, as a result of extensive sensory-motor experience and concrete manipulations of environmental objects, the child begins to think in terms of groups and classes and slowly acquires the understanding of such concepts as space, time, number, and the conservation of weight and volume. Eventually, mental structures develop from the integration and organization of acquired skills that enable the person to deal with the abstractions of symbolization and propositional-hypothetical thinking (Flavell, 1966).

Considerable research and curriculum development have been done using Piaget's model. Several studies have attempted to determine the influence of specific educational training on accelerating or furthering the acquisition of cognitive operations. One such project by Kingsley and Hall (1967) demonstrated that young children could be taught conservation of weight and length through an experimental task program involving clay and measuring scales. Many similar studies have shown that mental operations can be facilitated by systematic instruction. A few studies such as that of Caruso and Resnick (1972) have focused on the task structure and teaching methods used in helping children to acquire such thinking skills as double classification.

Numerous early childhood education programs and commercial learning kits have been created from this model. One of the most extensively used is the Early Childhood Curriculum by Lavatelli, which includes instructional materials for teaching classification, number, seriation, etc. (Lavatelli, 1970). Most commercial school supply companies have now produced various kinds of classification and seriation kits similar to that of the Learning Readiness System.* A few districts, for example, the New York City Schools, have also contracted with research and development firms such as the Educational Testing Service for the development of teaching guides and materials based on Piaget's theory (*Let's Look,* 1968). Parts of these programs will be discussed in more detail in Chapter 6.

Taxonomy of cognitive objectives

The first major classification of educational objectives in the cognitive domain of learning was done by Benjamin Bloom (1956) and his associates. This classification system consists of six major levels of cognitive functioning, beginning with *knowledge* and proceeding hierarchically through *comprehension, application, analysis, synthesis,* and *evaluation.* Each of the six major cognitive levels can be conceptualized as a complex structure of thinking skills and tasks.

Handbook I of the taxonomy presents a classification of cognitive objectives with detailed examples of how they might be measured through a variety of objective multiple choice test items. Most of the test items presented in the handbook relate to secondary school subject matter. However, the same ap-

---

*2500 Crawford, Evanston, Ill.

proach has now been adapted for measuring cognitive skills in elementary and special education children.

The six major cognitive skills are behaviorally defined by their component subtasks. Thus knowledge is comprised of "specific facts," "ways and means" of organizing knowledge (such as the *classification* of animals, foods, and other natural things), and universal "principles or theories" of knowledge. Each of these levels and its subcategories are presented below. It should be noted that the third level, application, has no subcategory, since application is a single unitary skill involved in all problem-solving situations. The highest order cognitive skill is evaluation, which utilizes all prior skills and criteria in decision making.

The most widely accepted use of this taxonomy has been as a model for curriculum planning. Many schools have organized instructional units to teach children how to acquire knowledge and comprehension skills, to apply them in projects, and then to analyze, synthesize, and evaluate the intellectual product (project, paper, experiment, etc.) itself. The taxonomy has been widely used as a guide for teaching gifted children. It has also been incorporated as a structural model in many science programs. More recently, these cognitive skills are being used as criterion references for evaluating the thinking processes of learning–handicapped children and in the planning of prescriptive remediation of cognitive deficiencies.

COGNITIVE TAXONOMY

1.0 Knowledge

1.1 Specifics
    1.11 Terminology
    1.12 Specific facts
1.2 Ways and means
    1.21 Conventions
    1.22 Trends and sequences
    1.23 Classifications and categories
    1.24 Criteria
    1.25 Methodology
1.3 Universals and abstractions
    1.31 Principles and generalizations
    1.32 Theories and structures

2.0 Comprehension

2.10 Translation
2.20 Interpretation
2.30 Extrapolation

3.0 Application

4.0 Analysis

4.10 Elements
4.20 Relationships
4.30 Organizational principles

5.0 Synthesis

5.10 Production of unique communications
5.20 Production of a plan of operations
5.30 Deriving abstract relations

6.0 Evaluation

6.10 From internal evidence
6.20 From external criteria

For example, diagnostic-prescriptive specialists using the taxonomy for initial evaluation purposes may decide that some pupils lack specific skills in being able to synthesize selected information or data. This may lead to a directive instructional unit providing varied practice in synthesizing knowledge, which may include such low-level activities as working with simple puzzles to such higher level processes as verbal synthesis of abstract relationships.

Most science kits and programs provide training in these cognitive skills. So do artistic projects of all kinds. Many commercial games and programs such as Attribute Games and Problems, Wff'n Proof, Husker Du, and Master Mind are widely used in cognitive therapy and prescriptive special education. Most teachers, however, tend to use a variety of educational materials (integrated with their own approach to developing these skills) to meet the unique needs of their pupils.

Basic learning abilities model

The basic learning abilities model is a curricular criterion model derived from an empirical analysis of the basic skills and abilities required in the process of school learning. Fifty-three basic learning abilities are classified into six developmental levels (Valett, 1969). These levels are labeled gross motor, sensory-motor, perceptual-motor (including auditory, visual, and visual-motor skills), language, conceptual, and social skills.

Each of the 53 subskills and abilities has been operationally defined for purposes of pupil evaluation, task analysis, and subsequent prescriptive programming. Since it is a broad developmental task model, it includes much more than the traditional cognitive skills. Because some of the most important motor, sensory, and perceptual components of higher order cognitive processes have been described in some detail, this model is widely used among special educators and developmental teachers.

The six major levels and subskills are outlined on p. 37. A single descriptive explanation or criterion reference is provided in parentheses for illustrative purposes. An accompanying inventory and pupil workbook present numerous developmental learning tasks that can be used as a taxonomic source of prescriptive objectives (Valett, 1968).

The most important cognitive abilities are classified on level 3 (perceptual-motor skills), level 4 (language development), and level 5 (conceptual skills). For example, auditory sequencing and visual memory are both considered to be perceptual-motor skills that are also fundamental parts of the cognitive process that we commonly refer to as reading. Obviously, verbal fluency, writing, and spelling are all advanced cognitive language skills. Such conceptual skills as arithmetic reasoning, classification, and comprehension are illustrative of other higher order cognitive abilities.

This basic learning ability model is widely used as a structural curriculum guideline in developmental and special education and in other forms of clinical

BASIC LEARNING ABILITIES

Level 1: Gross motor development

- Rolling (controlled)
- Sitting (erect)
- Crawling (smoothly)
- Walking (coordinated)
- Running (course)
- Throwing (accurately)
- Jumping (obstacles)
- Skipping (alternately)
- Dancing (eurythmy)
- Self-identification (name awareness)
- Body localization (part location)
- Body abstraction (transfer, generalization)
- Muscular strength (sit-ups, leg-ups, bends)
- General physical health (significant history)

Level 2: Sensory-motor integration

- Balance and rhythm (games, dance)
- Body-spatial organization (mazes)
- Reaction-speed dexterity (motor accuracy)
- Tactile discrimination (object identification)
- Directionality (right-left, etc.)
- Laterality (hand-eye-foot)
- Time orientation (lapse and concept)

Level 3: Perceptual-motor skills
Auditory

- Acuity (functional hearing)
- Decoding (following directions)
- Vocal association (imitative response)
- Memory (retention)
- Sequencing (patterning)

Visual

- Acuity (Snellen chart)
- Coordination and pursuit (tracking)
- Form discrimination (association)
- Figure-ground (differentiation)
- Memory (visual recall)

Visual-motor

- Memory (designs)
- Fine muscle coordination (designs)
- Spatial-form manipulation (blocks)
- Speed of learning (coding)
- Integration (Draw-A-Man)

Level 4: Language development

- Vocabulary (word knowledge)
- Fluency and encoding (use and structure)
- Articulation (initial, medial, final)
- Word attack skills (phonic association)
- Reading comprehension (understanding)
- Writing (expression)
- Spelling (oral, written)

Level 5: Conceptual skills

- Number concepts (counting)
- Arithmetic processes ($+ - \times \div$)
- Arithmetic reasoning (problem solving)
- General information (fund of knowledge)
- Classification (relationships)
- Comprehension (commonsense reasoning)

Level 6: Social skills

- Social acceptance (friendship)
- Anticipatory response (foresight)
- Value judgments (ethical-moral sense)
- Social maturity (gross problem solving)

teaching. If initial evaluation discloses many task difficulties or skill deficiencies in one or more of the basic learning abilities, it can then be suggested that the child has a possible learning *disability*.

This model is correlated with a curriculum guide entitled *The Remediation of Learning Disabilities* (Valett, 1974); this guide also contains developmental-remedial prescriptive lessons, commercial programs, and instructional material resources helpful in teaching each of the basic learning disabilities.

Language (verbal concepts) model

Another developmental task criterion approach is to be seen in the specific language "verbal concepts" models. The underlying rationale for this kind of model is that all persons must develop skills required for understanding the basic verbal concepts that are fundamental to higher order abstract thinking. This kind of model is a very narrow one in that it only focuses on the operations inherent in selected expressive language concepts. It is criterion referenced to curricular expectations in the lower primary grades, where children are taught these words and ways of thinking.

The *Boehm Test of Basic Concepts** is an example of an evaluation device that has been based on this kind of model. The Boehm test specifies 50 verbal concepts classified into the four categories of space, quantity, time, and miscellaneous. It can be seen that these are commonly recognized developmental concept classifications derived from Piaget. However, these are the most important verbal concepts, which should be learned by the end of the first grade. Standardization studies of 2000 pupils show that there is almost 100% achievement of these concepts by the end of the second grade.

The chart on p. 39 lists the concepts by category. There are 23 space, 18 quantity, 4 time, and 5 miscellaneous verbal concepts. The words in italics represent a number of related verbal concepts (largely "opposite constructs") from other sources that I have also found to be of fundamental importance in early childhood education (Valett, 1970).

A model such as this is very useful for remedial or special education teachers. For primary school and older children who have obvious language problems, it is essential to evaluate the actual kinds and categories of conceptual difficulties they are experiencing. Every child in elementary school should be systematically taught those verbal concepts that they have not yet acquired. For those exceptional children with learning disabilities, an intensive experiential remedial program for developing constructs of space, quantity, time, number, etc. may be needed.

Several structural language programs are used in public schools. One of the more successful developmental-remedial ones has been designed by Engelmann (1969); this approach emphasizes the importance of teaching the rules involved

---

*The Psychological Corp., New York, 1967.

VERBAL CONCEPTS MODEL

Space (location, direction, orientation, dimension)

Top	Over	Below	*Up and down*
Through	Between	Right	*In and out*
Away from	Nearest	Forward	*On and off*
Next to	Corner	Above	*Front and back*
Inside	Behind	Separated	*High and low*
Middle	Row	Left	*Under and over*
Farthest	Center	In order	
Around	Side		

Quantity (including number)

Some (not many)	As many	*First and last*
Few	Not first or last	*Full and empty*
Widest	Medium-sized	*Big and little*
Most	Zero	*Tall and short*
Whole	Every	*Light and heavy*
Second	Pair	*All and none*
Several	Equal	*Whole and part*
Almost	Third	*More and less*
Half	Least	

Time

After	*Minute*	*Early and late*
Beginning	*Hour*	*Fast and slow*
Never	*Ending*	*Moving and still*
Always	*On time*	*Night and day*

Miscellaneous categories

Different	*Similar*
Other	*Loud and soft*
Alike	*Hot and cold*
Match	*Round and square*
Skip	*Light and dark*

---

in each thought process and of highly programmed techniques to teach the actual concepts the child has failed to learn. Other language development programs also use operational behavior approaches with learning-handicapped children.

PSYCHOMETRIC APPROACHES

The psychometric models of cognitive skills and abilities are based on the statistical analysis of test results obtained from large numbers of people. Statistical theory assumes that a normal distribution or spread of skills and abilities will appear in representative populations. For example, empirical evidence shows that on any ability we may select (running, balancing, drawing, reading, computing, etc.) almost all measures will show that some persons perform very well with few errors, some do very poorly, but most are in the middle range between these two extremes.

The statistical range of normality is between plus and minus one standard deviation from the mean score; 68% of the population measured scores in this range. A standard score indicating that a person's performance falls more than one standard deviation below the mean reflects achievement in the lowest 16% of the population. Obviously, such low scores on tests of cognitive abilities should be cause for concern and demands that we examine the exact kinds of errors made to determine if remedial education is necessary to improve the child's performance.

Literally hundreds of standardized tests have been developed to measure all kinds of skills and abilities. Most tests of cognitive skills and abilities are based on some kind of model that lends itself to psychometric investigation, research, and validation. Five such models will be briefly considered here: Thurstone's primary mental abilities, Guilford's structure of intellect, the Wechsler constructs, a psycholinguistic model, and an academic skills model.

Thurstone's primary mental abilities

A number of years ago, Lewis Thurstone of the University of Chicago began a series of statistical experiments with psychological tests to determine their basic characteristics (Thurstone, 1938). Using factor analysis, he broke down the component parts of cognitive ability tests into several fundamental elements. Six major kinds (or factors) of cognitive skills were discovered; these were referred to as the primary mental abilities.

- VERBAL: Vocabulary and verbal comprehension (synonyms: "Still is to quiet as loud is to _____.")
- NUMBER: Basic arithmetic computations and problem solving ("What comes next in this series? 3, 5, 8, 12, 17, _____.")
- SPATIAL: Visual form relationships as in symbols, designs, and abstract pictures ("Mark those like the circled one."):

- MEMORY: Rote memory for words, numbers, sentences, etc. ("Repeat after me: 2, a, d, 5, m, 1.")
- REASONING: Understanding rules and similarities between concepts ("In what way might stone be superior to wood in building homes and garages?")
- WORD FLUENCY: Rapidly thinking of and using appropriate words ("Quickly tell me as much as you can about this picture.")

Using this factor model of primary abilities, it is possible to design relatively pure evaluation and instructional materials. A test of primary mental abilities has been designed with different forms available for primary-, elementary-, and secondary-aged pupils*; this test can best be used as a criterion measure for teaching specific kinds of primary skills rather than as a valid measure of general cognitive abilities. Continued research has shown that there are many other kinds of basic or primary abilities in addition to the six described. However, this is a fairly simple model that lends itself quite easily to direct educational programming. Several developmental education programs have been created using this model; the most widely known and used is the Learning To Think Series† by Thelma Gwinn Thurstone.

Guilford's Structure of Intellect

Beginning with the findings of other psychometricians and factor analyists, J. P. Guilford of the University of Southern California devised a much more complex model of cognitive abilities. This model is a three-dimensional structure constructed from the interactional probabilities of component factors, or cells. The three structural dimensions are content, operations, and products (Guilford, 1967).

This model presents four different kinds of intellectual *content:* figural, symbolic, semantic, and behavioral. Almost any intellectual thinking skill or ability can be classified in one of these four content areas.

There are five major intellectual *operations* by which content is demonstrated in action. These are referred to as cognitive, memory, divergent productions, convergent productions, and evaluative operational abilities. Each of these operations are expressed through distinctive forms of content. For example, a cognitive figural operation would be one concerned with recognizing and understanding a design such as a blueprint or abstract painting.

There are also six distinctive *products* of intellectual thought: units, classes, relations, systems, transformations, and implications of thought. A class product of a cognitive figural operation would be to recognize a blueprint as belonging to a specific architectural classification. There are, of course, numerous kinds of intellectual products that we encounter in real life. Guilford has identified more than 120 highly unique Structure of Intellect (SOI) cells that represent specific skills and abilities that can result from the various combinations of intellectual content, operations, and products.

The outline on p. 42 attempts to define and illustrate these components of Guilford's model. In studying the outline it is usually helpful to think of some real product such as a window that might be conceptualized in different ways by each component. It is easy, for instance, to figurally visualize a distinctive kind of window that we have experienced by living with it as part of our room or home. We can also sketch this window (symbolically), describe it semantically with words, and even attempt to portray it behaviorally through charades, etc.

---

*Tests of Primary Mental Abilities, Science Research Associates, Chicago, 1953.
†Science Research Associates, Inc., Chicago, 1967.

STRUCTURE OF INTELLECT MODEL

Kinds of intellectual content and expression

- Figural: Visual (incomplete words, pictures) and auditory (morse code, scrambled digits)
- Symbolic: Visual (spelling) and auditory (sound-letter associations, phonics)
- Semantic: Vocabulary
- Behavioral: Nonverbal information involved in human interactions in which awareness of perceptions, feelings, moods, intentions, and actions of other persons and ourselves is important

Specific intellectual abilities and operations

- Cognitive: Awareness, recognition of information, comprehension and understanding
- Memory: Retention of information (visual memory, paired associates, span memory for digits and letters, music)
- Divergent production: Elaboration, fluency, flexibility, originality in use of information (for example, divergent production from stimulus figure)
- Convergent production: Determination of unique answers and specific inferences (for example, "What is the opposite of *hard?*")
- Evaluative abilities: Process of comparing a product of information with known information according to logical criteria (for example, selecting logical mathematical alternatives)

Intellectual products of intellectual ability and unique expression

- Units: Items or bits of information equivalent to the gestalt "figure-on-ground"
- Classes: Sets of items of information grouped by virtue of their common property (for example, cows, horses, dogs)
- Relations: Relations between units of information (for example, verbal analogies)
- Systems: Organized or structured aggregate of items of information, a complex of interacting parts (for example, rhythms, melodies)
- Transformation: Changes of various kinds of information in its attributes or use (for example, folded paper cutouts)
- Implications: The fact that one item of information leads naturally to another—expectancies, anticipations, predictions (for example, figural mazes and route problems requiring foresight)

Operationally, we can remember certain different kinds of windows we have encountered, and we can even produce a divergent sketch of any given form of window we care to focus on; when done, we can carefully evaluate it using a number of different criteria available to us. If we concentrate on the window frame or a certain material used in its construction, we are dealing with specific units. French and Italian windows are different classes of windows. We might even think about transforming some of our knowledge about window units and construction into the creation of some new design or system for building windows for homes of the future.

It is important to recognize that this is largely a theoretical model, not a factor-pure one. There is much overlap between the various components, and each part can only be understood relative to the other elements in each cell. Nevertheless, Guilford has presented us with a useful way to consider what "thinking" actually consists of and what its forms and final products may be. He has also shown that each of these skills or abilities can be evaluated and developed through special training and practice. It is possible, for example, to improve a student's ability to remember classes of architectural blueprints (figural memory for classes) through personal effort and the appropriate kinds of learning activities.

There have been many attempts to apply this model to educational evaluation, programming, and curriculum development. Meeker was the first person to analyze traditional intelligence test items, such as those from the Stanford-Binet, into the structure of intellect components and then to provide lessons and worksheets for use in remedying deficits.* Since then, similar programs have been created and experimented with in several school districts, for example, Glendora, California.† The model has also been used in the development of large-scale commercial curriculum programs; the most notable and successful example is the Thinking Skills Language Program.‡

Wechsler constructs

While working as a clinical psychologist in a hospital setting, Wechsler recognized the need for a test that would evaluate an individual's performance skills and abilities as well as verbal ones. Accordingly, Wechsler proceeded to accumulate what he considered to be the most important cognitive skills and abilities. Some of these were classified as being primarily verbal tests such as vocabulary, general knowledge and information, and oral arithmetic problem solving. Others were classified as performance tests and included tasks like manipulating small wooden blocks, arranging picture puzzle sequences, and drawing designs.

Over the years, several forms of this test have been devised for use with adults, schoolchildren, and preschool youngsters. Most forms of the test have used the original test constructs such as vocabulary, arithmetic, and block design. which have been arranged in subtests. For example, the Wechsler Intelligence Scale for Children—Revised (WISC-R) is widely used with children to help in the diagnosis of learning disabilities. (A WISC-R profile and subtest items for one student are illustrated and discussed in Chapter 7.) The Wechsler constructs are organized into the following 12 subtests on the WISC-R:

---

*SOI Institute, 214 Main St., El Segundo, Calif. 90246
†Title VIB project No. 19 64576 3029-5-01, Glendora Unified School District, Glendora, Calif. 91740.
‡Innovative Science, Inc., 300 Broad St., Stamford, Conn. 06901.

Verbal tests

- INFORMATION: General knowledge from cultural experience and education
- SIMILARITIES: Understanding abstractions, relationships, logical associations
- ARITHMETIC: Computation, problem solving, attention to details
- VOCABULARY: Word knowledge, verbal fluency, expressive language
- COMPREHENSION: Commonsense reasoning, practical thinking, social awareness and judgment
- DIGIT SPAN: Attention, concentration, sequential rote memory

Performance tests

- PICTURE COMPLETION: Visual memory of common objects, alertness to details
- PICTURE ARRANGEMENT: Social interpretation, sequencing cartoon pictures, visual alertness
- BLOCK DESIGN: Visual-motor perception, reproducing abstract block designs from patterns
- OBJECT ASSEMBLY: Reproducing familiar picture puzzles from memory
- CODING: Speed, accuracy, and motor control in learning and drawing meaningless symbols
- MAZES: Visual-motor planning and control

The WISC-R was standardized on a representative population of more than 2200 children ranging from 6½ through 16½ years of age. On this test a score of 100 is average; scores of 85 and 115 correspond to one standard deviation below and above the mean, respectively. Each subtest has a mean scaled score of 10 and a standard deviation of 3 points. With these statistics it is possible to compare subtest strengths and weaknesses by contrasting standard scores. Accordingly, this test and its subtest scales are an important instrument for determining differences in acquired skills and abilities.

The clinical interpretation of the WISC may result in the selection of test-criterion task items useful in designing prescriptive remediation or developmental education programs. Many school and child psychologists and special educators use the WISC profiles in this way and devise psychoeducational prescriptions as recommended by Glasser and Zimmerman (1967), Ferinden and Jacobson (1969), and others (*Psychoeducational Interpretation*, 1975).

It should be remembered that the Wechsler constructs are nothing more than pragmatic classifications of important cognitive skills. All of the listed skills and abilities are acquired ones and subject to development and change as a result of maturational growth, cultural experience, and specific educational training. The test constructs are limited and not all of equal importance; for example, the digit span (memory) and maze (motor planning) subtests are not judged to be as important as the other subtest skills. Many other essential cognitive skills, such as figural relationships and classification, and reading processes are not measured. As a prescriptive teaching guide, however, the Wechsler constructs and test profiles are invaluable aids to special educators and cognitive therapists.

Psycholinguistic model

Starting with Osgood's principles concerning the communication process (Osgood, 1957), Samuel Kirk developed a psycholinguistic model that could be used as a basis for evaluating and differentiating various facets of cognitive ability. Kirk's intent was to devise a systematic diagnostic device that could be used to "delineate specific abilities and disabilities in children in order that remediation could be undertaken if needed" (Kirk, McCarthy, and Kirk, 1968, p. 5). The result was the Illinois Test of Psycholinguistic Abilities (ITPA), which has been revised several times.

The unique aspect of this model is that it centers on the essential components of the human language-communication process that is so important in elementary education. The model specifies 12 psycholinguistic functions, which consist of different kinds of acquired skills and abilities. These psycholinguistic functions are classified as being part of the receptive language process, the organizing process, or the expressive process; the 12 functions are also cross-referenced on "representational" (mediational-symbolic), and "automatic" (habitual-conditioned) levels of response. The model has been sharply criticized as being obtuse, and many factor analysis studies have shown that there is considerable overlap between the 12 functions.

The ITPA was standardized on a restricted sample of children, and normative data are available for age groups from 2 years 4 months through 10 years 3 months. For each of the 12 subtests the mean performance is equal to a score of 36 with a standard deviation of 6 points. A profile of functional abilities can be constructed using scaled scores. By examining the low subtests, special educators can teach those psycholinguistic skills on a prescriptive basis; posttest scaled scores usually rise following appropriate remediation. Subtest performance can also be totaled to give a psycholinguistic age, which has some developmental comparison value. The 12 subtests are outlined on p. 46 with brief examples.

From an examination of the subtests we can see that many of these skills and abilities are nearly identical to constructs found in other models. For instance, auditory association tasks correspond to similarities and analogies on the Binet and WISC tests, and auditory sequential memory is almost the same as the Binet and WISC digit span tests; in other words, these are merely new labels for old cognitive abilities. However, the ITPA model does put many of the old constructs in a newer developmental-remedial perspective. Also, the psycholinguistic functions of grammatic closure, verbal expression, auditory closure, and sound blending are unique to the ITPA and present us with another important dimension of cognitive development that is closely associated with many school learning tasks.

Most diagnostic-prescriptive educators and psychologists have found the ITPA model to be a useful one as a supplemental guide for curriculum planning.

Subtest	Content	Example
Auditory reception	Vocabulary meaning and comprehension	S responds yes or no to questions: "Do cats bark?"
Visual reception	Visual memory and generalization	S finds similar objects in a picture (electric fan—tree, leaf, hand fan, toy)
Visual sequential memory	Memory for design chips presented in 5 seconds	╱ □ ○ ♋ o|o
Auditory association	Verbal completion of sentences	Grass is green: Sugar is _____ .
Auditory sequential memory	Verbal sequencing of digits	2, 7, 3; 3, 4, 7, 3; 1, 6, 2, 9, 5
Visual association	"Common" picture association and comprehension	What goes with this? (matches—pen, hat, cigarette, magnifying glass)
Visual closure	Figure-ground differentiation of hidden pictures	Find all the fish you can in this picture.
Verbal expression	S responds to concrete objects with descriptive vocabulary	Tell me all you can about this (block, etc.).
Grammatic closure	Grammatical responses to pictures	Here is a dress. Here are two _____ .
Manual expression	S demonstrates through gesture the use of pictured objects	Hammer, guitar, etc.
Auditory closure	S listens to incompletely pronounced words by E and then repeats them in complete form	airpl/ (airplane)
Sound blending	S listens to words divided into successive sounds and responds by blending them together	Listen: d–og? What word is that?

Most often, remedial programs are developed according to the child's test profile considered in the context of other available information. A few commercial programs have been created on this model and are currently in fairly wide use. The MWM Program for Developing Language Abilities* is one that presents highly sequenced activities for developing psycholinguistic abilities that are considered essential to academic achievement. Another similar curriculum, but devised for preschool and kindergarten children, is the GOAL Language Development Program,† which includes numerous ITPA task cards and developmental activities.

Academic skills model

Perhaps the most pragmatic model of cognitive abilities is an academic skills achievement model. This kind of model assumes that school curricula are designed to gradually and systematically increase a student's competency in dealing with certain academic skills and objectives. Examining a large number of these academic learning tasks in the cognitive domain make it possible to determine and appropriately order and classify the developmental-sequential skills. Of course, these skills and abilities will vary by age, grade, or other forms of developmental placement in the school system. If the most important cognitive skills at each developmental level are specified, they can be operationally defined, measured, categorized, and then used as a basis for curriculum evaluation, improvement, and remedial instruction.

Well-designed standardized school achievement tests are usually constructed on this sort of rationale and then validated in part through curriculum-referenced content items. The Comprehensive Tests of Basic Skills (CTBS) provide a good example of an instrument that was built on this kind of rationale and then designed to tap the five following areas (which are similar to those found in Bloom's taxonomy of the cognitive domain) (*CTBS Level 1,* 1974, p. 1):

- RECOGNITION: Ability to recognize or recall information
- TRANSLATION: Ability to translate or convert concepts from one kind of language (verbal or symbolic) to another
- INTERPRETATION: Ability to comprehend concepts and their interrelationships
- APPLICATION: Ability to apply techniques, including performing fundamental operations
- ANALYSIS: Ability to extend interpretation beyond stated information

To evaluate these abilities, several different test forms were designed at each developmental level. Two examples are presented below. The CTBS level A measures important cognitive skills that should be learned during kindergarten and the initial part of first grade. These skills are as follows:

---

*Minskoff, E., Wiseman, J., and Minskoff, J. The MWM Program for Developing Language Abilities, Educational Performance Associates, Ridgefield, N.J., 1972.

†Karnes, M. GOAL Language Development Program, Milton Bradley Co., Chicago, 1972.

- LETTER FORMS: Matching capital letters with the same lowercase letters
- LETTER NAMES: Selecting letters named aloud by the teacher from four choices
- LISTENING FOR INFORMATION: Matching pictures with vocabulary and verbal concepts
- LETTER SOUNDS: Identification of consonant and long and short vowel sounds
- VISUAL DISCRIMINATION: Choosing words or shapes that match a visual stimulus
- SOUND MATCHING: Identifying whether words read aloud are the same or different
- LANGUAGE: Identifying whether sentences read aloud by teacher are correctly or incorrectly phrased
- MATHEMATICS: Numeration, basic foundations of measurement, time, and money

It can be seen that these are all critical cognitive functions that are essential for success in later learning. Each form of the test continues and extends this same pragmatic approach. The CTBS Level 1 form covers the basic skills to be acquired during the middle elementary grades (middle of second through fourth grade) and begins to organize them into the following traditional subject content areas:

- READING VOCABULARY: Choosing synonyms for underlined words
- READING COMPREHENSION: Interpreting reading passages
- SPELLING: Recognizing misspellings
- LANGUAGE MECHANICS: Punctuation and capitalization skills
- LANGUAGE EXPRESSION: English usage, syntax, diction, organization
- MATHEMATICS COMPUTATION: Addition, subtraction, multiplication, division
- MATHEMATICS CONCEPTS AND APPLICATIONS: Recognizing concepts and problem solving
- REFERENCE SKILLS: Dictionary use, parts of books, using library reference cards
- SCIENCE: Classification, evaluation of data, prediction of outcomes or trends, hypothesis formulation
- SOCIAL STUDIES: Social, political, economic, historical analysis, problem solving

More than 130,000 students in kindergarten through grade 12 were included in the CTBS standardization sample, which was representative of the national population. Scores are reported in percentiles, stanines (a standard score on a scale from 1 to 9; 9 is the highest level, representing the top 4%, and scores between 4 and 6 include the middle 54%), and grade equivalents. Through individual and group test results analysis, it can be decided whether or not students have achieved curricular cognitive objectives and, if not, "whether more training is needed in a particular skill or skills area" (*CTBS Test,* 1974, p. 93).

Academic skills models of cognitive abilities are the most widely used ones in public education. They are generally appropriate for teaching the majority of students in the public school population. These models are inadequate by themselves for use with learning-handicapped and cognitively disabled children because they fail to specify the more fundamental developmental cognitive skills that are prerequisites to higher order abstractions required in academic functioning. But these academic content models, test constructs, classifications, and test items can and should be used by all special educators who are concerned with closely relating or integrating diagnostic-prescriptive instruction with the actual cognitive task demands of the normal school curriculum.

SYNTHESIS

In this chapter we have considered a number of different models of cognitive skills and abilities and how they have been used in prescriptive education and curriculum development. Although it is not possible or desirable to fully synthesize or integrate these models into a single system, it can be seen that there is considerable overlap of component skills.

It is helpful, however, to recognize that cognitive skills can be ordered and classified according to developmental stage sequences and objectives. Such an organization is presented on p. 50. This organizational schema can be conceived of as an instructional taxonomy of major cognitive skills. Most of the skills and abilities in the models discussed have been placed here. Adaptations have been made in some aspects of the models for purposes of integration. The cognitive objectives column, for instance, is largely from Bloom (1956), but it has been modified to incorporate some aspects of Guilford's model. The cognitive objectives column lists parallel skills arranged according to Piaget's developmental stages.

All of the cognitive skills and abilities listed here have instructional correlates and programs. For example, most of the sensory-motor adaptive skills are taught through infant stimulation and clinical home-training programs. Most of the preoperational intuitional skills are taught and acquired through informal educational programs in the home, preschool, and kindergarten. The concrete manipulative skills form the content of most elementary school curricula, and this chapter has already mentioned several instructional programs in wide use. Formal operational skills are largely developed and taught in the upper elementary and secondary grades. Chapter 6 describes some special instructional programs and curricula being used to teach these advanced cognitive operations.

It should also be remembered that these skills and abilities have been defined operationally on many different forms and instruments such as criterion-referenced and standardized tests. Accordingly, they can be evaluated and measured for purposes of individual prescriptive instruction and cognitive development.

Theoretical models such as these present us with a structural foundation for experimentation and program development. They are all admittedly incomplete and will undoubtedly be incorporated into, and superseded by, other models yet to be created. With all of their limitations, they have provided us with new and different ways of looking at, understanding, and influencing the development of thinking and cognitive processes in children—and with such a guide we can proceed with some confidence to meet the challenging educational tasks before us.

COGNITIVE SKILLS INSTRUCTIONAL TAXONOMY

Cognitive objectives	Sensory-motor adaptations (birth to 2 years)	Preoperational intuitions (2 to 7 years)	Concrete manipulations (7 to 11 years)	Formal reversible operations (11 years and older)
Knowledge: Conditioned responses, terms, facts, conventions, methods, classes and relations	Reflexive assimilations, visual-motor accommodations, schematic organizations and co-ordination	Perceptual-representative judgment, irreversibility, intuitional abstractions	Receptive vocabulary, general information, number concepts	
Comprehension: Elements, rules, translation, interpretation, extrapolation	Experimental discovery	Single property classification, correspondence of sets, visual generalizations, simple seriation	Seriation of pictures and patterns, quantitative seriation, conservation of quantity and space, arithmetic computation, multiple classification, reading vocabulary, general comprehension	Time, reversibility
Application: Semantic, figural, symbolic, behavioral	Invention	Manual expression, perceptual-motor coordination, visual-motor memory	Mathematical reasoning, language mechanics, expressive vocabulary	Reality problem solving, creative divergency, social competency
Analysis: Units, relationships, organizational principles	Listening and attending, visual organization and closure		Auditory-vocal sequential memory, word attack skills, spelling, reference skills	Propositional thinking
Synthesis: Integration, planning, originality, theorizing	Motor planning, visual-motor integration	visual-motor patterns,	Sensory integration, auditory vocal closure, reading comprehension, similarities	Figural-symbolic abstractions and relationships
Evaluation: Self-criticism, external validation, implications	Self-awareness		Analogies, social interpretation, self-correction	Hypothetical-deductive reasoning, self-actualization

DISCUSSION QUESTIONS AND ACTIVITIES

1. What is the major difference between a "developmental task taxonomy" and the "psychometric approach"?
2. At approximately what age is a child expected to be able to think in terms of reversibility of cognitive operations?
3. Give an example of how and when reversibility might be taught to a learning-handicapped person.
4. Write a behavioral objective with minimal performance standards for a pupil who is experiencing great difficulty in the analysis of knowledge and acquired information.
5. Give an example of how a child might be taught to evaluate his or her own performance by comparison with some widely accepted external criterion.
6. How might sensory-motor dysfunction (such as directionality and time orientation disabilities) interfere with higher cognitive operations?
7. Write a specific task that would help evaluate a pupil's language development of specific word attack skills.
8. Design a picture or poster for teaching the verbal concept similar (but not alike). What kinds of perceptual-motor experiences could be used with children to teach this concept?
9. Suggest some other kinds of primary mental abilities that appear to be missing in Thurstone's model.
10. One unique aspect of Guilford's structure of intellect model is that it recognizes a behavioral component in intellectual expression. Of what importance is this for educational curriculum development?
11. How might you proceed to develop semantic divergent thinking in an elementary schoolchild?
12. Compare the Wechsler constructs with Piaget's developmental stage model. What cognitive abilities and skills are included in both models? How do they differ?
13. How might you incorporate phonics training as part of an ITPA prescriptive program?
14. Select a standardized achievement test that you think would be an appropriate one for use with a learning-handicapped pupil. Administer and score the test, and then devise three prescriptive objectives based on actual skill deficits indicated by the test results.
15. How might the cognitive skills instructional taxonomy best be used in prescriptive education?

Photo by Michael Hayman, Image, Inc., Nashville, Tennessee.

CHAPTER 4

Sensory and perceptual components of reading

Over the past 10 years there has been a rapid growth in programs for children with learning disabilities. There is every indication that this growth will continue in the foreseeable future. The purpose, of course, has been to provide more appropriate education for learning-disabled children so that their achievement will improve and they will be able to actualize their unique human potential. Reading performance and achievement have always been important skills of concern to educators. Undoubtedly, most special educators have devoted much of their time and effort to the amelioration of specific language problems, including such disabilities as aphasia, dysphasia, alexia, and dyslexia.

It is important to have some rationale for approaching such problems and for designing and implementing remedial instruction and strategies. A controversy exists, and will certainly continue to exist for some time to come, as to the efficacy of sensory and perceptual-motor training for persons with severe reading problems. Traditionalists insist that if we define reading as attributing meaning to written language through a decoding process, then remedial instruction should focus directly on the process itself through such means as concentrated phonic instruction, drill, and practice. On the other extreme we find the radical sensory-perceptual theorists and practitioners such as Delacato and others who insist on emphasizing motor and perceptual training activities as the essential elements in a remedial reading program. In my opinion and experience, both extremes are untenable positions; the in-between, or moderate, position is essentially a more rational and defensible "developmental" one.

DEVELOPMENTAL THEORY AND RESEARCH

There is considerable clinical and experimental evidence to support developmental theory and its approach to the remediation of reading problems and related learning disabilities. Although the evidence is not incontrovertible, it is ample to convince one of the necessity of making a careful developmental assessment (including a task analysis of reading performance) of learning-handicapped children. Theoretically, Piaget (1952) has provided the basic structure for developmental evaluation and treatment with his finding that conceptual development in children is dependent on the gradual acquisition of such concrete operations as auditory and visual manipulation, verbal discrimination, and classification, as well as systematic ordering of experiences, and that all such operations are based on more fundamental sensory-motor and tactile experiences.

It also seems that the neuropsychological theory of Hebb (1949) is relevant here and has been substantiated by much research. Hebb posited that as the neural axons of brain cells repeatedly fire and excite related cells, some growth process or metabolic change occurs that increases the efficiency of the entire process. Through repeated practice and exercise, "synaptic knobs" develop and increase neurological integration and functioning. The work of Diamond et al. (1966) and Rosenweig (1966) with rat litters provides sound experimental support of Hebb's theory. In her classic study of 21 pairs of litter mate rats, Diamond found that an "environmental complexity and training" program consisting of exploratory activities with toys, climbing ladders, platforms, wheels, boxes, etc. produced a 6.4% (significant) increase in the depth of the visual cortex and a 14% greater glia/neural ratio in the 80-day experimental group. Kretch (1970) has summarized these studies with the comment that "by manipulating the environment of the young we can make a 'lame brain' with lighter cortex, shrunken brain cells, fewer glia cells, smaller blood vessels, and lower enzymatic activity levels—or we can create a more metabolically active and healthy brain." It should also be pointed out that these researchers have acknowledged the importance of language as the species-specific behavior of humans and the impossibility of duplicating their studies on human subjects; nevertheless, I concur with their conclusions that many of these findings can be generalized to human beings.

We can then argue that specific sensory-motor and perceptual training of reading-disabled children may result in improved neuropsychological functioning. If cortical functioning is "immature" (as suspected in developmental dysphasia) or impaired (as is implied by "traumatic alexia"), then highly prescriptive and intensive training should result in positive metabolic changes furthering sensory-perceptual integration and language behavior.

Recent research by Ingvar and Schwartz (1974) has disclosed that reading activities activate the blood flow pattern in the dominant hemisphere of the brain and that sensory-motor centers are also activated simultaneously. Clinical evidence with humans also supports the idea of psychoneurological correlates to reading. The work of Drew (1956) showed that such a thing as congenital word blindness does exist and that delayed development of the parietal lobes disturbs the gestalt recognition and integration of visual patterns, causing this condition. But Luria's extensive clinical research (1966), with brain-damaged and language-impaired patients is even more relevant. Luria found that difficulties in phonetic analysis and synthesis may result from lesions in the auditory cortex of the temporal region. He pointed out that the person who is unable to discriminate between simple and more complex auditory stimuli (such as grapheme-phoneme correspondence) or who cannot blend sounds and deal with phonetic values of words will unquestionably have difficulty using a phonic approach to reading. In such cases, it is obvious that compensatory visual and kinesthetic education must be provided along with whatever remedial auditory training is possible.

THE REEDUCATION OF BEVERLY

At this point, it would be best to illustrate some of these developmental principles through their application to an actual case. Beverly, an 8½-year-old normal girl, was an excellent student, independent and responsible in completing assignments and able to read above grade-level expectancy. She suffered brain damage in an automobile accident and consequently began having seizures and was comatose for several weeks.

When she regained consciousness, she could not speak and had regressed to infantile levels. Gradually, she left her bed and awkwardly began to explore her environment, suffering many falls and bruises as she did so. Then speech therapy was initiated for her aphasia, and very slowly her language reappeared developmentally. After a few months she was discharged from the hospital but obviously was unable to return to a school of any kind, as her functional abilities were approximately at the 3-year level. It was then that she began individual psychoeducational therapy with the goal of getting her back into school as soon as possible.

Of course, Beverly could not read. She had "lost" this ability and was truly alexic. However, the fact that she had already regained much of her speech was an encouraging sign. Therefore a therapy plan was designed in accord with developmental theory. It was assumed that her speech and language centers were permanently damaged but that with special training she could regain much of her functioning, including her ability to read. It was also assumed that the training should follow normal developmental progressions with emphasis on the integration of compensatory visual and kinesthetic abilities with her residual auditory processing skills. More than 60 individual prescriptive teaching sessions (each about 45 minutes long) plus 22 small group sessions were held over a 6-month period. The details of this case have been presented elsewhere (Valett, 1974a), but some of the treatment procedures are particularly relevant to this discussion.

As any good practitioner knows, it would have been futile to begin formal reading instruction with Beverly. Her reading skills were checked and found to be on a preschool level, with no letter or sound recognition and no sight vocabulary. Both visual and auditory memory were significantly deficient, and she had great difficulty in listening and following even the simplest directions. Her visual-motor skills were characterized by crude drawings of a circle and scribblings. Similarly, her sensory-motor abilities were such that she had little balance or gross motor coordination and was even unable to place large wooden blocks sequentially on the table without dropping them on the floor.

Prescriptive training began with reinforcement of her listening and attention skills; then it proceeded through gross motor and sensory-motor integration training, with almost everything taught kinesthetically. Gradually, auditory discrimination of sounds and auditory association tasks were introduced. Then these were combined with visual discrimination, sequencing, and memory instruction. Finally grapheme-phoneme associations were taught using tactile-kinesthetic materials, and then she relearned a few sight words. At this time, she was placed on limited-day attendance in a special education class and reintroduced to a structured reading program. Supplemental prescriptive teaching was continued with supportive home training by the parents. Step by step, Beverly recovered many of her skills and developed some new ones. Over a 2-year period, she moved along quite rapidly to the point that supplemental aid was discontinued. She began attending her special education program full-time and is now reading again, although there is no indication she will ever be able to function in accord with her former potential.

This is not an atypical description of the application of developmental theory and its remedial applications. Those persons who have severe reading problems (whether or not they are alexic or dyslexic) and who are functioning significantly below their known potential should be provided with specific sensory-perceptual assessment and training. Let us now consider what both clinical and experimental research have to say about the relevance of this training.

RESEARCH ON RELEVANT SKILLS

This section will briefly describe a few selected studies that show the importance of specific sensory-perceptual training for reading-handicapped pupils. No attempt is made here to present conflicting or nonsupportive studies, as they abound in the literature and this is not intended to be a complete or unbiased review of the research. These are also numerous ways of labeling or classifying the prerequisite skills and abilities for reading, and the one that follows is purely arbitrary but in accord with developmental theory.

Listening and attending

Most teachers would concur that listening and attending to task are essential prerequisites to reading. Poor readers have long been described as inattentive and having poor attitudes and little interest or motivation for reading. One way to approach this problem is with behavior modification programs with positive token and social reinforcement systems. Another way is to provide specific sensory-motor inhibition, relaxation, and attention-training programs.

One such model program was experimented with by McCormick and Poetker (1968). Forty-two underachieving first grade pupils were assigned to matched groups. The experimental training group met for 45-minute sessions, twice a week, for 7 weeks. Although some motor activities were provided, the program emphasized Luria attention-training tasks such as listening, visualizing, verbalizing, and following self-directions in exploring the immediate environment. Results showed a significant difference on the Lee-Clark Reading Tests in favor of the experimental training group.

Krippner (1966) conducted a 5-week summer reading clinic for 49 children who received 10 hours of remediation each week. Hypnosis and positive auto-suggestion techniques were used to decrease tension, increase motivation, develop concentration and attention, and foster interest in reading. Positive suggestions were also used to facilitate revisualization and reauditorization of graphic and spoken symbols. Posttest gains on the California Reading Tests disclosed a significant gain of more than 5 months for the pupils treated with hypnosis.

Sensory-motor stimulation was combined with hypnosis in an experiment by Jampolsky (1970) to aid children making reversals. This was an intensive clinical study, but control subjects were also included. Ten intensive treatment periods of positive suggestion, relaxation training, and concomitant vibratory, touch, and muscle memory exercises ("drawing" on the back and forehead, finger tracing in stencils, etc.) completely eliminated reversals in the experimental group.

These and other studies seem to show that listening and attending skills can be significantly improved. Certainly such programs should be given careful consideration as the initial phase of a developmental program for children with reading and associated language problems.

Kinesthetic-tactile training

After many years of clinical practice and research, Fernald (1943) reported that a larger percentage of extreme reading disability cases are due to the use of methods that omit or actually suppress kinesthetic factors such as motor adjustments of lip, throat, and hand movements. Fernald thought that when these vital learning mechanisms are inhibited, thwarted, or undeveloped, the result is inappropriate visual and auditory perceptions such as discriminatory problems, inversions, reversals, and other "confusions" in reading and writing.

Some experimental studies have combined tactile-kinesthetic training with other sensory-motor activities such as vestibular and reflex training and postural and visual-motor puzzle exercises. In one of the many studies in this field done by Ayres (1972), 148 learning-disabled children were separated into 40 experimental and control groups. Training was provided for 25 to 40 minutes per day, 5 days per week, for about 6 months. The treatment program was individually prescribed according to pupil needs and produced significant increases on the Wide Range and Slosson Reading Tests.

A classic clinical study using Fernald kinesthetic techniques to teach a child with Down's syndrome was reported by Seagoe (1965). The child began receiving prescriptive education at 7 years of age and slowly began to learn to read and write. At age 11 he began to keep a personal diary, and a follow-up evaluation when he was 43 years old showed a reading performance at the seventh grade level. Could it be that intensive prescriptive kinesthetic training such as Seagoe described produces a psychoneurological change that increases the ability to process and integrate the auditory-visual stimuli inherent in reading?

Auditory processing

Much research has been done on the auditory correlates to reading. Although much of it remains controversial, some data support the idea that specific auditory training for poor readers is important, and the data do have direct educational implications.

For example, the ability to hear a particular sound pattern such as a series of taps on a table (hand claps, drum beats, etc.) and then to repeat them correctly and visually match them with stimulus cards (tap-tap/tap-tap/tap-tap-tap = ++ ++ +++) is highly related to reading performance in the primary grades, but the importance declines by fourth grade (Birch and Belmont, 1965). However, Corkin (1974) established that inferior readers at all ages studied had significant serial-ordering deficits; these deficits should be remedied as much as possible.

Recently Hammill and Larsen (1974) reviewed 33 statistical studies containing 292 separate coefficients of the relationship of auditory discrimination, memory, blending, and auditory-visual integration to reading. Although most of their findings failed to support the supposition of these significant correlates, several were discovered. For example, the coefficient for sound blending was only 0.31 for grades 1 through 3 but was much more significant (0.47) for grades 7 through 12. This is what might be expected because of the multisyllabic words and advanced reading materials in the higher grades. Interestingly, the correlation of auditory-visual integration skills with word recognition was 0.24 and with reading comprehension was 0.37. The coefficient for correlation of auditory memory skills with word recognition was only 0.22. Phonemic auditory discrimination skills had correlation coefficients of 0.34 for word recognition and 0.26 for reading comprehension.

These findings generally confirm Chall's idea of the importance of auditory association and blending. Chall (1967) reported on a survey of 17 major studies on predictive reading abilities and established that, in primary grade children, knowing the sound values of the letters and being able to hear similarities and differences in the spoken words are a much more reliable indicator of future reading achievement than any other predictive measures. The Hammill and Larsen study gave further support to this; they found that on the Roswell-Chall Auditory Blending Test an overall correlation of 0.47 quite significantly indicated that auditory blending in first grade foretold reading performance in third grade.

My interpretation of these and other studies is in accord with the conclusions of Johnson and Myklebust (1967), who specified the following as the critical auditory skills related to reading.

- Auditory discrimination of letter sounds
- Auditory discrimination of initial and final sounds
- Auditory memory of patterns, sequences, and words
- Blending letter sounds into words
- Remembering details of oral directions and stories and the central ideas involved

Accordingly, I have attempted to delineate many developmental and remedial auditory training activities in these areas, together with prescriptive examples (Valett, 1974b). Such training should be made a fundamental part of any special education program for pupils with reading disabilities.

Visual perception

The critical visual skills and abilities related to reading are visual discrimination and analysis, visual memory, visual closure, visual coordination, visual integration, and comprehension. Both experimental and clinical research confirm the importance of prescriptive education in these areas for poor readers.

In 1922 Gates reported research on visual perceptual analysis and concluded that the "sight word" method of teaching reading resulted in "inappropriate methods of observing words"; this difficulty occurred among reading-disabled pupils, including those of superior intelligence (with no known organic or physical defects that could be discovered) who were also anxious to learn. The implication was that remedial training in visual analysis and discrimination of word parts was essential. Subsequent research has continued to support this position.

One of the most recent and extensive statistical studies on these skills if that of Satz and Friel (1974). A second year follow-up study of 497 white kindergarten children was made to determine the ability of selected neurological tests to predict reading performance for high-risk and low-risk children. A total of 22 variables were involved in the study; the three most discriminate skills were finger localization, recognition-discrimination, and alphabet recitation, which can be combined as a single sensory–perceptual–motor–mnemonic predictive factor. It was concluded that the high correlation of these visual-discriminative processes to later reading achievement illustrated the importance of early acquisition of such skills.

The earlier work of Kass (1962) is also relevant here. Using the ITPA she found that children with reading disabilities differed significantly from normal readers; they had greater difficulties in reproducing visual symbols, predicting a whole from a part, manually representing visual images from memory, and visually comparing detailed figures rapidly and accurately. The importance of accurate visual discrimination of symbolic material is further confirmed by the research reports of Groff (1974) and his conclusions that visual discrimination and memory training for letters and specific letter clusters are essential cues for word recognition.

Visual closure—the ability to rapidly perceive varied visual stimuli and to meaningfully organize them—was found to be the most significant factor correlating with reading ability as reported in studies by Goins (1958). Similarly, the clinical neurological studies of Goldstein (1948) clearly demonstrated that damage to the occipital lobe or other parts of the brain can cause varied and complex visual disorders interfering with reading, since primary reading disturbances are related to the analysis and synthesis of visual stimuli. Visual coordination, tracking, and length of the visual perception span are also involved here; this idea is supported by such early research as that of Gray (1922). These studies showed that older and better readers have fewer eye movement pauses per line, shorter pauses, and fewer regressive movements and that both reading rate and comprehension are positively correlated with the length of the span of perception.

From these and other studies it is possible to arrive at some logical conclusions regarding teaching procedures. If, as Luria (1966) has pointed out, the visual cortex is damaged (as in cases of literal alexia) and the integrated perception of graphemes and the visual differentiation of those signs with cue value is so disrupted that either the letters lose their meanings altogether or their identification becomes highly unstable, *the cue value needs to be increased.* This can be done through the use of kinesthetic color-coded letter cards, reading skills, and markers, as well as numerous other forms of multisensory training. These techniques have long been described in the literature in the detailed teaching reports of such early clinicians as Itard (1894/1962). It behooves us to remember that Itard wrote that he began to work with the wild boy Victor by attempting to develop his senses of sight and touch. After some months of training, Victor could read and write a series of words passably well; he then learned to analyze the words, mentally comparing all of the letters in the words. From that point, Itard succeeded in making Victor distinguish objects and letters by touch and *"develop the symbols of thought."*

Auditory and visual integration

Reading involves the simultaneous perception of abstract visual symbols and their auditory associations, which are immediately integrated meaningfully with one's experience. Although initial remedial programs can and do separate the auditory and visual processes, they are soon brought together for higher level training. Most of the studies referred to in this chapter have both visual and auditory components, although one skill may have been emphasized for research purposes. A number of studies have been done, however, that deliberately attempt to determine the value of combined or integrative forms of remedial treatment.

After a 10-year period of intensive study of language disorders, Orton (1937,

p. 145) concluded that the one common factor in cases of specific language disability was the difficulty on the part of pupils in "rebuilding the order of presentation, sequences of letters, of sounds, or of units of movement." This problem of perceptual integration has been further substantiated by such researchers as Katz and Deutsch (1963). They established that when a number of visual, auditory, memory, and reaction time tests were given to first, third, and fifth grade children, the poor readers had greater difficulty in differentiating between qualitatively different visual *and* auditory stimuli; as they grew older, however, poor readers faced with tasks of increasing complexity did least well with auditory stimuli.

On the other hand, Myklebust's cumulative research (1968) on visual dyslexia established the unique sensory and perceptual characteristics for this syndrome:

- Confusion of similar words and letters
- Frequent letter reversals and inversions
- Difficulty in following and retaining visual sequences
- Visual memory problems
- Problems with visual analysis and integration
- Tendency to avoid games requiring visual integration

Although most poor readers cannot be said to be either auditory or visual dyslexics, there is no doubt as to the importance of these integrative processes in higher level language functioning.

An example of exemplary research in this area is the study of Halliwell and Solan (1972) with 105 first graders with potential reading problems. One experimental group received integrative perceptual training in 45-minute sessions, twice a week, for 7 months *plus* regular reading instruction. The training consisted of activities designed to improve the following specific skills: visual memory, auditory discrimination, form constancy, visual-motor integration, listening, visual tracking, and following tactual-auditory commands. A second experimental group received regular reading plus special traditional remedial reading instruction; a control group was provided with the regular reading program. Significant differences in favor of the group who received experimental training were found on the reading comprehension subtest of the Metropolitan Achievement Test.

The implications of all this are fairly clear. A developmental remedial prescription should provide highly specific sensory and perceptual training, which should gradually become more integrative and symbolic as the program proceeds. The systematic organization of such a transitional program and instructional materials* for young children has shown the techniques to be quite successful

---

*Valett, R., and Valett, S. The Valett Perceptual-Motor Transitions to Reading Program, Academic Therapy Publications, San Rafael, Calif., 1974.

for use with individual children with reading disorders. The principles of this kind of prescriptive instruction, which are now fairly well established by both research and practice, are summarized in the following section.

DEVELOPMENTAL REMEDIAL READING

The basic prerequisite to reading is general language development and experience. Briefly summarized, the developmental steps in the remedial reading process are as follows:

1. EXPRESSIVE LANGUAGE: Through gross motor and sensory stimulation, the child is taught to babble, to imitate, to act out and express his feelings, to label, to manipulate, and to attempt to describe his environment orally.
2. SERIAL LANGUAGE: The child is taught to organize and seriate his language to accurately describe his experiences. If necessary, direct baseline language samples are tape recorded, appropriate developmental word and sentence targets are selected, and they are systematically introduced, taught, and reinforced.
3. IMMEDIATE EXPERIENCE: The pupil is provided with immediate concrete experiences or engaged to discuss his previous experiential interests, concerns, etc. He is helped to select words he would like to learn to read and use.
4. VOCABULARY DEVELOPMENT: Multisensory tactile-kinesthetic techniques are used to create, write, and develop a personal (and colorful) basic vocabulary card file.
5. MULTISENSORY FEEDBACK: Numerous opportunities are provided for the pupil to create, experience, use, and feel his basic words by using media such as sand, glue, rope, wood burners, electric vibrators, finger paint, chalk, paper cutting, clay, tape recording, and body movement.
6. STORY TELLING: The pupil creates stories with his basic vocabulary and uses drawings, coloring, painting, dramatic play, and recording methods, including taping, writing, and typing of stories.
7. VISUAL-AUDITORY DECODING: Elementary decoding and associative training are begun using words and stories selected from the pupil's experiences. Basic visual-auditory discrimination, seriation, memory, and integrative skills are taught.
8. FORMAL PHONICS TRAINING: Remedial phonics training using tactile-kinesthetic and body movement techniques is introduced. The pupil is gradually moved into a more formal symbolic training program.
9. INFORMAL READING: Reading is initiated from basic vocabulary language experience units and the pupil's own stories about current happenings, news, and events.
10. STRUCTURED READING: A good developmental sequential structural reading series can be introduced at this point. Of course, this should be supplemented with student-selected, high-interest–appropriate-vocabulary reading materials and related experiences.

It must always be remembered that reading is essentially a restructuring of personal experience. Reading is dependent for meaning on the person's concrete involvement in and struggle to understand and order his environment. In the final analysis, true reading is a uniquely human, culture-bound act of conceptualization of personal and vicarious experience. Through the manipulation of and association to this highly symbolic form of visual, auditory, and kinesthetic stimuli, we form our impressions of reality and act accordingly. The entire process is a learned one and can be taught to all who are interested and motivated to do so. Although further research will enable us to better understand and teach the acquisition of these skills, we already have sufficient evidence on which to construct effective prescriptive education programs for individuals with significant reading and language disabilities.

DISCUSSION QUESTIONS AND ACTIVITIES

1. Define reading.
2. What is a "synaptic knob?"
3. Discuss Kretch's quotation as it relates to the results of Heber's Milwaukee project (presented in Chapter 2).
4. Discuss some of the implications of Luria's findings for reading instruction.
5. What is the difference between alexia and dyslexia?
6. How can autosuggestion be used to improve reading performance?
7. In what way might "kinesthetic cues" be suppressed by teachers?
8. Discuss the importance of the Roswell-Chall Auditory Blending Test in predicting reading performance.
9. List three of the most important auditory skills required in reading.
10. How might visual perceptual training improve reading performance?
11. Critique Itard's program for helping Victor develop "the symbols of thought."
12. Which of Myklebust's characteristics of visual dyslexia do you think is the easiest to evaluate? Why?
13. Critique Halliwell and Solan's study of the effects of integrative perceptual training on reading comprehension.
14. Discuss the pros and cons of introducing formal phonics training at an earlier stage in the developmental reading process.
15. How can reading be construed as a distinctive cognitive ability?

Photo by Mike Borum, Image, Inc., Nashville, Tennessee.

CHAPTER 5

A perceptual-linguistic approach to conceptualization

All developmental models of cognitive behavior acknowledge the importance of sensory input and experience. We have already reviewed the experiments of Kretch, Rosenzweig, and Bennett (1966) and others, which have demonstrated that highly specific sensory-perceptual training stimulates changes in brain chemistry and actually produces measurable neurological changes in the cerebral cortex. These findings tend to support the theory of neurological organization and cell assembly developed by Hebb (1949). The work of Piaget (1952) has specified the origins of intellectual operations to be in these fundamental sensory-motor adaptations, which provide for the concrete manipulation of the environment and the eventual development of abstract thought.

Strauss and Kephart (1955) were pioneers in the psychopathology of perception and in showing how it related to language and concept formation; from their work we now understand that expressive language is dependent on the ability of the person to construct and organize relatively permanent perceptions, which then permit initial communication with oneself to take place. Later, Kephart (1960, 1964) showed how special education could be used to stimulate perceptual and cognitive development in learning-disabled children. The extensive clinical work of Johnson and Myklebust (1967) with the auditory and visual correlates of psycholinguistic dysfunctions has further influenced both educational practice and continued research. Similarly, Orton's early clinical investigations of the psychoneurological basis for language disorders influenced Gillingham and Stillman (1965) to develop an outstandingly successful remedial training program for children with specific disabilities in reading, spelling, and penmanship.

RELATED RESEARCH

Of course, much research and development remain to be done to clarify our understanding of the interrelationship of perception, psycholinguistics, and conceptualization. But recent studies have already demonstrated the value of certain kinds of sensory-perceptual training programs to cognitive development.

For example, McCormick and Schnobrich (1971) found significant differences in experimental groups of preschool children given perceptual-motor training to increase attentional processes, concentration, and accuracy of movement. In a similar study Keim (1970) found significant improvement in school readiness skills of kindergarten children with visual-motor deficiencies when they were provided with highly specific training. Other experiments, such as those of Jensen and King (1961), have shown how highly specific visual-motor training (tracing, matching, rearranging, etc.) can be used with kindergarten children to help them discriminate and read words.

The efficacy of perceptual-motor training in helping older pupils to become more linguistically proficient is also beginning to be demonstrated. The study by Halliwell and Solan (1972) is frequently cited as one that specifies how relevant visual and auditory training tasks can significantly improve reading comprehension in children achieving at low levels. McCormick, Schnobrich, and Footlik (1969) have also reported a study in which significant gains on the Metropolitan Reading Test were made by underachieving children following perceptual-motor training that emphasized self-verbalization of commands and self-correction. Other research, such as that conducted by Heath, Cook, and O'Dell (1976), indicates that improvement of visual convergence and tracking skills in poor readers is another form of relevant perceptual training that improves efficiency and reading achievement. In a recent summary by Sartain (1976) of the causes and correlates of reading disability it is again emphasized that a dysfunction in the mental processing of language symbols is the root cause to be considered in remedial planning.

Considerable effort has been made to refine the diagnosis of and prescriptions for those perceptual and psycholinguistic functions that appear to be most important for school success and higher order cognitive learning. ITPA* is a major instrument that was devised for this purpose. Numerous educational programs and materials have been developed for, or correlated with, the ITPA subtests (Rupert, 1970). However, the extensive research summarized by Hammill and Larsen (1974) has clearly indicated that the ITPA is not a very valid instrument since most of the subtest items do not correlate directly with linguistic tasks and constructs experienced in academic learning. The same research discloses that remedial programs based on the ITPA subtest scores fail to show that such training is beneficial in improving the educational task performance of the children involved. Related research on psycholinguistic training as summarized by Minskoff (1975) points out the importance of valid diagnosis and the essential nature of task-relevant education if training is to be helpful to the learning-handicapped child. There is no doubt but that some so-called psycholinguistic skills do not relate directly to the symbolic reading process. However, most of these skills are of such a distinctive symbolic nature that they require the use

---

*Kirk, S., McCarthy, J., and Kirk, W. The Illinois Test of Psycholinguistic Abilities, University of Illinois Press, Urbana, 1968.

and interpretation of specific auditory and visual stimuli—and it is about these perceptual tasks and skills that we need to be most concerned.

A THEORETICAL SPECULATION

We have already considered several major models of cognitive development. We have also seen how certain motor, sensory, and perceptual skills contribute to the eventual organization and expression of cognitive operations. It is also helpful to understand something of the nature of the psychoneurological process itself and its implications for developmental and prescriptive education.

The model that follows is a simplified synthesis of many "mental processing" theories. But it is sufficient to present the critical elements involved in the process of thinking and cognitive expression. This is a "perceptual-linguistic conceptualization" model, and it is presented below in schematic form.

Initially, a person receives varied sensory input through the major visual, auditory, kinesthetic (tactile), and visual-motor (movement-vestibular) channels, If these channels of communication are intact and open, sensory stimuli proceed directly to appropriate mind-brain centers for psychoneurological processing and organization. Pearce (1976) has reminded us that our mind-brain system is designed for functions that transcend current usage in that we actually have an astonishing capacity for creative intelligence built into our genetic makeup, and it gradually expands as we encounter the proper environmental stimuli.

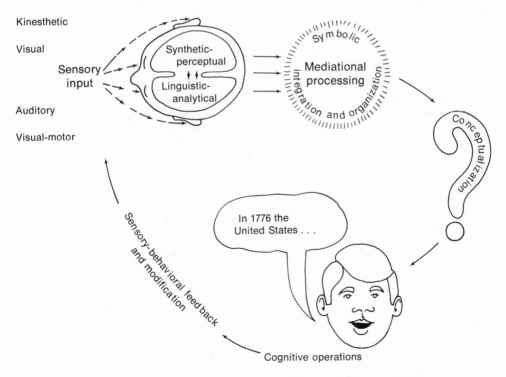

A PERCEPTUAL-LINGUISTIC MODEL OF CONCEPTUALIZATION

Within the brain itself, sensory data are processed by being transmitted to the appropriate centers where the input is stored, associated, and related to prior data. We also now know that both hemispheres of the brain have unique processing functions that must be harmonized for total human development to occur. Ornstein's summaries (1973) of brain research show that the left hemisphere is concerned with linguistic-analytical processes such as reading and mathematics and the right hemisphere synthesizes visual-spatial perceptual information and processes. It appears that primary perceptual form discrimination is integrated on the right side of the brain and then labeled and given linguistic meaning through associative relations with other brain centers.

Once stimulus information has been "registered" and interrelated within the brain, mediational processing begins to occur. Mediational processing consists of the "in-between" computer-like brain operations of organizing and integrating current data of immediate concern and then producing symbols of thought that have particular relevance and meaning. For example, a person may have seen many pictures of things that occurred in the year 1776, heard various stories about the American Revolution, and so on. But it is not until these visual impressions, stories, etc. are sifted, interconnected, and associated in a particular way that the year 1776 begins to develop a symbolic connotation that can then be conceptualized and expressed in several different ways.

Through mediational processes we begin to "talk with ourselves" and to develop a bank of inner symbols (signs, figures, words, etc.). These symbols, in turn, are manipulated abstractly in such ways that certain concepts are produced that can be used in problem-solving situations. Most often, cognitive operations are expressed in spoken or written language forms such as sentences and mathematical numeration. For meaningful linguistic conceptualization to develop, the perceptual input and integration must consist of the visual forms, patterns, and sounds that are an integral part of the actual symbols to be mastered and manipulated. Thus the visual parts and sounds of visual-kinesthetic designs and drawings such as graphemes, letters, and signs must be a concrete part of the sensory input to be processed, integrated, and finally conceptualized into some form of meaningful synthesis and expression.

VALETT PERCEPTUAL-LINGUISTIC INVENTORY

On pp. 69 to 70 is an inventory of the six most important perceptual-linguistic abilities that are directly related to abstract/symbolic functioning. The Valett Perceptual-Linguistic Inventory (VPI) covers auditory decoding, visual conceptualization, auditory-vocal association, auditory-visual memory, kinesthetic symbolization, and basic expressive language.

Each of the six parts of the VPI begins with an operational definition of the given ability. This is followed by a list of criterion instruments that correlate closely with the tasks listed in the inventory; the following abbreviations are used:

CTBS/A: Comprehensive Test of Basic Skills, Form A
Slingerland: Slingerland Tests of Specific Language Disability

VALETT PERCEPTUAL-LINGUISTIC INVENTORY

Pupil's name _____ School _____ Age _____

Teacher _____ Grade/program _____

Inventory administered by _____ Date administered _____

Perceptual-linguistic skills	Very strong	No concern	Weak	Needs remediation
I. Auditory decoding A. Following simple directions				
B. Interpreting sentences				
C. Number seriation				
D. Alphabet/time sequencing				
E. Letter-sound discrimination				
II. Visual conceptualization A. Picture-object matching				
B. Symbol matching				
C. Figural association				
D. Word matching				
E. Visual closure				
III. Auditory vocal association A. Picture interpretation				
B. Sound pattern organization				
C. Word rhyming				
D. Similarities and analogies				
E. Grammatical completion				
F. Sound blending				
G. Letter-sound associations				
IV. Auditory/visual memory A. Visual sequential memory				
B. Visual memory for word symbols				
C. Auditory sequential memory				

Continued.

VALETT PERCEPTUAL-LINGUISTIC INVENTORY—cont'd

Perceptual-linguistic skills	Very strong	No concern	Weak	Needs remediation
V. Kinesthetic symbolization A. Copying symbols				
B. Reproducing symbols from memory				
C. Writing symbols from dictation				
D. Writing letters of initial/final sounds				
VI. Basic expressive language A. Oral fluency				
B. Body language				
C. Reading				
D. Writing				
E. Spelling				

Special strengths:

Special weaknesses:

Priority teaching objectives:

Comments:

Wepman: Wepman Auditory Discrimination Test
ITPA: Illinois Test of Psycholinguistic Abilities
PIBLA: Psychoeducational Inventory of Basic Learning Abilities
Binet: Stanford-Binet Intelligence Scale
WISC: Wechsler Intelligence Scale for Children
Spache: Spache Diagnostic Reading Scales
Frostig: Frostig Developmental Test of Visual Perception

The VPI is for direct use with young children with suspected perceptual-linguistic problems of symbolization that may interfere with reading and other higher forms of expressive language.

Since these are the primary perceptual-linguistic tasks required in reading and expressive language, the VPI should be used with primary-aged school children who are suspected of having such difficulties. Each task should be presented to the child *and supplemented* by other similar tasks as deemed necessary by the evaluating teacher or learning specialist.

If the child has displayed competency in the task, his actual response should be noted and dated accordingly. Those tasks that are missed should be carefully considered as possible learning targets for prescriptive teaching or developmental instruction.

VALETT PERCEPTUAL-LINGUISTIC INVENTORY

I. AUDITORY DECODING

Sound reception and discrimination, listening, understanding, comprehending auditory information, and verbal concepts and symbols

> *Criterion instruments*
> CTBS/A: Listening
> Wepman: Sound identification
> Slingerland: Individual auditory tests
> ITPA: Auditory reception
> PIBLA: Auditory decoding

A. Following simple directions

Point to your nose, mouth, feet, eyes.
Point to the bottom of page 7 in this book.
Show me the Table of Contents in this book.

B. Interpreting sentences

Does a book fly?
Can a teacher read?
Can a pencil be used to write with?
Can a desk run?
Does a sentence contain words?

C. Number seriation

What number comes after 1?
What number comes before 8?
What number is between 11 and 13?

D. Alphabet/time sequencing

What is the first letter in the alphabet?
What is the last letter in the alphabet?
What day comes after Wednesday?
What letter in the alphabet comes before f?
What month comes before February?

E. Letter sound discrimination

Listen carefully and tell me if these sounds I say are the *same* or *different* (lips hidden).

T–T	tap–cap	2–2
zoo–shoe	boy–doy	kuh–kuh
bub–bub	cl–cl	boat–boot
toes–does	a–ah	sp–sp
pan–ban	fox–fox	fuh–tu

Raise your hand when you hear a *different* sound.
boy–boy–boy–goy–boy
tu–bu–tu–tu–bu
take–lake–take–lake–lake
pu–pu–ku–pu–pu

II. VISUAL CONCEPTUALIZATION

Identifying and interpreting picture stories, figural associations, and visual symbols by simple nonverbal means

> *Criterion instruments*
> CTBS/A: Visual discrimination, letter forms
> Slingerland: Visual discrimination
> Raven Progressive Matrices: Figural relationships
> ITPA: Visual reception, visual association, visual closure
> PIBLA: Visual form discrimination, visual figure-ground differentiation

A. Picture-object matching

Point to the book in this picture.
Go and point to the largest thing in this room.
Get a book and show me the second word in the first paragraph you can find.
Look around this room and show me some things that go together like a pencil goes with paper.

B. Symbol matching

Draw a line between those symbols that look alike.

```
M
9              G
X        )         b           W
A                        A
A      3    X    Q        &
4
b              9         4
)         M       d
Q           (
&
```

C. Figural associations

Check the figure in the box that is similar to the first one.

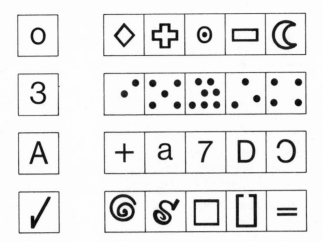

D. Word matching

Draw a line between those words that look alike.

To   BOY
boy   WAS   men   saw
saw   to   was
       man   To   boy
DOG   Man
man

E. Visual closure

Name the things you see below.

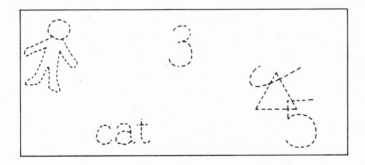

Point to all the little words in this big word below.

TOGETHER

III. AUDITORY-VOCAL ASSOCIATION

Putting together and integrating sound-symbol associations and interpreting them in proper context

> *Criterion instruments*
> CTBS/A: Letter name, letter sounds, sound matching
> ITPA: Auditory association, grammatic closure, sound blending, auditory closure
> PIBLA: Auditory-vocal association
> Binet and WISC: Similarities and analogies
> Spache: Phonics tests

A. Picture interpretation

Look at your clothes and describe them for me.
Look at this picture and tell me what the children are doing.
Look outside and tell me what the weather is like.

B. Sound pattern organization

Clap your hands three times.
Make a noise like a dog.
What object sounds like "tick, tick, tick, tick"?
Make a sound like the wind blowing.

C. Word rhyming

The word "red" rhymes with the word "bed." Tell me some words that rhyme with

boat	tall	bed
dog	cake	nap

Tell me as many other words as you can that begin with the same sound.

gr : great	ju : jump
buh : boy	ru : run
hu : hike	

D. Similarities and analogies

Fish swim down; airplanes fly _____.
Boys become men; girls become _____.
The opposite of in is _____.
A rabbit is fast; a turtle is _____.
The opposite of young is _____.
A is to B as 1 is to _____.
A pencil is to paper as chalk is to a _____.

E. Grammatical completion

Yesterday we talked; today we are ta _____.
Last week Billy ran fast. This morning he ran even _____.
Here is one finger, and here are three f _____.
Imagine we have four cookies here. This cookie is not very good; this cookie is good; this cookie is even better; and this last cookie is the very _____.

F. Sound blending

Listen very carefully; say these *sounds* after me; then put them together and tell me what they mean.

h–i (hi)   m–e (me)   g–o (go)
f–oot (foot)   c–ar (car)   b–o–a–t (boat)

G. Letter-sound associations

Listen carefully and tell me the name of the letter you hear at the beginning of these words.

*m*an   *b*aby
*g*arage   *d*ime

Tell me the *sound* of each letter you hear.

a   f   n
b   g   p
d   j   r

This time tell me the *letter* of the sound I say.

ah (a)   hu (h)   sss (s)
khu (c/k)   lu (l)   vu (v)

IV. AUDITORY-VISUAL MEMORY

Recalling extended sound-symbol associations, serial patterns, nonsense sentences, formulas, and operations

Criterion instruments

Slingerland: Visual-perceptual memory, auditory association
ITPA: Visual sequential memory, auditory sequential memory
Binet and WISC: Digit span
PIBLA: Auditory memory, auditory sequencing, visual memory

A. Visual sequential memory

In just a minute I will show you a card with some symbols on it. After I take the card away I want you to take these symbol cards and arrange them in the order you saw them on my card.

X ◇ C 5

X M + •

– B □ 6

a • A d

S ÷ Q = 7

MY DOG

B. Visual memory for "word" symbols

In just a minute I am going to ask you to look carefully at a word I will point to. Then I will cover that word, and I want you to pick out the word you saw in the box that follows.

me		ew	em	me	we

saw		was	mas	saw	sam

fb		th	fb	df	bt

9d		6d	9b	6b	9d

hold		hold	dolb	holb	bold

C. Auditory sequential memory

Listen carefully and repeat after me.

I have a little dog.
I like to play outside in the water.
tap/tap/tap/tap–tap (Tap desk.)
toot/toot/bang/toot
quack–quack/oint–oint/quack–oint
1–3–7
1–a–5
a–c–x
c–3–buh

square–square–circle–5
diamond–circle–square–cross
6–t–kuh–7
ju–uh–mp
ru–uu–un
ca–nn–dy
s–m–i–l–e
5–c–p–6–period

Count the numbers from 1 to 20 aloud for me.
Recite the alphabet for me.

V. KINESTHETIC SYMBOLIZATION

Drawing, copying, and writing meaningful designs and symbols

Criterion instruments

Slingerland: Copying, visual-perceptual-memory-kinesthetic, writing auditory sounds, auditory-kinesthetic recall
Frostig: Visual-motor skills
PIBLA: Tactile discrimination, visual-motor memory

A. Copying symbols

Look at the symbols and copy them in the boxes below.

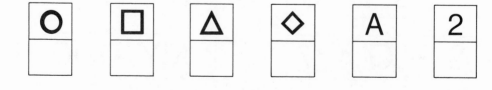

Copy these words and write in your name.

My　　　　name　　　　is

_____　_____　____　_____

B. Reproducing symbols from memory

Look carefully at the cards that I am going to show you one at a time, and then draw the symbols on your paper when I take the card away.

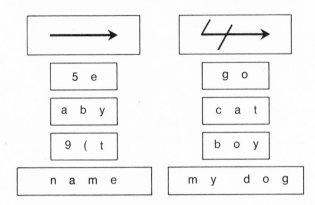

5　e		g　o
a　b　y		c　a　t
9　(　t		b　o　y
n　a　m　e		m　y　　d　o　g

C. Writing symbols from dictation

Listen carefully and write the words, letters, and numbers you hear me say.

a–b–c　　　1–7–b–t　　　man
4–7–8　　　s–i–h–c–a　　cat
k–o–q　　　　　　　　　　dog

D. Writing letters of initial and final sounds

Listen carefully and write down on your paper the letter of the sound that you hear at the *beginning* of each word I say.

*b*read　　　*m*other
*c*ow　　　　*w*eather

Listen carefully and write down on your paper the letter of the sound that you hear at the *end* of each word I say.

fathe*r*　　　bo*y*
schoo*l*　　　ma*n*

VI. BASIC EXPRESSIVE LANGUAGE

Formal expression of basic linguistic symbols in oral, written, and gestural context

> *Criterion instruments*
> CTBS/A: Language
> Binet and WISC: Vocabulary
> ITPA: Verbal expression, manual expression
> PIBLA: Vocabulary, fluency and encoding, articulation, word attack skills, writing

A. Oral fluency

Describe this room for me in as much detail as you can.
Tell me about your favorite games and other things that you like to do.
Tell me a joke or riddle you have heard.

B. Body language

Show me what you do with a basketball.
Show me how you use a book.
Show me how happy people might act.
Show me how you use a telephone book and telephone.

C. Reading

Read these letters for me.
    R Q   Z   A   K   U   P   G
Read these words for me.

| in | black | cat | finger |
| eat | cliff | open | |

Tell me what each word you just read means.
Get your current reading book and read something for me.

D. Writing

Write your name and address for me.
Write your telephone number.
Write the name of this school.
Write something else for me.

E. Spelling

Spell your name out loud for me.
Spell the name of the street you live on.
Show me some of the words you are spelling in school.

EXAMPLES OF EDUCATIONAL PRESCRIPTIONS

Children who lack specific perceptual-linguistic skills need to be provided with appropriate prescriptive education if symbolization and subsequent conceptualization are to be developed.

Two examples are presented here. The first is a prescriptive lesson plan for an 8-year-old child who is unable to identify and name the letters of the alphabet (a common linguistic-conceptual disability of young learning-handicapped children). The main purpose of this illustration is to specify the sequential order and structure necessary for teaching children with significant disabilities such as these.

The lesson proceeds from a statement of the priority target objective through a pretest, several sequential teaching tasks, and an evaluation and critique of what was tried and accomplished.

PRESCRIPTIVE LESSON PLAN

1 PUPIL'S NAME: Betty Harris   AGE: 8   DATE OF LESSON: March 4, 1977
2 PROGRAM: Learning Disability Resource   TEACHER: T. Clemons

3 PRIORITY TEACHING OBJECTIVE: For Betty to be able to identify and name the letters of the alphabet

3.1 EDUCATIONAL DOMAIN: Perceptual-motor and cognitive

3.2 SPECIFIC LEARNING ABILITY PROGRAMMED: Visual form discrimination of letter symbols, verbal naming of letter symbols

3.3 RATIONALE: It is essential that Betty learn these fundamental skills to learn to read.

4 PRETEST (ENTRY SKILLS) TASKS: Betty was presented cards with the following letters on them laid out on the table in the sequence shown. She was then given a duplicate pack of cards and asked to match her cards, one at a time, with those on the table.

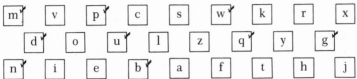

4.1 PRETEST RESULTS: Of the 26 letters presented, Betty was able to correctly match 17; the 9 missed are checked above.

---

5 MINIMUM PERFORMANCE EXPECTATIONS: On completion of this lesson Betty will be able to match and name 9 of the following 10 lowercase wooden cutout letters: m, o, d, n, q, u, p. w. b, g

---

6 INSTRUCTIONAL MATERIALS REQUIRED: Lowercase wooden cutout letters, cardboard box, letter cards

7 SPECIFIC TEACHING PROCEDURES

7.1 TEACHER EXPLANATION: "Betty, in this lesson I want you to learn to identify and name the letters of the alphabet. Listen carefully to me, watch what I do, and then follow my directions."

7.2 TEACHER DEMONSTRATION: "See this wooden letter? It is the letter 'a', so I say 'a' and pick it up and put it right on top of the other wooden 'a' here on the table."

7.3 PUPIL VERBAL INTERPRETATION AND IMITATION (Teacher says, "Now Betty, tell and show me what you are to do."): "I'm to pick up a letter like you do, say its name, and place it on top of another letter that looks like it."

7.4 TEACHER REINFORCEMENT OF PUPIL (explanation of system): "Good! Now for each letter that you get correct in the following exercises you will receive a point on your reward card."

7.5 SEQUENTIAL LEARNING TASKS:

TASK A. ALPHABETICAL ARRANGEMENT AND NAMING

"O.K. Betty, look at all the wooden letters spread out on this table. Now look at the one in my hand; it is the letter 'b.' See how I feel it and then place it on the other b here on the table. Now you feel it, say its name, and place it on the other letter like it."

Sequence: b, c, d, e, f, g, . . . No errors were made.

TASK B. KINESTHETIC MATCHING AND NAMING

"You did really well, Betty. This time I want you to feel and identify the letters I name that are hidden in this cardboard box. See, the box has holes cut in each end so you can put your hands through. Put your hands in and feel the letter and tell me what it is."

"It feels like the letter 'o.'"

"That's right, it is the letter 'o.' Now take it out of the box with one hand and say its name again and put it here on the table. Good. Now I will put three different letters at a time in the box. Put your hands back in and give me the letter 'b.'"

Sequence: o, *b*, t/*m*, v, c/*p*, c, s/*d*, r, x/*u*, l, z/*q*, y, l/*i*, *n*, e. Errors made were naming p for d, q for g, and n for u.

TASK C. "TOTAL KINESTHETIC ALPHABET NAMING"

"This time, Betty, I have placed all of the wooden letters of the alphabet in the box. Reach your hand in, take one, and feel it carefully with both hands. Name it, take it out, and look at it. If you are correct, place it aside; if you missed it, look at it again and name it and place it on top of the other wooden letter on the table that looks just like it."

Sequence: random selection. Error made was naming b for d.

8 JOINT EVALUATION

8.1 TEACHER COMMENTS: "Very good Betty! You did quite well and made very few mistakes—do you remember what they were?"

8.2 PUPIL COMMENTS: "Yes, I still get mixed up on the letters that look and feel alike such as b, d, p."

8.3 POSTTEST AND RESULTS: The same pretest task cards were presented again in the same sequence. The only mistake was to name d as b.

9 TASK ANALYSIS AND CRITIQUE

9.1 TASK APPROPRIATENESS: Very appropriate. All of the learning tasks were relevant and demanding.

9.2 QUANTITATIVE ACHIEVEMENT: Altogether Betty earned 57 points on her reward card. The total lesson took about 25 minutes. On the posttest she made only one mistake.

9.3 PUPIL ATTITUDE AND MOTIVATION: Betty showed good interest and a positive attitude during this lesson. Although she was hesitant at first, the use of wooden letters and the kinesthetic activities in the cardboard box captured her attention and concentration.

9.4 PUPIL PERFORMANCE RATING: Very good. Apparently this lesson was effective in helping Betty to learn the letters she has been having trouble with, and she was able to transfer what she learned to the posttest letter cards with success.

9.5 IMPLICATIONS FOR EXTENDED PRESCRIPTIVE TEACHING:

Betty obviously needs continued practice with the commonly reversed letters, such as b and d. Letter cards should be used that have visual discrimination cues such as a "tail" on the letter "d."

Follow-up activities should include using sand trays and finger paints to reinforce kinesthetic learning of letters and symbols.

The second prescriptive example consists of programmed lesson materials for children with perceptual-linguistic disabilities.

This lesson is concerned with teaching the "t" sound and appears as the sixth lesson in a series of 26 used to teach the visual-auditory-kinesthetic symbols to young children. The supplemental lesson requires symbol drawing and integrates the sounds of the letters learned in the first five lessons (a, b, f, i, h).

The value of such materials is in their structure and systematic presentation, which also requires motor-kinesthetic involvement as part of the learning process. The provision of immediate feedback and self-correction is another important aspect of programmed approaches to learning and helps to increase attention, concentration, and intrinsic reinforcement.

Although all lessons in this particular program consist of 20 learning tasks, the actual tasks vary from lesson to lesson. Multisensory learning tasks and activities are presented to stimulate perceptual organization and conceptualization.

PERCEPTUAL-MOTOR TRANSITIONS TO READING (Lesson 6)*

Name _____ Date _____

☐ 1. Look at the picture card with the rough letter "t" on it. Watch how your teacher traces the letter "t" with her finger. Now, you trace the letter "t" with your finger three times. Then, check the box.

☐ 2. Look at this letter: Its *name* is "t". Say "t" and check the box.

☐ 3. Look at this picture. The letter "t" is used at the beginning of the word *turn*. Say *turn* and check the box.

☐ 4. The words and picture say to turn around. Do as it says and then check the box.

Turn around

☐ 5. Listen to the teacher say the *sound* of the letter "t". Now, you say the *sound* of "t" and check the box.

☐ 6. Color the picture that says "turn around." Check the box.

☐ 7. Make up your own sentence using the word *turn*. Say the sentence out loud and check the box.

☐ 8. Use your *finger* to trace over this letter 6 times. The arrows will show you which direction to go. As you trace the letter, first say its *name* and then its *sound,* as in *turn*. Check the box.

*From Valett, R., and Valett, S. Perceptual-Motor Transitions to Reading Program. San Rafael, Calif.: Academic Therapy Publications, 1974.

☐ 9. Now, use your pencil to trace over the above letters. Say the *sound* of the letter as you trace it. Check the box.

☐ 10. Copy the letter "t" 5 times, in the boxes provided. Say the letter's *sound* as you copy it. Check the box.

t					

☐ 11. Now, turn around, while you say the "t" sound 5 times. Check the box.

☐ 12. Write the letter "t" 5 times from memory. *Don't* look at the one you just finished writing. Say the sound as you write each "t". Check the box.

_____

_____

☐ 13. Look at your writing. If you wrote all the letters correctly, check the box.

☐ 14. Draw a picture in the space below of something that begins with the *sound* of the letter "t". When you have finished, check the box.

☐ 15. Tell your teacher 3 more words that begin with the "t" *sound*. Check the box when you have given 3 words.

☐ 16. Close your eyes. Listen to your teacher read these words. Clap when you hear one that begins with the "t" sound.

turn	act	itch	top	taffy
bounce	toss	tank	fall	tease

If you clapped your hands at all the "t" sounds, check the box.

☐   17. Can you toot on your tuba? As you pretend to toot on your tuba, say the "t" sound 5 times. Check the box.

☐   18. Use a crayon to color in this letter. Now cut two pieces of paper and cross them to make a letter "t" like this. Check the box.

☐   19. Now, trace the rough letter "t" on the picture card again with your finger 3 times, while you say the *sound* of "t". Check the box.

____ 20. Count the number of checks you have earned, and write it on the line.

Supplemental lesson—after letter "t" is introduced

Ask your teacher to help you put these letter sounds together to make words. After you have sounded out the word, trace it, and then write it and say it two times.

tab

hat

fat

REMEDIAL PROGRAMS

In this chapter we have considered the nature of perceptual-linguistic processes and their importance in the development of symbolization and eventual conceptualization. A detailed specification of the primary skills involved in these processes has been presented in a perceptual-linguistic inventory. Two prescriptive lessons were also presented to emphasize the importance of the systematic approach needed to help children acquire the symbolization that is essential for higher order cognitive operations and thinking.

Numerous learning materials and programs are available to help children develop their perceptual processes and linguistic skills. A few of the ones in wide use are listed here.

Developing Learning Readiness (Webster Division, McGraw-Hill Book Co., 1221 Avenue of the Americas, New York, N.Y.)

Peabody Language Development Kits (American Guidance Service, Publishers' Building, Circle Pines, Minn.)

Auditory Discrimination in Depth (Teaching Resources, 100 Boylston St., Boston, Mass.)

SEMEL Auditory Processing Program (Follett Publishing Co., 1010 W. Washington Blvd., Chicago, Ill.)

DISTAR Language and Reading (Science Research Associates, Inc., 259 E. Erie St., Chicago, Ill.)

Phonics We Use game kits (Lyons & Carnahan, 407 E. 25th St., Chicago, Ill.)

Cuisenaire rods (Cuisenaire Co. of America, 9 Elm Ave., Mt. Vernon, N.Y.)

Of course there are literally hundreds of other programs available. Those listed above are merely representative of the kinds of programs that stress the development of perceptual-linguistic symbolization and basic conceptualization. Many other similar programs are listed in the resource book *The Remediation of Learning Disabilities* (Valett, 1974). In addition, there are numerous formal reading programs of all kinds available, and many of these stress fundamental linguistic skills; however, since we are not directly concerned with the teaching of formal reading in this book, the reader must consult other sources for this kind of information.

Chapter 6 presents other types of cognitive development programs and materials. The programs to be presented pick up where perceptual-linguistic materials leave off. For successful teaching of learning-handicapped children, both perceptual-linguistic and cognitive development programs must be used on a diagnostic-prescriptive basis.

DISCUSSION QUESTIONS AND ACTIVITIES

1. Discuss Hebb's theory of cell assembly.
2. Write a book review of Kephart's classic *The Slow Learner in the Classroom*.
3. Research and critique the Orton-Gillingham method.
4. Outline a lesson that would help improve a child's attention and concentration.
5. Why is self-verbalization so important in remedial education?
6. Write a critique of the research on the ITPA.
7. Discuss mediational processing.
8. Outline the various functions of the right and left hemispheres of the human brain.
9. Use the VPI with a young primary schoolchild and write a case report of your findings.
10. List several supplemental perceptual-linguistic tasks you devised and used with the VPI as part of your case study.
11. Design and teach a lesson using the prescriptive lesson plan outline.
12. Suggest several other commercially available remedial programs that could be used to develop specific perceptual-linguistic skills.

Cognitive development programs

Many cognitive development materials and programs have been devised, published, and widely used in educational systems of all kinds. Many of these programs have been created from a particular model of cognitive development. Some materials have even appeared from the pragmatic experience of various practitioners and are not based on any theoretical model.

At this point we need to carefully consider the nature and contents of several major programs. The intent here is to present a representative sample of widely used programs and materials that are currently available to professionals interested in cognitive development and remediation.

The first section will present some of these major programs. Then a few games, typical of the many now being used in cognitive training, are listed. A brief list of learning kits and associated materials is presented last. Program sources, addresses, and some related information are given after materials are described. All prices listed are approximate. Specific information concerning learning games, kits, and associated educational materials should be obtained from school supply catalogs, local toy stores, and library resources.

PROGRAMS
Thinklab

Thinklab is a thinking and reading skills program kit developed by K. Weber of the University of Toronto. It consists of some manipulative materials, 125 color-coded cards containing logical problem-solving activities, and a teacher's guide and answer key.

The Thinklab was developed to provide students with experience in genuine problem solving. Its contents have been designed to stimulate unmotivated, slower learning students in an age range from approximately 11 years to the late teens. The program is organized to teach the following five basic types of problem solving, which have been taken from Bloom's taxonomy (1956).

- OBJECT MANIPULATION: Ways and means of dealing with specific data (blue cards)
- PERCEPTION: Extrapolation from given data (orange cards)

- ABSTRACT RELATIONSHIPS: Developing insight from given data (green cards)
- PATTERN ANALYSIS: Perceiving image patterns and structure (red cards)
- HYPOTHESES TESTING: Logical analysis and use of data in planning a set of operations (purple cards)

All of the problem-solving cards are sequenced in units of 10 in order of difficulty, which allows for pacing and programming different cycles of instruction. This progression in cognitive difficulty has also been correlated with reading level; the first 20 cards require a third grade reading performance with sequential progression of difficulty to the last 20 cards, which are on the seventh grade level.

Students usually begin at card 1 and work through the problems sequentially. Multiple copies of each card allow several students to work at any given level. A student progress card is also provided and is maintained by each pupil as evidence of visible achievement and for motivational purposes. An example of a similar problem-solving card on the extrapolation of data is presented below.

(orange color)	7C

Why is this woman a fraud?

"Look what I have!" said the woman excitedly. "This is a magic wand! You can see it in my hand! It will dissolve anything you touch with it in mere seconds, and it only costs $5.00."

Since the problem-solving cards are nonacademic and designed with a puzzle-like format, they are appealing to reluctant students. The cards include brief statements of the problem with accompanying pictures, designs, etc. Additional cards can be created by the teacher, made by students, or added from many other sources. This kit is incomplete as a total program for cognitive development, but it is recommended as a supplemental resource for teaching the specified skills on an individualized basis. (Science Research Associates, Inc., 259 E. Erie St., Chicago, Ill. 60611. $50.)

KELP program

KELP is a unique learning and evaluation program for preprimary and kindergarten children developed by Wilson and Robeck (1966) through the University of California at Santa Barbara. The actual program consists of a large attractive kit of varied learning materials, pupil evaluation sheets, and a text-manual for teachers. This is one of the very few well-developed programs based on the original cognitive constructs presented by Binet (Binet and Simon, 1961).

KELP is an acronym for Kindergarten Evaluation of Learning Potential. In reality, however, the KELP materials and the teacher's guide provide a curriculum for developing cognitive skills and remedying cognitive dysfunctions as they are determined on intelligence tests such as the Standford-Binet.

The program kit itself consists of eleven different kinds of instructional items and activities grouped under these headings: skipping, color identification, bead design, bolt board, block design, calendar, number boards, safety signs, printing, auditory perception, and social interaction. As an example of the materials, the auditory perception items consist of 18 small toys, the names of which begin with one of three consonants, for use in naming, articulation, and auditory association training. All of the materials and activities are test and curriculum referenced.

The following are some of the major purposes of the KELP materials.

1. To teach the skills by which a child may be evaluated
2. To give the teacher clear guides for individualized teaching
3. To provide opportunities for slower starting children to develop their strengths without threat

Although the KELP program materials have been available now for a number of years, this kind of precision prescriptive teaching has not been widely used in the public schools. However, with more recent trends toward the individualization of instruction for all children, this program and other similar program materials will gain wider acceptance. It should be part of the curricular resources available to all teachers of young learning-handicapped children. (Webster Division, McGraw-Hill Book Co., New York.)

Piaget Early Childhood Curriculum

The Early Childhood Curriculum is one of the very few well-organized programs developed on the Piaget model. The curriculum consists of three large boxes of learning materials to teach (1) classification, (2) number, measurement, and conservation of space, and (3) seriation. All materials and the accompanying textbook (Lavatelli, 1970) and teacher's guides were created by a developmental psychologist, Celia Stendler Lavatelli.

Designed for use with 4-, 5-, and 6-year-old children and with others who have not acquired these thinking skills, the objectives and associated learning materials for each kit are as follows.

Classification

- SIMPLE SORTING: Grouping objects according to a single property that is perceptually apparent, such as color, size, or shape
- EMERGENCE OF TRUE CLASSIFICATION: Abstracting the common property in a group of objects and finding that same property in other objects in the group
- MULTIPLICATIVE CLASSIFICATION: Classifying by more than one property at a time and recognizing that an object can belong to several classes at the same time
- ALL-SOME RELATION: Distinguishing classes on the basis of a property belonging to some members of the class (in a display of red squares and red circles, for example, recognizing that all the shapes are red and that only some are circles)

- CLASS-INCLUSION RELATION: Forming subclasses of objects (a class of red beads and a class of yellow beads) and including the subclasses in a larger class (the class of wooden beads)

There are eight sets of materials for teaching these classification skills. Materials consist of beads, matrix puzzles, planes and trucks, animals, miniature toys, rings and geometric figures, dolls, and train cars. The materials are systematically used to teach properties of objects, complementary classes, subclasses, intersections of classes, pairs and combinations.

Space and number

- PHYSICAL CORRESPONDENCE OF OBJECTS ON A ONE-TO-ONE BASIS: Establishing equality between two sets of objects when the objects correspond visually
- ONE-TO-ONE CORRESPONDENCE WHEN PHYSICAL CORRESPONDENCE IS DESTROYED: Recognizing equality between sets of objects even in the absence of spatial equivalence
- CONSERVATION OF QUANTITY: Recognizing that a particular quantity, whether of a liquid such as water or of discrete objects such as beads, does not vary when the quantity is moved so that it occupies a different space (that 10 is 10 regardless of whether the 10 objects are in a low, flat container or a tall, thin one, whether spread out in space or bunched together).
- CONSERVING THE WHOLE WHEN THE ADDITIVE COMPOSITION OF ITS PARTS IS VARIED: Understanding that 8 objects divided into sets of 4 and 4 are numerically equivalent to 8 objects divided into 1 and 7.
- CONSERVATION OF AREA: Recognizing that area is conserved even though its appearance may change, provided nothing is added or taken away
- TRANSFORMATION OF PERSPECTIVE: Ability to picture how an object would look when viewed from a different vantage point or to turn things around in the mind to visualize how they would look after a transformation in space

There are nine different sets of materials for teaching number and space concepts. The materials consist of toys and pennies, cupcake cubes, lemonade, marbles, water-level jars, parking cars, towers, table settings, and a toy house, garage, and tree. These are used to teach conservation of number, volume, direction, surface area, length, one-to-one correspondence, spatial transformations, and visualization.

Seriation

- ORDERING OBJECTS IN A SERIES ACCORDING TO ONE PROPERTY: Ability to put objects in order from shortest to tallest (or some other property) and to include all the objects to be ordered
- ORDERING OBJECTS IN TWO SERIES INVERSELY RELATED TO ONE ANOTHER: Ability to think of two relations at once and to reverse the order of arrangement from shortest to tallest or thinnest to fattest
- SERIATION OF GEOMETRIC SHAPES: Ordering a set of geometric shapes increasing in area and number of sides
- SERIATION OF VISUAL REPRESENTATIONS: Ability to draw a picture of objects one has arranged in a series and later to draw the picture before arranging the objects

There are five different sets of materials for teaching seriation. These include flower pots, dolls and umbrellas, oblong strips, geometric shapes, and irregularly shaped cards. The materials teach seriation of size, sets of objects, length and color, transitivity, and multiple seriation.

These early childhood curriculum materials provide the teacher with the structure and behavioral objectives to actually put Piaget's theory into practice. The kits and materials are colorful, well organized, and appealing to young children. The teacher's guide and reference books are very well done. The kits are expensive and some materials lack durability. There is also a danger that these materials could be inappropriately used in a mechanical way with groups of children, some of whom would not be ready for such an experience. However, for developmental instruction as part of a diagnostic-prescriptive education program, this is an excellent source of aids and ideas. (Lavatelli, C. S. Early Childhood Curriculum—A Piaget Program, American Science & Engineering, Inc., 20 Overland St., Boston, Mass. 02215. Three kits, $300.)

Let's Look at First Graders

During the 1960s the Educational Testing Service worked with the New York City schools in developing a first grade project to teach critical cognitive skills. The project was based on Piaget's developmental model and four assumptions:

1. Intelligence is essentially a set of developed skills rather than an inherited characteristic.
2. Intellectual skills develop as a result of the child's continuous interaction with his environment.
3. Children are inherently motivated to explore and master their environment.
4. Intellect develops through a sequence of related stages that produce *qualitative changes* in the way children think and are able to deal with the world.

These theoretical assumptions were then put to work through the development of a teacher's guide and related materials and instructional manuals. The guide translates theory into behavioral terms and pupil objectives, and it presents classroom illustrations for teaching the following developmental concepts.

Auditory discrimination and attention
Listening comprehension
Learning to communicate
Language for thinking
Learning shapes and forms
Spatial perspective
The notion of time
Logical classification
Concepts of relationship
The conservation of quantity

One-to-one correspondence
Number relations
Understanding cause and effect
Reasoning by association
Reasoning by inference
Growing awareness and responsiveness
Directed activity
General knowledge
Developing imagination

A series of written lesson sheets and exercises includes shapes and forms, spatial relations, time concepts, mathematics, communication skills, and logical reasoning. A sequence card game kit includes sets of four cards showing various kinds of sequences, which the child puts in correct order to tell a logical story;

the cards vary in nature, purpose, and difficulty level. A "directions" card game kit completes the materials and consists of symbolic playing cards that teach the child to classify and follow directions. All of the materials have individual answer sheets or built-in feedback allowing self-correction.

This program was first experimented with in 25 New York City elementary schools. Since the cognitive skills taught are not confined to the first grade curriculum, the program has focused on younger children. It has also been widely used in a variety of special education settings in which intensive cognitive training can be provided as needed. (Educational Testing Service, Princeton, N.J., and Board of Education of the City of New York. $35.)

Attribute games and materials

The set of Attribute games and materials was developed by William Hull for use in developing thinking skills in elementary schoolchildren. It is specifically concerned with teaching classification and the relationships between classes. Although originally designed for fifth grade children, it has been adapted for use in the early primary grades and is also used as part of many elementary school science units.

A variety of materials are provided for direct instructional use with children. These include the following.

- Box of colored wooden shapes and sizes
- Box of colored cubes
- Box of plastic tiles with drawings of people
- Set of classification "creature cards"
- Set of stickers for mapping problems and making puzzle cards
- Teacher's guide

There are many different ways to use these materials, ranging from free play and discovery activities to creative problem development and innovative games. Besides classification, the materials can be used to teach simultaneous or associative thinking, seriation, sequential thinking, analysis, and evaluation. A representative simple puzzle block card is shown on p. 92.

From such a simple matrix as this, the 39 problem cards for use with the attribute blocks become increasingly more complex. At the advanced level the cards and blocks teach intersecting sets using 32 blocks, three loops, and both positive and negative verbal attributes. The color cubes are used in a similar way but also allow for color seriation, pattern analysis, and Latin square problems.

A box of people pieces contains tiles with colored pictures of boys, girls, men, and women. These are used to teach the following attributes and their values.

Attribute	Value
Color	Red, blue
Age	Adult, child
Sex	Male, female
Girth (fatness)	Fat, thin

People pieces can also be arranged in Latin squares and matrix problems. They can also be used in teaching sets and subjects in combination with the block and cube materials.

The 15 creature cards are highly attractive and stimulating to most children. Beginning with simple classifications similar to that in card A below, they increase in difficulty to the level represented in card Z and beyond. Children are then taught to create their own creature cards and to sequence them by concept and difficulty.

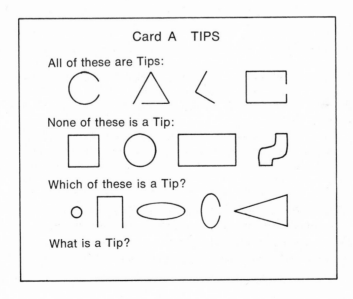

Continued.

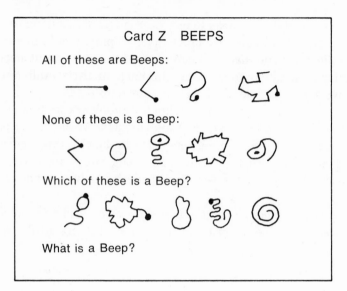

Children who use Attribute games are encouraged to extend them to other materials. Such common things as nails, marbles, buttons, toys, and pictures of all kinds can be used. One of the advantages of this kind of approach is that creative and divergent thinking can also be taught along with the development of basic classification skills. (Webster Division, McGraw-Hill Book Co., New York. Manual and materials, $20.)

Think—A "Thinking Skills" Language Program

Think is an advanced learning system for improving the language and intellectual capabilities of students. The entire program has been based on Guilford's cognitive model and attempts to develop the following thinking and reasoning skills.

- THING MAKING: Mental process of becoming aware of things and giving them a name
- QUALIFICATION: Process of recognizing unique characteristics in a thing—sensory, emotional, or logical aspects of the thing
- CLASSIFICATION: Process of sorting things into groups according to their common qualities
- STRUCTURE ANALYSIS: Process of dividing things into their parts
- OPERATION ANALYSIS: Process of dividing events into phases or stages
- SEEING ANALOGIES: Process of recognizing a similarity between relationships

This extensive curriculum consists of nine programmed instruction books, 45 developmental reading taped lessons, 123 language analysis tapes, and answer sheets, plus pupil progress records, test pads, and teacher guides.

Each Think learning module is structured to emphasize three levels of abstraction: physical and perceptual characteristics of things, primary uses of things, and the implied or creative uses of things. The reading level of lessons and materials ranges from pre–first grade through the ninth grade. The program is a very highly organized one and is most widely used with upper elementary and secondary students who are slow learning and conceptually handicapped.

This is one of the few cognitive development programs with available research data. The results of numerous junior and senior high school experimental studies show a significant improvement beyond normal expectation in language analysis and reading skills. Since the program is a complete learning laboratory approach, it is necessary to use it as a whole over a concentrated period of time to obtain desired results. (Innovative Sciences, Inc., 300 Broad St., Stamford, Conn. 06901. Costs vary according to program components.)

Reading-Thinking Skills

Reading-Thinking Skills instructional materials were created by Ethel S. Maney for use by classroom teachers of elementary schoolchildren. They have been developed to supplement the regular reading program by emphasizing the following thinking skills.

- CLASSIFYING IDEAS: Classifying picture objects, adding members of a class, refining a classification, oral to written classification, and classifying in outline form
- DEVELOPING SENTENCE SENSE: Detecting inconsistencies, completing a pictured sequence, completing a printed sentence, and rearranging scrambled words
- UNDERSTANDING MULTIPLE MEANINGS: Matching pictures of same label and matching word meaning with context
- MAKING INFERENCES: Inferring from a picture, inferring from oral context and pictures, inferring from reading context, and using context clues to solve puzzles
- RELATING PRONOUNS AND ANTECEDENTS: Associating pronouns with pictures, recognizing pronouns in reading context, substituting pronouns for antecedents, and identifying antecedents for pronouns
- DETERMINING ANALOGOUS RELATIONSHIPS: Completing a picture analogy, completing a picture-word analogy, and completing a word analogy
- ORGANIZING IDEAS ACCORDING TO TIME ORDER: Arranging pictures in sequence, arranging sentences in sequence, and arranging story segments in sequence

The materials in this program consist of 37 colorful overhead transparencies for introducing each skill to be taught, a total of 384 thinking-skill lessons presented in 16 liquid duplicating sets or in eight individual pupil workbooks, and teacher's guides and manuals.

Lesson materials begin at the early first grade level and proceed sequentially through the sixth grade level. The materials for grade 2 level 2 are typical of those in the entire program and can be used for illustrative purposes. These lessons teach classifying, generalizing, and determining relationships. One such lesson requires the pupil to label and explain how 20 different words in a series are all alike (for example, "barn, house, store"). Another lesson contains 24 groups of words with instructions to cross out the word that does not belong (for example, "kitten, puppy, hen, baby"). More advanced lessons require verbal analysis, writing, and oral interpretation (for example, "Complete the simile: As furious as _____.").

Most of the thinking-skill lesson material is directly relevant to the elementary school curriculum. The teacher's guide for the overhead transparencies contains pupil objectives, step-by-step teaching procedures, and a number of suggested follow-up learning activities. The critical thinking skills involved in the reading process on the elementary level are presented and taught in a number of interesting ways. This material has long been used by special educators and is recommended as supplemental lessons to other remedial reading programs. (The Continental Press, Inc., Elizabethtown, Pa. 17022. $70 per transparency set, 50 cents per workbook.)

Learning to Think Series

The Learning to Think Series is a series of four developmental workbooks and accompanying sensory-motor materials by Thelma Thurstone. It is for use with primary and elementary schoolchildren. All of the workbooks have been devised to provide direct training in the following primary mental abilities.

- VERBAL MEANING: Ability to understand ideas expressed in words
- SPACE: Ability to think about objects in two or three dimensions
- REASONING: Ability to solve logical problems, to foresee, and to plan
- QUANTITATIVE THINKING: Ability to work with quantitative concepts rapidly and accurately
- WORD FLUENCY: Ability to write and talk easily
- MEMORY: Ability to recall past experiences
- MOTOR: Ability to coordinate eye and hand movements
- PERCEPTION: Ability to recognize likenesses and differences accurately and quickly

These lessons and accompanying sensory-motor activities are said to help prevent potential failure in the early primary grades if they are used early enough. Some research studies demonstrate that after training many children show marked improvement in their ability to solve problems involving the primary mental abilities. Emphasis placed on the development of motor coordination and perception for young children and on reasoning, quantitative thinking, and verbal fluency for older ones.

The developmental lessons are provided in four different colored workbooks: green, red, blue, and gold. Each workbook consists of more than 1200 pictures and drawings for use with individual children. Each lesson is planned to take from 10 to 20 minutes. The material in each book presents a daily lesson for one half of the school year. A great deal of the material is devoted to the development of verbal-meaning ability, as this is fundamental to all other school learning. This material can also be used in conjunction with the Primary Mental Ability tests available from the same publisher. (Science Research Associates, Inc., 259 E. Erie St., Chicago, Ill. 60611. Less than $1 per workbook. Other materials sold separately or in packages.)

Structure of Intellect programs

A number of cognitive development evaluation materials and programs have been based on Guilford's model (1959), which classifies intellectual factors according to content, operations, and products. Mary Meeker (1969) devised a means of profiling individual intelligence test results using the Structure of Intellect (SOI) approach and published the first book on its interpretation and use. Since then, computer analysis and printouts have been devised, such as the one available from Computer Applications to Education, which produces individual pupil profiles covering the following SOI dimensions.

- CONTENTS: Figural (F), symbolic (S), and semantic (M)
- OPERATIONS: Cognition (C), memory (M), evaluation (E), convergent production (N), and divergent production (D)
- PRODUCTS: Units (U), classes (C), relations (R), systems (S), transformation of information (T), and implications (I)

Profiles such as these present a graphic picture of the pupil's cognitive strengths and weaknesses; a list of specific prescriptions is then recommended to help remedy the weaknesses and to build on the student's strengths. Printouts and individual test scoring templates can be obtained for use with all of the Wechsler intelligence scales in addition to the Stanford-Binet. (Computer Applications to Education, P.O. Box 146, University Station, Syracuse, N.Y. 13210.)

Remedial workbooks on cognition, evaluation, memory, convergent production, and divergent production, with related materials, can be obtained from the SOI Institute. Each workbook contains teacher orientation, instructions for use, objectives, and pupil worksheets. The worksheet lessons are well organized and vary in length from 8 to 27 pages for each SOI ability. Some of the worksheets contain pretests that have been developed for teachers who do not have diagnostic test information available. The divergent production workbook includes a rating scale for creative potential. All of the lessons are of high interest and intriguing to most students. However, they do need to be supplemented with other learning activities and more varied materials. (SOI Institute, 214 Main St., El Segundo, Calif. 90246.)

The Glendora Unified School District has conducted longitudinal research and development using and adapting the SOI model. Over several years of applied research the Glendora staff has devised numerous short tests to measure a variety of SOI skills, and norms have been developed in regular classrooms with children from 5 to 12 years old. A battery of 17 tests is individually administered, a profile is made, and a prescription is written. The material has also been extended to include a self-concept component; the enhancement of poor self-concepts through special classroom lessons and materials, and through parent education discussion groups, is a unique aspect of this project.

The Glendora project has produced an interesting array of tests, curriculum materials, activities, and games for remedial use with children with SOI deficits.

Initial research results indicate significant increases in test criterion scores for pupils enrolled in SOI programs. Of special interest is the fact that many educationally handicapped and retarded students improved their cognitive skills in this program to the extent that they reached mastery levels of performance and were returned to regular classrooms. (Dissemination of Learning How to Learn, Title VIB project, Glendora Unified School District, 352 N. Wabash Ave., Glendora, Calif. 91740.)

GAMES

Mastermind

Mastermind is a battle of wits and logic between two players. The code maker secretly sets up a line of code pegs behind a shield, and the code breaker has up to 10 opportunities to duplicate the colors and exact positions of the hidden code pegs without seeing them. (Invicta Plastics, Ltd.)

Battleship

Battleship is a strategy game for two players. Each player commands his own fleet of authentic-looking plastic ships that range from aircraft carriers to submarines. The game requires extensive use of graphing and planning skills. (Milton Bradley Co.)

Solitaire

Solitaire is a marble and board game in which one marble is left out of the middle and the player must figure, through logic, how he can jump one at a time and end with only one marble on the board. (Reiss Co.)

Password

Password is a vocabulary development game for two teams of two players each. One player on each team receives a card with the password and gives his partner one-word clues to enable him to guess the password. The game develops associative thinking. (Milton Bradley Co.)

Husker Du

Husker Du is a memory game that requires players to match symbols on a playing wheel. It is of high interest to young children. (Products International Co.)

Scrabble

Scrabble teaches sequencing, logical planning, vocabulary, and spelling skills. (Selchow & Righter Co.)

Inquisitive Games

The Inquisitive Games are a series of sensory-motor games to enable preprimary and kindergarten children to explore the concepts of number and space through movement activities requiring observation, classification, comparison, decision making, problem solving, and the organization of information. (Science Research Associates, Inc.)

Jeopardy

In the game of Jeopardy the answer is supplied and the players must use logic to decide on a question that would match the answer. This develops the concept of reversibility. (Milton Bradley Co.)

Science Games and Activities

Science Games and Activities is a handbook of 160 games and learning activities requiring elementary hypotheses formulation, experimentation, and deductive reasoning. An extensive list of related resource material is included. (Teachers Publishing Corp., Darien, Conn.)

LEARNING KITS AND MATERIALS
Concept Building

Concept Building is a set of matrix cards and activity and picture books for developing skills in classifying data. (Developmental Learning Materials.)

Reading, Thinking, and Reasoning

Reading, Thinking, and Reasoning is a set of colorful workbooks to teach critical thinking skills for the first through sixth grade. (Steck-Vaughn Co.)

Choose and Check

Choose and Check consists of four manipulative programmed learning boards for teaching verbal concepts, cause-effect relationships, and analogous thinking. (Scott, Foresman & Co.)

The Thinking Box

The Thinking Box is a collection of learning materials for young children; it teaches such critical thinking skills as logical comprehension and classification. (Benefic Press.)

Language Patterns

Language Patterns is a kit of varied materials for identifying categories, establishing attributes, making descriptions, and determining sequences and outcomes. (Creative Teaching Associates.)

Cognitive Development Intervention Cards

Cognitive Development Intervention Cards are a set of 280 colored cards for teaching reasoning by visual analogy. (Developmental Learning Materials.)

The Productive Thinking Program

The Productive Thinking Program is an extensive kit of materials for use with young children. (Educational Innovations, Berkeley, Calif.)

Invicta/Instructo programs

Invicta/Instructo programs include the following materials: Classification Activity Kit, Opposite Concepts, Attribute Sets, Logical People, and Concept Builders Study Prints. (Available through school supply houses such as Ideal and Lakeshore.)

Creative Thinking Activities

The Creative Thinking Activities are contained in a series of handbooks of games and cognitive development activities for primary children. A similar series, Tricks and Teasers, is also available. (Highlights for Children.)

Mind Expanders

Mind Expanders is a set of problem-solving cards that provide key elements of a story and pose imaginative questions. (Educational Insights, Inc.)

Concepts and Inquiry

Concepts and Inquiry consists of learning activities and lessons for teaching logical analysis. The material was developed by the Educational Research Council Social Science Program. (Allyn & Bacon, Inc.)

Try—Experiences for Young Children

Try is an excellent set of sensory-motor materials for teaching basic concepts of discrimination and classification to young children. Geometric shapes, design blocks, and alphabet tiles and trays are each provided with their own teaching guide. (Noble & Noble.)

Matrix Games

Matrix Games is a series of carefully sequenced sets of pictures and instructions to be used with groups of young children to give them systematic practice in language concepts. (Appleton-Century Crofts)

SOME CAUTIONS

We have considered a fairly representative sample of programs, games, kits, and associated learning materials now being used in cognitive development and remediation. The brief descriptions presented here are necessarily incomplete. For full and complete information the reader must consult the basic source itself and become personally acquainted with the material or program.

There is no single "complete" cognitive development program. Each of the programs and materials presented here has something distinctive to offer teachers of all kinds. But, like all tools, they are only as good as the person who uses them. Considerable caution must be exercised in both the selection and the use of any such material or program.

There is no doubt, however, that instructional tools and materials such as these do have their proper place in education and therapy. What that place is and how they are to be best used must be determined by each professional person after considering the distinctive needs of his or her pupils. When wisely used as a part of the total psychoeducational program, they can contribute much to the cognitive development of children.

DISCUSSION QUESTIONS AND ACTIVITIES

1. Design a problem-solving card of your own that you could use as an addition to Think-lab.
2. How do you think the Piaget Early Childhood Curriculum might best be used in special education?
3. Design two different attribute matrix cards of varying difficulty using different shapes and colors.
4. Present the Tips and Beeps creature cards to a child and discuss the principles involved. Have the child design another card of his or her own.
5. Which of the major programs presented here appear to have research validation?
6. Select one of the skills in the Reading-Thinking Skills program. Write or design a learning task that could be used as part of a lesson to teach this specific skill.
7. Which of the programs presented here is directly derived from a factor analysis of mental abilities?
8. Create an SOI lesson with tasks that would teach figural memory for relations.
9. Visit a toy store and list several games, puzzles, etc. that might be used in a cognitive development program.
10. Select one of the major cognitive development programs presented here, prepare a written critique of it, and then demonstrate the program to your class or group.
11. Visit a school system instructional materials center. Review and describe a program available to teachers that is not described here. Review current school supply catalogs and describe some new material and its use.

CHAPTER 7

Task analysis and the Larry P. case

In 1971 several black children in the San Francisco City School District were experiencing great difficulty in learning. Their teachers referred them for psychological evaluation to determine if they needed special education. When it was found that the children scored below 75 on IQ tests the district decided that they should be placed in classes for the educable mentally retarded (EMR). The parents, however, were not convinced that this was in the best interest of their children; the parents collaborated with the Bay Area Association of Black Psychologists in a suit alleging that the children had been inadequately examined by school psychologists and that they were misdiagnosed and prejudiciously placed in classes for the retarded (Moriarty, 1972). This class action suit became known as the "Larry P." case and has raised serious questions about the proper use of intelligence testing in schools.

On June 20, 1972, United States District Judge Robert F. Peckham issued a preliminary order that for all practical purposes stopped the use of standardized intelligence tests with minority students in the state of California. In essence, the order required the California State Department of Education and the professional psychological associations to demonstrate the validity of IQ testing for special education placement. By implication this order also required the development of new and more rational procedures and guidelines to enable children with significant learning problems to be properly evaluated, have their difficulties diagnosed, and receive whatever kind of additional or special education that they require (Stickel, 1976).

The need for reform in the use (or misuse) of IQ tests has been professionally recognized for some time. There has been no question but that too much importance has been attributed to single IQ scores. This was formally recognized as early as 1971 when the California Association of School Psychologists and Psychometrists (CASPP) adopted a resolution to condemn reliance on test scores as the sole criterion for the initial placement and classification of any pupil in special classes or programs. The CASPP also called for an immediate moratorium on such use of test scores and then endorsed the use of "achievement and performance evaluations, tests, and tasks as placement criteria instead of intelligence test scores" (*Executive Board Minutes,* 1971).

TASK ANALYSIS

For some time now, psychologists and diagnostic-prescriptive specialists of all kinds have stressed the fundamental importance of behavioral observation and the collection of baseline performance data. It is now widely recognized that all psychoeducational evaluations must begin at this point. This requires a systematic observation of the child in his or her actual learning situation, be it the classroom, home, or playground. The purpose of this observation is, of course, to determine the situational demands on the child, including the teacher's task expectations of the pupil and the specific kinds of errors and difficulties the child is having in learning and achieving.

The major questions to be answered in part through task analysis include the following.

1. What are the learning objectives, tasks, and expectations?
2. Are they reasonable ones for the child to attain?
3. Are they clearly understood by the child and others concerned?
4. Is the teaching-instructional situation conducive to task achievement and performance, or are there situational barriers or hinderances to learning?
5. What is the final criterion that will be used to determine pupil achievement (achievement tests, projects, rating scales, papers, etc.)?

In most cases, answers to these questions are obtained through the combined behavioral analysis of classroom observation data and teacher referral information, which should include a detailed description of the learning problem accompanied by actual work samples that illustrate the kinds of errors being made. After all of these are reviewed, it is then (and only then) possible to determine if additional testing is required and, if so, just which psychoeducational tests might be the appropriate ones to supplement the basic observational data on hand. The analysis of all such information can then lead to a meaningful understanding of the child's learning problem and a diagnostic-prescriptive plan for improving the pupil's performance and achievement.

Let us consider some data for Larry P.,* a 10-year-9-month-old boy in a regular fifth grade class who has been referred for possible placement in a special education class. His record is one of poor grades, limited motivation, and low achievement in reading, writing, spelling, and arithmetic. On the WISC-R (Wechsler Intelligence Scale for Children-Revised) he scored a full scale IQ of 75, with a verbal scale IQ of 72 and a performance scale IQ of 82. Most of Larry's teachers have thought that he is retarded since he has not been able to do the work in their classes; therefore they have recommended that he be moved from the regular program to a self-contained class for the educable mentally retarded.

By itself this referral information about Larry is extremely limited and of little value in helping plan a prescriptive or "special" education program for him. In fact, we have no real baseline information, as we do not know what is actually being required of Larry in his present class. For example, we do not know the

---

*All data and descriptions of Larry P. are hypothetical.

kind of reading program he is in, the kinds of reading materials he is using and the errors he is making, or what arithmetic operations he is having difficulty with. This vital information can best be obtained through classroom visitation and observation and through the collection of relevant work samples. It is also possible to get some of this data through the use of systematic teacher referral forms of various kinds (Valett, 1969, pp. 66-68; Valett, 1972).

There is no evidence, however, that indicates that any attempt was made to obtain the necessary baseline data. In fact, many school districts do not have policies that require teachers to submit detailed referral data. Also, many districts do not allow diagnostic-prescriptive specialists, psychologists, or allied professionals to conduct actual classroom observations or to consult with the referring teacher during an on-site visit. When these policies are justified in the name of administrative expediency, they are short-sighted and may result in serious legal and ethical problems. California law, for instance, is quite specific in its standards for the individual evaluation of pupils with suspected educational handicaps as it requires that the psychoeducational study include the following.*

- The developmental history, school history, and educational progress of the pupil
- The specific steps taken to assist the pupil *in the area of his school difficulty and the results of such assistance*
- Observation of the pupil in his regular school situation and an evaluation of the environmental factors and peer and teacher interactions affecting his functioning in the regular school program
- Specific measurements of the pupil's levels of potential academic functioning, including reading
- Appraisal of the pupil's intellectual capacity for potential cognitive learning
- Appraisal of the economic, social, cultural, and language factors that may have an effect on school functioning of the pupil

If these steps had been followed in the evaluation of Larry P., it is quite probable that teacher and parent involvement with the psychoeducational consultant would have produced sufficient data for task analysis and educational programming. It would have also enabled the school district to take a closer look at the regular curriculum and classroom organization to consider alternative forms of remedial education.

TEST ANALYSIS

Of what value is IQ testing in the Larry P. case? How can such test information be used to actually help children like Larry P. learn and achieve? These are two basic questions that can only be answered through the process of test analysis. This process demands that we carefully study the specific items on the test that were missed to determine subtest strengths and weaknesses and what they mean for remediation when correlated with baseline information.

By itself, an IQ of 75 tells us that Larry is currently learning significantly more

---

*California Administrative Code. Title V, Chapter 2, Article 3, Section 3231. Sacramento: State Printing Office.

slowly than most other children his age. Of course, we also know that he is some-what stronger in performance skills and abilities than in verbal abilities. But we need to study the subtests in detail to determine what might be done to help such a child improve. Larry's WISC-R profile is presented below. This is a profile of standard scaled scores on which a score of 10 is average; scaled scores between 7 and 13 represent the lower and upper ranges of statistical normality (which means that 68% of all children Larry's age score between 7 and 13).

An immediate survey of the profile shows some real differences between verbal and performance subtests. The similarities and comprehension subtests are this boy's most significant verbal weaknesses, and these items and skills require careful analysis and programming; he also scored very low on information, vocabulary, and the coding subtest, which requires him to perform by writing symbols as quickly as he can.

The WISC-R profile lists the subtests across the top of the form. The scaled score for each subtest is recorded in the appropriate box and marked on the sheet.

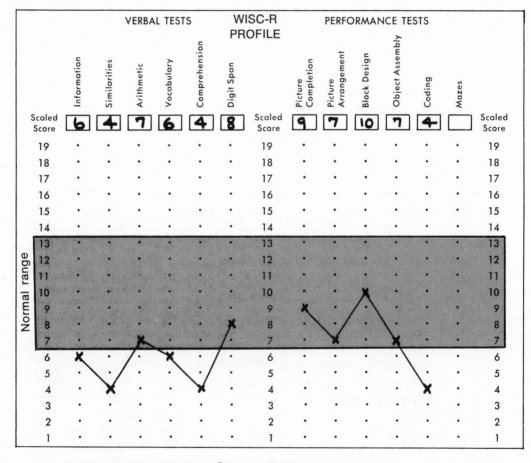

Since scaled scores are standardized scores, they can be compared to indicate real differences in subtest skills and abilities. If retesting is done following remediation, the new profile should indicate growth in thinking and cognitive skills relative to the nature of the prescriptive program, its duration, and intensity. This profile indicates that, although Larry has several very weak cognitive skills, he also has two or three relatively normal abilities with great educational significance.

What then does this profile tell us are some of the more obvious skills that Larry needs to learn? The simplest way to respond to this question is to list one or two of the easiest items missed on selected subtests. By actually teaching the concepts reflected by each item and using the items as guides for remedial curriculum planning, much can be done to help Larry improve his problem-solving skills and school achievement. Listed by priority, these items are as follows.

- SIMILARITIES: Understanding common relationships, elements, and likenesses between things
  How are these alike, or the same?
  Beer and wine   Elbow and knee
  Cat and mouse   Eye and mouth
  Horse and donkey
- COMPREHENSION: Practical knowledge, judgment, reasoning, and understanding logical relationships
  What are some reasons why we need policemen?
  What is the thing to do if you lose something you borrowed from one of your friends?
  Why should dogs wear license tags?
- CODING: Speed and accuracy in learning and reproducing meaningless symbols
  Look at the numbers and their symbols below and then write in the symbols in the missing boxes.

1	2	3	4	5	6
⊤	C	O	⊥	M	Λ

1	3	4	2	5	3	6	2	5	1	4

- INFORMATION: Memory of acquired general information from natural experience and education
  What are the four seasons of the year?
  Who discovered America?
  Who is president of the United States?
- VOCABULARY: Word knowledge, verbal fluency, and expressive vocabulary
  Explain what these words mean and tell me as much as you can about them.
     diamond   gamble   nonsense   prevent

- ARITHMETIC: Knowledge of basic arithmetic operations and their application in problem solving, concentration and attention in reasoning and dealing with abstractions
  At 8 cents each, what will three candy bars cost?
  If a boy had 26 comic books and sold 11 of them, how many would he have left?

The WISC profile also tells us something about Larry's strengths. The block design subtest indicates average ability in being able to reproduce abstract design with colored wooden blocks from a pictorial model; from this test we know that Larry can perceive and understand figural abstractions and relationships that are basic to most learning situations. He also has normal visual memory and awareness, at least as it is reflected in the picture completion subtest, which requires the person to be alert to the details of things in the natural environment by indicating missing parts in pictures of things such as animals, clothes, people, tools, and other common objects. Larry also does fairly well on the digit span subtest; he was able to sequence numbers (5–2–1–8–6), which reflects attention, concentration, and memory.

On the other two subtests he scored 7 scaled points, a low normal score. The picture arrangement subtest requires the proper sequencing of several cartoons that, when put together, comprise a story such as a man going fishing, or a burglar being caught; by misplacing one card on two different items he indicated a different style of social interpretation, which resulted in a lower score. Similarly, on the object assembly subtest Larry was clearly able to see that the cut-up pictures represented objects such as a girl and a horse, but he was penalized because he had to proceed very slowly in putting them together.

Taken as a whole, the WISC-R test results are most valuable and helpful in that they clearly show that Larry does not have the typical low and relatively flat profile of mentally retarded children. Although his total IQ of 75 may superficially appear to indicate borderline mental retardation, an analysis of subtest items contradicts this immediate interpretation. When test analysis is then considered along with the meager information available—namely, that Larry is from a poor minority family of very limited cultural and educational background where English is spoken with a noticeable dialect—mental retardation can almost certainly be ruled out.

CRITERION EVALUATION

It has long been recognized that the single most important criterion for judging mental retardation is that of social competency and incompetency. The following are relevant questions to be considered here.

- How well does Larry get along with his peers?
- Does he participate in games and related activities, and to what extent is he involved?
- How does he care for his own basic personal needs such as dressing, eating, and bathing?
- To what extent does he move about his neighborhood and community without supervision?

These questions can all be answered through interviews with parents, teachers, and significant others who have known Larry for some time. Some direct observation of Larry at home and school is necessary to substantiate interview results.

When this kind of pragmatic evidence is considered, it is apparent that Larry is actually quite socially competent in that he receives fairly positive ratings on all of the above social skill criteria. He is, however, a slow and somewhat apathetic boy who tends to be a follower. In school, his attention wanders, and he clearly lacks self-confidence and quickly loses interest in verbal abstractions beyond his immediate comprehension. It is always best to begin the evaluation of children like Larry P. with a home visit and parent interview using some instrument for determining social competency such as the Vineland Social Maturity Scale,* The Developmental Task Analysis,† or the Revised School Version of the American Association of Mental Deficiency Adaptive Behavior Scale.‡ Since an initial evaluation of this kind of primary social-adaptive criteria was not made for Larry P., the diagnosis was incomplete and invalid.

If evidence of social competency and several average cognitive abilities exists, it may rule out mental retardation, but it does not dispel the fact that Larry is an educationally handicapped child with many learning problems. What, then, is yet to be considered to determine the more exact nature of Larry's educational difficulties? In the school learning situation, the answer to this question is to be found in an analysis of Larry's responses to his assignments and other critical cognitive tasks. The most common school learning criteria are functional performance in the language arts, such as reading and communication skills. That is the reason, of course, that most state laws and local school district policies require periodic evaluation of reading and language achievement of all children and demand that it be done as part of the initial evaluation of children referred for possible remedial or special education.

The evaluation of reading and language skills always requires the use of some standardized test as well as direct work samples that clearly indicate the kinds of errors being made in classroom performance. Through the use of standardized tests and related criterion instruments, Larry's reading vocabulary, comprehension, fluency, and phonetic skills and achievement levels must all be determined before a meaningful remedial plan can be developed. In addition, there are many sensory and perceptual components of the reading process that may require more in-depth study and diagnostic appraisal, since many children like Larry P. have highly specific learning and language disabilities. These skills and their relationship to cognitive functioning are discussed in more detail in Chapter 8.

Again, there is no indication that this kind of thorough cognitive and language skills evaluation was conducted with those children who became part of the Larry P. case. What these children really required, of course, was a more complete diag-

---

*American Guidance Services, Circle Pines, Minn.
†Fearon Publishers, Inc., Belmont, Calif.
‡American Association on Mental Deficiency, 5201 Connecticut Ave. N.W., Washington, D.C.

nostic evaluation of their overall learning strengths and weaknesses. And such an evaluation should have involved the task analysis of both tests and associated school learning criteria to arrive at a logical diagnosis and prescription. Since Larry was not mentally retarded, arbitrary placement in an EMR class would have been ethically irresponsible and may well have resulted in personal harm and detriment.

FEASIBLE ALTERNATIVES

There are numerous slow-learning and educationally handicapped children like Larry. Conservative estimates based on statistical studies of standardized test results indicate that at least 10% of schoolchildren are functioning on low achievement levels similar to that of Larry P. In an earlier study of 743 pupils placed in EMR classes, I disclosed that the majority of them were actually slow learners with specific cognitive and educational problems whose causes could be found in cultural deprivation, socioeconomic disparities, and minority differences of psycholinguistic expression (Valett, 1965). If the solution to these children's learning problems is not to be found in EMR placement, what are the more rational and feasible alternatives for helping them? Although each Larry P. must be considered and prescribed for on the basis of individual study and diagnosis, several general alternatives are readily apparent.

First, it must be recognized that the school system cannot by itself "cure" or completely remedy learning handicaps of this kind. If Larry P. (and others like him) is really handicapped by living in a poor home with an unemployed father, inadequate food and nutrition, and little or no cultural stimulation, this must be recognized for the socioeconomic problem that it clearly is. School welfare, nursing, counseling, and remedial services may be of some help in these cases, but it should be obvious that much more is needed. So-called full-employment legislation, minimal income family support systems, national health insurance, and similar programs may be essential requisites for ensuring successful learning of deprived children.

Second, schools must provide more flexible developmental and achievement placement for pupils of all kinds. Children must be allowed to make continuous progress in school at their own rate and with their own style of learning. Individualized instruction of different kinds must be provided for within the organizational context of the *regular* school curriculum. Such instruction must include practice in the development of critical thinking and cognitive skills basic to all learning. A number of commercial cognitive development programs such as the Meeker Structure of Intellect materials, the Science Research Associates Thinklab, the Continental Press Reading-Thinking Skills program, and many others should be an intrinsic part of the curriculum. (See Chapter 6 for information about such programs.) Cognitive and language arts training for slow-learning children should emphasize listening, auditory processing, phonetic analysis, and the interpretation of meaningful reading materials. Intensive structural language and remedial reading programs for those in need should ensure mastery of the fundamental sensory-perceptual and conceptual skills inherent in the reading process.

All schools should also provide learning resource centers and programs to supplement the regular flexible developmental achievement grouping of pupils. Resource and clinical teachers should work as members of the total school staff to help design more effective learning programs and systems both in and out of the regular classroom. Children like Larry P. need to be taught by several teachers working together to meet prescriptive objectives, and their efforts should be coordinated by a resource specialist trained in special and remedial education who is also experienced in the regular school curriculum.

The Larry P. case has taught us much. It has shown us how test results can be used inappropriately. But it has also shown us how tests and other forms of psychoeducational evaluation should be properly used in a diagnostic-prescriptive manner. It would be a tragic mistake for educational and psychological specialists not to use the tools of task analysis, behavioral observation, and tests of all kinds that are now available to us to help children learn.

DISCUSSION QUESTIONS AND ACTIVITIES

1. What would your reaction be if you were suddenly informed by a school psychologist that one of your own children was mentally retarded?
2. To what extent do you agree or disagree with the CASPP test score moratorium and endorsement of other placement criteria?
3. What might be a teaching-instructional "situational barrier" to learning? How might such a barrier be removed or reduced to facilitate learning?
4. Design a two-page teacher referral form that would provide you with the minimum information necessary to initiate a psychoeducational study.
5. How would you decide who, what, and when to observe in a classroom visitation?
6. Outline a 15-minute lesson that would *teach* Larry to comprehend the similarities in specifically selected verbal concepts.
7. What might be done to help Larry improve his poor performance skills and low subtest scores? How might verbal fluency and related abilities be included in "performance lessons"?
8. Assume Larry is reading functionally in books and materials at the low third grade level. What standardized reading test would you use to help diagnose his reading problems and difficulties? What phonic skills are evaluated by this test?
9. How would you best determine which verbal abstractions are beyond his "immediate comprehension"? What might then be done to help teach him some of these abstractions?
10. Design a modified extension of the WISC coding subtest tasks that would relate more directly to the normal reading decoding process.
11. In what way might EMR placement be detrimental to children like Larry P.?
12. Suggest at least one alternative form of school organization that would have furthered individualized continuous progress instruction in the elementary school you attended as a child.
13. Demonstrate part of a commercially available cognitive development program that you think might be useful with Larry P.
14. Select and discuss another case of your own that you believe is similar to that of Larry P.

CHAPTER 8

Critical thinking skills

It has long been assumed (and rightly so) that schools should be concerned with teaching children how to think and solve real-life problems. Of course, schools are also concerned with many other things as well, such as the transmission of knowledge and cultural values, the development of character, and enhancing personal health. The basic skills such as reading, writing, and arithmetic have universally been included in school curricula since they have been recognized as essential tools for the communication of ideas and for problem solving. But there are many other fundamental skills that contribute to the functional ability of the person to think and convey ideas. These other skills have been defined and categorized in many different ways, but seldom have they been given their proper place in the curriculum. However, their acquisition is essential for achievement in life and in the traditional subject matter areas such as literature, science, the arts, and social studies.

BASIC CONCEPTS

Let us consider some of the basic concepts and assumptions underlying our concern with teaching what we will call the critical thinking skills.

"Thinking" refers to the mental processes of conceiving, manipulating, and dealing abstractly with ideas. In turn, ideas are nothing but notions, thoughts, and impressions of things that are being integrated and meaningfully organized in the brain of the person doing the thinking. A particular concept or idea appears in the conscious mind of the thinker as a result of a unique combination of maturation, cultural experience, and highly specific education.

If we want children to be able to formulate ideas and then to use them in meaningful problem-solving situations, we need to be aware of the mental processes involved and how the required skills may be enhanced through proper education. We know, of course, that most ideas can be described in such functional terms that they can be recorded and then conveyed to others through varied kinds of educational experiences and methods. Historical records and archives, libraries, and scientific laboratories are among the more common depositories of important ideas and their consequences when applied in given life situations.

In this context we are concerned with isolating certain thinking "skills." A skill may be best comprehended as a highly specific form of behavior that has been acquired through proper education, continued practice, and much effort. For example, riding a bicycle, playing the piano, operating a calculator, writing a story, and swimming are all examples of functional skills that are acquired through highly specific education, practice, and effort. And each of these skills requires the manipulation of rather unique concepts in several mental processes. Skills can also be thought of as highly differentiated segments of broader abilities. For example, most persons have some physical and musical abilities (which, like all abilities, vary greatly between persons), but the way in which we are educated to use such abilities determines whether we become specialized athletes, musicians, or just persons with some interest and rather minor proficiency. (This proficiency, however, may still be sufficient to bring us much pleasure and enjoyment in life!)

The skills required for most jobs and tasks can be observed, identified, isolated, and operationally defined. "Thinking skills" are those *ways of dealing with or manipulating abstract ideas* that make the idea or concept "meaningful" and thereby allow the person to use it in functional problem solving. Although all types or kinds of skills deal with the manipulation of relationships, physical and perceptual skills focus on the relationships between things or objects in the person's immediate environment. However, thinking or cognitive skills deal with the relationships of nonmaterial things or the remembered representations of the outer objective world, and these representations occur in mental pictures, words, formulas, images, and other abstract forms of thought.

Some thinking skills are much more important, or critical, than others. A critical thinking skill is one that is of decisive or significant importance in the life of the person. In this sense, critical thinking skills change according to life stages, growth, and development—and according to the actual tasks confronting the individual. A critical thinking skill of a 5-year-old differs significantly from that of an 11-year-old or a mature adult.

The life demands of the elementary schoolchild between 5 and 12 years of age are fairly well understood. We know, for instance, the developmental stages that children go through and how this affects their thinking (Inhelder and Piaget, 1958). We can also isolate the kinds of home, school, and community experiences of children and the expectations that are made of them at each developmental stage. Then we can specify the kinds of cognitive skills involved and do whatever is possible to ensure their development and proper acquisition.

Let us say, for instance, that we are fully aware of the curricular demands in the regular elementary school. That is, we know such things as what words, symbols, and concepts are used and taught at the different grade levels and we understand the relationships and mental processes involved. We also know which concepts and mental processes are sequential and cumulative, in the sense that understanding multiplication is dependent on the acquisition of addition concepts and operations, etc. Clearly, then, we must see to it that our pupils have acquired those fundamental mental processes and skills necessary for continued and future success. Critical thinking skills must have curricular validity in that they can be demonstrated to relate directly to school achievement and success and also must be able to transfer to similar life problem-solving situations, such as shopping.

Another basic element in considering the importance of specifying critical thinking skills in the elementary school is the possibility of remediation. Even the best designed and implemented developmental sequential curricula do not automatically lend themselves to individualization and continuous progress on the part of the child. When exceptional children or others with learning problems begin to experience significant difficulty, it is essential to be able to determine what faulty thinking processes and skills are involved and how these might possibly be remediated. What are these skills, and how might they be used by the teacher interested in curriculum modification or by the special educator in prescriptive teaching?

DEVELOPMENTAL SKILLS

As we have seen, it is possible to list and define hundreds of different learning skills. The *Mental Measurements Yearbook* (Buros, 1972) actually lists thousands of tests and instruments concerned with the evaluation of such skills and abilities. But the critical thinking skills of concern here are those that are most often seen in commonly used standardized tests for elementary schoolchildren. Our rationale is that if schools continue to use both individual and group achievement and ability tests (and to measure their own success according to test scores), then surely the very thinking processes and skills involved in such tests must be the basic criteria for any prescriptive or remedial instruction that may be necessary.

Following an extensive evaluation of currently used tests, 20 thinking skills have been identified as critical ones for elementary-age children. These 20 skills have been grouped into four categories according to Guilford's structure of mental content (1967); the term "mental content" refers to the *kinds* of abstractions that are being manipulated by the child. These are the following.

- BEHAVIORAL: Referring to the use of such personal and social skills as nonverbal communication, gestures, manners, and conventions
- SYMBOLIC: Referring to the use of signs and symbols and their interrelationships, including written language
- FIGURAL: Referring to the understanding and use of classifications and designs, and the relationships of figural parts and wholes
- SEMANTIC: Referring to the understanding and use of words and language

All persons use all four kinds of mental content and abstractions, but some persons are more proficient in dealing with behavioral abstractions than semantic ones. Similarly, others are more effective in dealing with symbolic or figural material. Most schools emphasize the importance of acquiring semantic skills.

But the others are of equal importance, as they are commonly required in daily problem-solving situations as well.

The operational definitions for each of the 20 critical thinking skills, as arranged categorically, are as follows.

Behavioral

1. SELF-EVALUATION: Self-analysis and constructive autocriticism
2. SOCIAL JUDGMENT: Analysis and interpretation of social situations and anticipation of logical consequences
3. MANUAL EXPRESSION: Nonverbal communication through gestures, body movement, sign language, charades, etc.

Symbolic

4. WRITING: Written expression and communication of ideas
5. AUDITORY VOCAL SYNTHESIS: Understanding and using auditory association, closure, and speech sounds in a meaningful context
6. ARITHMETIC PROBLEM SOLVING: Arithmetic applications and reasoning
7. SERIATION: Understanding a series of sequential patterns or symbolic relationships
8. SYMBOL DRAWING: Copying abstract designs and representations correctly and proportionally

Figural

9. FIGURAL RELATIONSHIPS/CLASSIFICATION: Understanding pictorial similarities and differences, logical classes, and relationships
10. VISUAL-KINESTHETIC MEMORY: Symbol reproduction from memory following brief exposure
11. MOTOR PLANNING/CODING: Perceptual-motor integration, anticipation, planning, and accuracy in motor decoding
12. VISUAL INTEGRATION: Organizing and meaningfully integrating visual stimuli, parts, and impressions and providing visual closure and generalizations

Semantic

14. ANALOGOUS THINKING: Understanding and application of relationships, inferences, and correspondence
14. DIFFERENCES AND OPPOSITES: Contrasting things according to differences and logical opposites
15. SPELLING: Correct oral and written expression of letter symbols and sound combinations
16. READING INTERPRETATION: Meaningful understanding and application of written language
17. COMMONSENSE INFORMATION: Factual information and knowledge, reference skills from experience and education
18. EXPRESSIVE LANGUAGE: Verbal expression and fluency of verbal concepts
19. VERBAL COMPREHENSION: General verbal reasoning and practical problem solving
20. RECEPTIVE CONCEPTUAL VOCABULARY: Understanding and nonverbal interpretation of spoken language

DIAGNOSTIC-PRESCRIPTIVE USE

A list of critical thinking skills is of primary value to the educator only if the actual tasks to be learned are clearly identified. This is always best done by making an actual in-depth item analysis of the kinds of specific problems a pupil is experiencing. Through such an analysis of regular unit test items and through special teacher-made or other specially selected tests, the teacher can usually plan the properly required remedial program. However, the teacher may recognize that a pupil is having difficulty in dealing with various kinds of problems and yet be unable to specify primary learning objectives.

At this point in the diagnostic-prescriptive process the teacher needs to conduct a survey of the pupil's critical thinking skills to determine those areas of primary concern. If the teacher has a number of different achievement and ability tests on hand, they may be used to obtain the desired information. Unfortunately, too often such tests or other basic criterion instruments have not been provided or are not available when needed. Even individual psychological reports that are available for most children requiring special education usually fail to provide the necessary information unless they contain actual item samples and highly correlated suggestions for prescriptive teaching.

CRITICAL THINKING SKILLS SURVEY

The critical thinking skills survey in Chapter 9 has been designed for direct use by diagnostic-prescriptive teachers. Twenty skills are presented in the survey. Each of the 20 skills has been operationally defined and categorized in one of the four educational domains of instructional concern—behavioral, symbolic, figural, or semantic. Each skills is also classified according to the taxonomy (RLD) given in the *Remediation of Learning Disabilities* (Valett, 1974), which provides specific psychoeducational resource programs and suggestions for use as the teacher thinks appropriate.

Each survey skill has a place for recording test criterion scores, listing the test names and the subtests that have been used to provide the criterion items included on the survey. In most cases, the actual item from the test has been slightly modified, but its basic form and content remain intact. In this way, the diagnostic-prescriptive teacher can see how and what each survey item represents, as indicated by the criterion tests listed. The special educator *should* have pretest scores available to use as a guide in prescriptive planning. Most of the actual criterion test scores are standard scores (although some may be raw scores or age scores), which are obtainable from the psychological reports available for practically all exceptional children.

For example, let us consider critical thinking skill number 18, expressive language. A teacher working with 7-year-old nonexpressive child would certainly want to note the pretest scores on the WISC, Boehm, ITPA, or some other test that was used. Certainly, some test scores should be recorded as valid pretests that are indicative of the need for developing the child's expressive vocabulary. By carefully considering the pretest scores available (and what they represent) and by obtaining a direct sample of the child's expressive language on the survey form, the teacher can begin to develop the remedial program. Later, if appropriate prescriptive teaching has been carried out, educational gains should be reflected in an increase on posttest criterion scores. Tests used in the survey as criterion measures and abbreviations are listed here.

- BG: Bender Visual Motor Gestalt Test (The Psychological Corp., 304 East 45th St., New York, N.Y.)
- Binet: Stanford-Binet Intelligence Scale L-M (Houghton-Mifflin Co., 110 Tremont St., Boston, Mass.)
- Boehm Test of Basic Concepts (The Psychological Corp.)
- Columbia Mental Maturity Test (Harcourt Brace Jovanovich, Inc., 757 Third Ave., New York, N.Y.)
- CTBS: Comprehensive Test of Basic Skills (CTB/McGraw-Hill Div., Del Monte Research Park, Monterey, Calif.)
- Detroit Verbal Opposites Test from Detroit Tests of Learning Aptitude (Bobbs-Merrill Co., 4300 West 62nd St., Indianapolis, Ind.)
- Draw-A-Person Test (Harcourt Brace Jovanovich, Inc.)
- Englemann: Englemann Basic Concept Inventory (Follett Corp., Chicago, Ill.)
- GFW: Goldman Fristoe Woodcock Auditory Skills Test (American Guidance Services, Publishers Building, Circle Pines, Minn.)
- ITPA: Illinois Test of Psycholinguistic Ability (University of Illinois Press, Urbana, Ill.)
- Key Math: Key Math Diagnostic Arithmetic Test (American Guidance Services)
- My Self Concept (Fearon Publishers, Inc., 6 David Dr., Belmont, Ca.)
- PIAT: Peabody Individual Achievement Tests (American Guidance Services)
- PPVT: Peabody Picture Vocabulary Test (American Guidance Services)
- Piaget Seriation Tasks (Center for Media Development, American Science & Engineering, Inc., Boston, Mass.)
- Raven Progressive Matrices (The Psychological Corp.)
- Slingerland: Slingerland Screening Tests for Identifying Children With Specific Language Disability (Educators Publishing Service, 75 Moulton St., Cambridge, Mass.)
- Spache Diagnostic Reading Scales (CTB/McGraw-Hill Div.)
- WRAT: Wide Range Achievement Tests (Guidance Associates, 1526 Gilpin Ave., Wilmington, Del.)

Prescriptive teachers and special educators should be provided with copies of any actual test forms that have been used with the pupil. In this way the teacher will be able to locate and evaluate actual items missed and to note any unique responses the child may have made. A qualitative analysis of the pupil's errors and style of thinking are invaluable for remedial planning.

Administering the survey

The survey may be administered in one or more sessions as the situation requires. If it is given in two or more sessions, a single content area such as symbolic skills can be completed at one time. As with all such evaluations, the child should be put at ease and introduced to the survey with a statement such as "I would like to have you do some of the things on this form so I can see what kinds of skills you have and how I might best help you." For young or hyperactive children, it may be necessary to take frequent breaks or to reinforce completion of several skill tasks with a small snack of some kind.

Each of the critical thinking skills is surveyed on four different levels: developmental ages 5, 7, 9, and 11. These four age levels have been selected because they correspond to the beginning, middle, and upper grades in the typical elementary school with kindergarten through grade 6. Each of these age groups has its own distinctive thinking style or stage, which is reflected in the school curriculum and teacher expectations. The 5-year-old's thinking is primarily at a transitional sensory stage in which much movement is necessary to provide needed sensory integration. The 7-year-old has advanced to the stage of perceptual organization in which auditory, visual, and kinesthetic modalities are of great importance. At 9 years of age the child's thinking style is shaped by his broadening social and community experiences. By the time the child reaches 11 years of age his thinking skills have matured to the stage at which he is becoming capable of dealing rationally, including the manipulation of more formal abstract mental operations.

The diagnostic teacher should begin the survey by administering the age tasks that he or she thinks are closest to the child's developmental age. If the child fails those tasks, the next lower ones should be tried; if the child passes a task, the next advanced one should be given. The teacher-evaluator should mark the plus column to indicate a pass and the minus column to indicate an error. It is extremely important to write in any comments the pupil may make that may disclose his style of thinking.

The form on pp. 124 and 125 should be completed after all the skills have been evaluated. For each skill, the highest age passed should be indicated by +. These can then be connected by lines to give a graphic profile of relative strengths and weaknesses. Pupil motivation and the approximate reliability and validity of the evaluation should also be checked and commented on if necessary. The diagnostic teacher should then review the pupil's responses to determine the selection of priority teaching tasks and objectives.

Possible teaching tasks and objectives are suggested within the context of the survey itself. For each developmental age, an "easy" developmental learning task is presented as a suggested teaching objective if the child has failed on that level. If the developmental learning task presented is too easy, the teacher should modify it by writing a moderate or more difficult one. It is very important that each developmental learning task be written so that it closely corresponds to the criterion test item. Of course, other tasks, lessons, and prescriptive programs should then be selected or devised from all available resources to help the child develop that critical thinking skill.

In most cases it is sufficient to select no more than three priority teaching objectives. This is usually adequate to focus on at any one time and is feasible for prescriptive planning. All priority objectives and tasks should clearly specify the skill involved and should state in detail exactly what the child is expected to do and what lessons and materials might be required.

Objectives should be revised periodically and prescriptive lessons changed accordingly. Other tests, such as required state and district achievement tests and textbook tests, should also be used as a criterion source of teaching objectives. We must always keep in mind, however, that whatever kinds of tests, inventories, surveys, or other evaluation devices are selected and used as criterion instruments, it is essential to formulate teaching objectives that focus on the content, skill, and mental processes involved, rather than on the single test item itself.

DISCUSSION QUESTIONS AND ACTIVITIES

1. List and discuss the basic tools or skills that you feel should be taught in all elementary schools.
2. What is "thought"?
3. Define "critical" thinking skills.
4. Select a test of some specific cognitive skill and discuss the test review in the most recent edition of the *Mental Measurements Yearbook*.
5. Discuss Guilford's four content areas and specify which one you think is the most neglected in the public elementary schools.
6. What other kinds of behavioral skills do you think could be specified for instructional purposes?
7. List two remedial sources or guides that might be used in providing prescriptive instructional tasks or ideas for teachers concerned with critical thinking skill deficits.
8. Suggest some other tests that might be added as source criterion items for the critical thinking skills.
9. In each of the four major content areas listed for the critical thinking skills, write a behavioral objective with minimum performance standards.

CHAPTER 9

Critical thinking skills survey

This chapter consists of the critical thinking skills survey, which was introduced in Chapter 8. The survey has been developed for use by diagnostic-prescriptive teachers as an aid in understanding the nature of various conceptual skill test items that are frequently used as criterion measures of cognitive growth and achievement.

The introductory part of the survey is a form for recording pupil information and performance. The following pages consist of 20 major behavioral, symbolic, figural, and semantic skills presented in a worksheet format for use by teachers and others concerned. Tests used as criterion measures (with abbreviations) are listed on p. 118.

Chapter 8 also contains instructions for administering the survey. The reader should carefully review the entire survey and then consider the discussion questions and activities. After the survey has been administered (in whole or in part), results and prescriptive learning tasks should be shared and discussed in detail with another person similarly concerned.

Since the primary purpose of the survey is to initiate help and practice in designing task-relevant prescriptive instruction, teachers should write and design the prescriptive tasks in behavioral terms. For actual instructional application the survey should always be used in conjunction with other forms of psychoeducational evaluation such as classroom baseline observation and achievement tests.

CRITICAL THINKING SKILLS SURVEY
A criterion evaluation instrument for diagnostic-prescriptive teaching

Pupil's name _____ Date _____

Address _____ Birthdate _____

School _____ Class/program _____ Age _____

Cognitive abilities and skills	Developmental stages and ages (in years)			
	Sensory 5	Perceptual 7	Experiential 9	Rational 11
Behavioral				
1. Self-evaluation				
2. Social judgment				
3. Manual expression				
Symbolic				
4. Writing				
5. Auditory vocal synthesis				
6. Arithmetic problem solving				
7. Seriation				
8. Symbol drawing				
Figural				
9. Figural relationships/ classification				
10. Visual kinesthetic memory				
11. Motor planning/coding				
12. Visual integration				
Semantic				
13. Analogous thinking				
14. Differences and opposites				
15. Spelling				
16. Reading interpretation				
17. Common sense information				

CRITICAL THINKING SKILLS SURVEY—cont'd
A criterion evaluation instrument for diagnostic-prescriptive teaching

Cognitive abilities and skills	Developmental stages and ages (in years)			
	Sensory 5	Perceptual 7	Experiential 9	Rational 11
Semantic—cont'd 18. Expressive language				
19. Verbal comprehension				
20. Receptive conceptual vocabulary				

Pupil motivation: Poor _____ Fair _____ Good _____ Excellent _____

How reliable and valid do you consider this evaluation to have been?

Poor _____ Fair _____ Good _____ Excellent _____

Priority teaching objectives and tasks (selected from this survey):

First:

Second:

Third:

Comments:

Signature _____

(Evaluator)

▶ Skill 1
SELF-EVALUATION
Pupil's name _____

Self-analysis and constructive autocriticism (personal strengths and weaknesses, accomplishments, appearance, goals, problems, etc.)

EDUCATIONAL DOMAIN: Behavioral   RLD TAXONOMY: Social maturity

Test criterion scores

Test	Pretest		Posttest	
	Date	Score	Date	Score
Vineland SA				
My Self Concept				
Other				

	Evaluation	
	Plus	Minus
DA 5 Are you a boy or a girl? How old are you?		
Developmental learning tasks		
EASY: Your name is _____. You are _____ years old. Say, "My name is _____. I am _____ years old."		
MODERATE:		
DIFFICULT:		
DA 7 What color are your eyes? What games can you play best?		
Developmental learning tasks		
EASY: Look at your hair in this mirror. The color of your hair is _____. Say, "The color of my hair is _____."		
MODERATE:		
DIFFICULT:		

	Plus	Minus
DA 9 What do you most need help with in school? What do you most need help with at home?		
Developmental learning tasks		
EASY: Here is a school assignment that you obviously need some help with. Show and tell me what kind of help you need.		
MODERATE:		
DIFFICULT:		
DA 11 Tell me about some work you have done for money and how well you did it.		
Developmental learning tasks		
EASY: Describe a job at home that you have done as part of your allowance or were specially paid for.		
MODERATE:		
DIFFICULT:		

▶ Skill 2

SOCIAL JUDGMENT   Pupil's name _____

Analysis and interpretation of social situations and anticipation of logical consequences (understanding cartoon and photo sequences, story endings, jokes, proverbs, etc.)

EDUCATIONAL DOMAIN: Behavioral   RLD TAXONOMY: Anticipatory response

Test criterion scores

Test	Pretest		Posttest	
	Date	Score	Date	Score
WISC—picture arranging				
Binet—absurdities				
Other				

	Evaluation	
	Plus	Minus

DA 5 If placed in proper order these pictures tell a story about growing flowers. Look at the pictures and point to the one that comes first, then second, then last. Tell me the story.

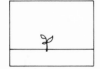

Developmental learning tasks

EASY: These pictures tell a story about a little tree that grew into a big tree. Point to the pictures and tell me the story.

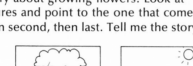

MODERATE:

DIFFICULT:

DA 7 Why is it silly for children to play tag on a busy street or highway?

	Plus	Minus

Developmental learning tasks

EASY: These children may
be injured. Show me
why this might happen.

MODERATE:

DIFFICULT:

DA 9   Tell me what is silly about this story: "Bill
Jones' feet are so big that he has to pull
his trousers on over his head."

Developmental learning tasks

EASY: Here is a pair of old pants. Try to put them on over
your head. See how they are upside down and will not
go down to cover your legs? Now you tell me why that
is a silly way to try to put pants on.

MODERATE:

DIFFICULT:

DA 11   Number these pictures from 1 to 5 to tell
the best story of a boy going fishing.

Developmental learning tasks

EASY: The first picture should be of the boy digging for
worms. Put an X on that picture and explain why this
is the first one in the story.

MODERATE:

DIFFICULT:

▶ **Skill** 3

MANUAL EXPRESSION   Pupil's name _____

Nonverbal communication through gestures, body movement, sign language, charades, etc. (basic feelings, use of tools, eating utensils, musical instruments, telephone, camera)

EDUCATIONAL DOMAIN: Behavioral   RLD TAXONOMY: Social acceptance

Test criterion scores

Test	Pretest		Posttest	
	Date	Score	Date	Score
ITPA—manual expression				
Informal charades				
Other				

	Evaluation	
	Plus	Minus

DA 5 Here is a picture of a hammer. Show me what you do with a hammer.

Developmental learning tasks

EASY: Watch me pretend to use a hammer. See how I take it in my hand and pretend to use it to hammer a nail in something. Now you show me how to do it.

MODERATE:

DIFFICULT:

DA 7 Look at this picture and think for a moment how you can use this. Now pretend you are using it—show me what you could do with it.

Developmental learning tasks

EASY: The object is a telephone. One thing you can do with it is to dial a number like this. You do it and then show me what else you might do with it.

	Plus	Minus
MODERATE:		
DIFFICULT:		

DA 9   Pretend you had two eggs, a frying pan, some butter, salt, and pepper. Show me in detail what you might do with these things.

Developmental learning tasks

EASY: Let's suppose we had a hot stove and we put the frying pan on like this; then we put butter in like this. What would you do next? *Show me.*

MODERATE:

DIFFICULT:

DA 11   This time pretend you are using sign language to tell an Indian that over a big hill to the East there are many buffalo that the tribe can hunt for food.

Developmental learning tasks

EASY: A sign for a big hill might be like this (demonstrate). What might a sign be for buffalo?

MODERATE:

DIFFICULT:

▶ Skill 4

WRITING   Pupil's name _____

Written expression and communication of ideas (words, sentences, paragraphs, punctuation, mechanics)

EDUCATIONAL DOMAIN: Symbolic   RLD TAXONOMY: Writing

Test criterion scores

Test	Pretest		Posttest	
	Date	Score	Date	Score
Slingerland				
WRAT—spelling				
CTBS—language mechanics				
Other				

	Evaluation	
	Plus	Minus

DA 5   Write your name in the box.

Developmental learning tasks

EASY: I have printed your name in the box. Copy over it and tell me the letters in your name.

MODERATE:

DIFFICULT:

DA 7   Write your address in the box.

Developmental learning tasks

EASY: I have written your address in the box. Copy it correctly.

	Plus	Minus
MODERATE:		
DIFFICULT:		

DA 9   Write the correct punctuation mark on the line at the end of the sentence.

> He went home____

Developmental learning tasks

EASY: A period is a dot that comes at the end of a sentence● Place an X on the period at the end of each of these sentences●

MODERATE:

DIFFICULT:

DA 11   Write this sentence in the box. "I go to _____ school and my teacher's name is _____."

> | |
> |---|

Developmental learning tasks

EASY: Your teacher's name is written on the chalkboard. Copy it in the box.

> | |
> |---|

MODERATE:

DIFFICULT:

AUDITORY-VOCAL SYNTHESIS   Pupil's name _____

Understanding and using auditory association, closure, and speech sounds in a meaningful context (consonants, vowels, blends, associations) grammar, integration

EDUCATIONAL DOMAIN: Symbolic   RLD TAXONOMY: Word attack skills

Test criterion scores

Test	Pretest		Posttest	
	Date	Score	Date	Score
Spache—phonics				
ITPA—grammatic closure				
ITPA—auditory closure				
ITPA—sound blending				
GFW—sound symbols				
Other				

	Evaluation	
	Plus	Minus
DA 5 Listen to the sounds I am going to say, put them together, and tell me what the word is: "ea–t" (eat)		
Developmental learning tasks EASY: Listen to the sounds "b–oy." When put together they say "boy." What is a boy? What do the sounds "b–oy" mean when put together? Say the sounds "b–oy" out loud. What do they mean?		
MODERATE:		
DIFFICULT:		
DA 7 Look—Here are lots of blocks. 		
Look—Here are even <u>(more)</u>. 		
Developmental learning tasks EASY: Look—I am holding up two fingers. Now you hold up three fingers. You are holding up one *more* than I		

	Plus	Minus

am. Now look at both of my hands. I am holding up even *(more)* fingers.

MODERATE:

DIFFICULT:

DA 9 How do these sound? What do they say?

b	tr	f	pl	j
sh	v	ing	m	ow

Developmental learning tasks

EASY: Place a circle around the first sound you missed in the above box. What is the name of the letter (or letters) in the box? The *sound* of that letter (or letters) is _____. Say the sound for me.

MODERATE:

DIFFICULT:

DA 11 Look—Here is a _____.

Look—Here are two _____.

Developmental learning tasks

EASY: We can always find the plural form of a word by using the dictionary. Look up the word *mouse* in the dictionary and write the word that is used to describe more than one mouse: _____.

MODERATE:

DIFFICULT:

▶ **Skill 6**

ARITHMETIC PROBLEM SOLVING Pupil's name _____

Arithmetic applications and reasoning (applied counting, measurement, purchasing, etc.)

EDUCATIONAL DOMAIN: Symbolic   RLD TAXONOMY: Arithmetic reasoning

Test criterion scores

Test	Pretest		Posttest	
	Date	Score	Date	Score
Key Math				
WISC—arithmetic				
PIAT—mathematics				
WRAT—arithmetic				
Other				

	Evaluation	
	Plus	Minus

DA 5 Show me four fingers.

Developmental learning tasks

EASY: Touch and count each of the fingers of my hand as I show them to you. Now show me your fingers and count them one at a time.

MODERATE:

DIFFICULT:

DA 7 John has 4 pieces of candy. Mary has 3 more than John. How many pieces of candy does Mary have?

Developmental learning tasks

EASY: Here are John's pieces of candy:

Mary has this much plus 3 more. Draw all of Mary's candy.

	Plus	Minus
MODERATE:		
DIFFICULT:		

DA 9 What does the sign in the circle mean?

$$6 \div 3 = 2$$

Developmental learning tasks

EASY: The sign in the circle above means to *divide*. Say "divide." If you divide an apple in half, how many pieces would you have? Write the sign that means to divide. _____

	Plus	Minus
MODERATE:		
DIFFICULT:		

DA 11 A boy had 24 comic books for sale. He sold 11 of them. How many did he have left?

Developmental learning tasks

EASY: Use the chalkboard to draw 24 comic books. Then circle 11 that were sold. Count those that are left.

	Plus	Minus
MODERATE:		
DIFFICULT:		

▶ Skill 7
SERIATION

Pupil's name _____

Understanding a series of sequential patterns of symbolic relationships (sounds, pictures, symbols)

EDUCATIONAL DOMAIN: Symbolic   RLD TAXONOMY: Visual and auditory sequencing

Test criterion scores

Test	Pretest		Posttest	
	Date	Score	Date	Score
Piaget Seriation Tasks				
WISC—digit span				
Slingerland—story telling				
Other				

	Evaluation	
	Plus	Minus

DA 5 Look at the balls in the box below. Draw a picture of the one that comes next. Explain your answer.

Developmental learning tasks

EASY: The first ball above is very small, the next one is big, the third is even bigger, the last one should be the *biggest*. Draw the last one.

MODERATE:

DIFFICULT:

DA 7 Fill in the numbers on the line in the box.

| 1 2 3 | A B__ | H I__ |

Developmental learning tasks

EASY: We can count and group things in order. Clap your hands once like this. Now clap twice like this. What would you clap next time?

	Plus	Minus
MODERATE:		
DIFFICULT:		

DA 9 Look carefully at the designs below. In the last box shade in the piece that comes next and explain why it comes next.

Developmental learning tasks

EASY: Think of these numbers: 2, 4, 6, 8. $2 + 2 = 4$; $4 + 2 = 6$; $6 + 2 = 8$. The next number in the series would be 10 because $8 + 2$ *more* $= 10$. What would the next number in the series be? Why?

MODERATE:

DIFFICULT:

DA 11 Look carefully at this series and then draw in the missing part in box number 3 below. Explain your answer.

Developmental learning tasks

EASY: In the picture above we take away one side at a time. In the third box we should have taken away two sides, which leaves only two sides left on the box. Draw in the two sides that should be touching one another.

MODERATE:

DIFFICULT:

◗ Skill 8
SYMBOL DRAWING

Pupil's name _____

Copying abstract designs and representations correctly and proportionally (symbols, pictures, people, objects).

EDUCATIONAL DOMAIN: Symbolic   RLD TAXONOMY: Visual-motor integration

Test criterion scores

Test	Pretest		Posttest	
	Date	Score	Date	Score
Binet				
Bender-Gestalt				
DAP				
Other				

	Evaluation	
	Plus	Minus

DA 5   Draw the pictures in the empty boxes.

Developmental learning tasks

EASY: Trace the circle (or box) above with your finger. Good! Now watch me draw a big one on the chalkboard. Now you trace that one with your finger and then make one like it with the chalk.

MODERATE:

DIFFICULT:

DA 7   Draw the pictures in the empty boxes.

Developmental learning tasks

EASY: Trace the diamond with this crayon. Now color it in. Draw one like it on a sheet of paper for me.

	Plus	Minus
MODERATE:		
DIFFICULT:		

DA 9   Draw the picture in the empty box.

Draw a picture of man or woman in the box.

Developmental learning tasks

EASY: Here is a clean sheet of paper. I want you to look at me carefully and draw a picture of me. Draw a whole and complete picture of me on the paper.

MODERATE:

DIFFICULT:

DA 11   Draw the picture in the empty box.

Developmental learning tasks

EASY: Use a ruler to measure each design and then copy it on a clean sheet of paper.

MODERATE:

DIFFICULT:

FIGURAL RELATIONSHIPS/   Pupil's name _____
CLASSIFICATION

Understanding pictoral similarities and differences, logical classes, and relationships (pictures of food, clothes, buildings, objects, symbols, abstract designs)

EDUCATIONAL DOMAIN: Figural   RLD TAXONOMY: Classification

Test criterion scores

Test	Pretest		Posttest	
	Date	Score	Date	Score
Raven Progressive Matrices				
Columbia Mental Maturity Test				
Other				

	Evaluation	
	Plus	Minus

DA 5 Point to the picture that does not belong and tell me why it does not belong.

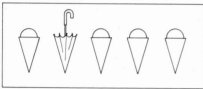

Developmental learning tasks

EASY: In the above picture there are four ice cream cones and one umbrella. The umbrella is not an ice cream cone; therefore it is different and does not belong with the others. Put your finger on the umbrella and tell me why it does not belong.

MODERATE:

DIFFICULT:

DA 7 Point to the piece that would complete the design and tell me why it would be the best piece.

	Plus	Minus

Developmental learning tasks

EASY: In the above picture the missing piece would make a circle if all parts were put together. Trace the circle with your finger. Now trace the pieces with your finger until you find one that matches the circle.

MODERATE:

DIFFICULT:

DA 9   Look at the symbols below and point to the one that does not belong. Tell me why it does not belong.

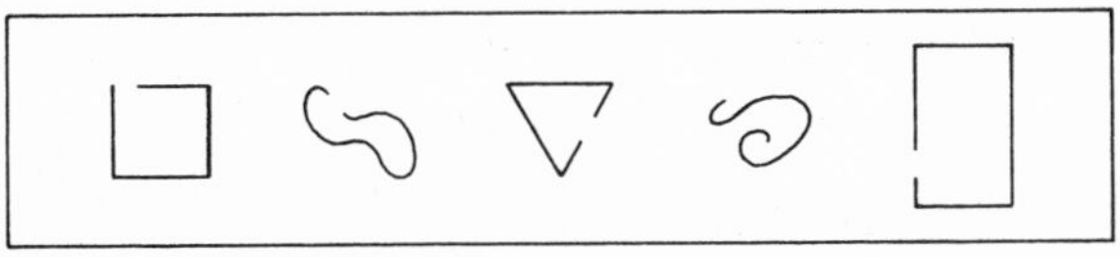

Developmental learning tasks

EASY: The first circle is different from the others. Trace each one with your finger and tell me why the first one is different.

MODERATE:

DIFFICULT:

DA 11   Which piece below will best complete the puzzle board? Why?

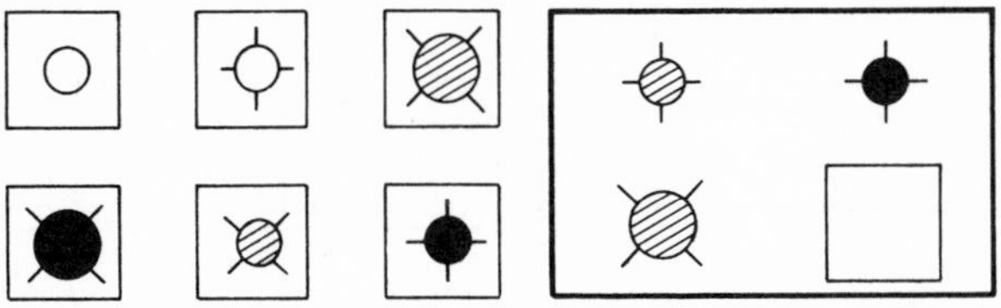

Continued.

	Plus	Minus

Developmental learning tasks

EASY: Draw the missing piece in the space and tell me why you drew it as you did.

MODERATE:

DIFFICULT:

▶ **Skill 10**

VISUAL-KINESTHETIC MEMORY   Pupil's name _____

Symbol reproduction from memory following brief exposure (figures, designs, letters, numbers, words)

EDUCATIONAL DOMAIN: Figural   RLD TAXONOMY: Visual-motor memory

Test criterion scores

Test	Pretest		Posttest	
	Date	Score	Date	Score
Slingerland—test 5				
Bender Gestalt—memory				
ITPA—visual sequencing				
Other				

	Evaluation	
	Plus	Minus

DA 5   Look at the design carefully because I want you to remember what it looks like and draw it in the empty box. (Show design for 10 seconds; cover design; *wait 10 seconds;* have pupil reproduce design in box.)

Developmental learning tasks

EASY: Use your pencil to shade in the designs. Now cover them with your hand and silently count to 10. Keep them covered while you draw them in the empty box.

	Plus	Minus
MODERATE:		
DIFFICULT:		

DA 7   (Same instructions as DA 5.)

Developmental learning tasks

EASY: Trace each design with your pencil. Now close your eyes and trace each design in your mind. Open your eyes and look carefully once more. Now cover the designs and draw them in the empty boxes.

MODERATE:

DIFFICULT:

DA 9   (Same instructions as DA 5.)

Developmental learning tasks

EASY: Use your pencil to trace each design. Now copy them three times on this clean sheet of paper. Now cover them and draw them in the empty boxes.

MODERATE:

DIFFICULT:

Continued.

	Plus	Minus

DA 11   (Same instructions as DA 5.)

67–WOULD–519	

Developmental learning tasks

EASY: Close your eyes and think of your birthday. Now open your eyes and write it in the box below.

MODERATE:

DIFFICULT:

▶ **Skill 11**

MOTOR PLANNING/CODING   Pupil's name _____

Perceptual-motor integration, anticipating and planning responses, speed and accuracy in understanding codes and reproducing figures (designs, letters, numbers, crossword puzzles)

EDUCATIONAL DOMAIN: Figural   RLD TAXONOMY: Speed of visual-motor learning

Test criterion scores

Test	Pretest		Posttest	
	Date	Score	Date	Score
WISC—coding				
Binet—mazes				
WISC—mazes				
Other				

	Evaluation	
	Plus	Minus

DA 5   Put your pencil on the boy in the middle of this room. Draw a line showing how you would get him out of the room without going through any walls.

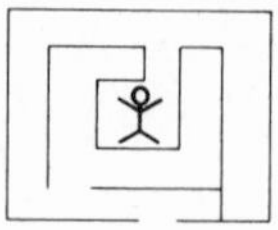

	Plus	Minus

Developmental learning tasks

EASY: Watch me as I show you how to get the boy out. Listen to what I say as I draw the path. Now you do it and tell me why you draw the line the way you do.

MODERATE:

DIFFICULT:

DA 7 Look at the lines in the figures below. Draw the same lines in the other figures.

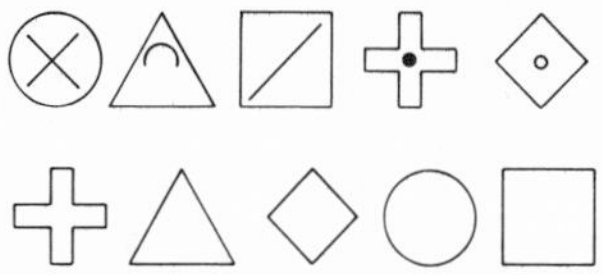

Developmental learning tasks

EASY: Look at the first figure above. It is a circle and has an X mark in it. Now place an X mark in the other circle above.

MODERATE:

DIFFICULT:

DA 9 Look at the figures below and fill in the missing boxes.

B	O	Y
	O	
		Y

Developmental learning tasks

EASY: In each empty box copy the letter in the box above it. What letter is in the middle box? What is the word?

Continued.

	Plus	Minus
MODERATE:		
DIFFICULT:		

DA 11 Look at the figures below. Copy them in the empty boxes as fast as you can.

1	2	3	4	5	6	7	8	9
●		/	+	∧	L	⊢	)	✓

9	4	1	7	5	8	3	6	2

Developmental learning tasks

EASY: Here is a clean sheet of paper. Make an easy code using the letters in your first name. Show me how it works.

MODERATE:

DIFFICULT:

◢ Skill 12
VISUAL INTEGRATION

Pupil's name _____

Organizing and meaningfully integrating visual stimuli, parts, and impressions; providing visual closure and generalizations (common objects: clothes, tools, utensils, symbols)

EDUCATIONAL DOMAIN: Figural   RLD TAXONOMY: Visual memory

Test criterion scores

Test	Pretest		Posttest	
	Date	Score	Date	Score
ITPA—visual association				
WISC—picture completion				
ITPA—visual closure				
Other				

	Evaluation	
	Plus	Minus
DA 5 Draw a line from the picture of the spoon to the thing that goes best with a spoon. Tell me why it goes best. 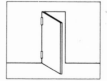		
Developmental learning tasks		
EASY: The first object above is a nail. Tell me what the other pictures are. The spoon does not go with the nail. What does it go with? Why?		
MODERATE:		
DIFFICULT:		
DA 7 Something is missing in this picture of a door. What is it?		
Developmental learning tasks		
EASY: Look at the door in this room where we are sitting. Tell me all the parts you see. What does that door have that is missing in the picture above?		

Continued.

	Plus	Minus

MODERATE:

DIFFICULT:

DA 9   Look carefully at the box below. Fill in the rest of the letters in your mind so it makes a complete word. What is the word?

Developmental learning tasks

EASY: Print your name for me. Now erase parts of it. Show it to another pupil. Could he or she identify it? Why or why not?

MODERATE:

DIFFICULT:

DA 11   Look at the first box; the two circles go together. If the circles go together, what goes with the box in the second picture? Why?

Developmental learning tasks

EASY: If the small shaded circle goes with the small white circle, then the small shaded box goes with the small

_____ _____.

MODERATE:

DIFFICULT:

▶ Skill 13

ANALOGOUS THINKING

Pupil's name _____

Understanding and application of similar relationships, inference of correspondence of parts, function, or class (animals, clothes, objects, persons)

EDUCATIONAL DOMAIN: Semantic   RLD TAXONOMY: Comprehension

Test criterion scores

Test	Pretest		Posttest	
	Date	Score	Date	Score
ITPA—auditory-vocal association				
Binet—analogies, proverbs				
WISC—similarities				
Other				

	Evaluation	
	Plus	Minus

DA 5   In what way are a wheel and a ball alike?

Developmental learning tasks

EASY: Look at these pictures. One is a ball and the other is a wheel. Describe them to me. Show me how they are alike.

MODERATE:

DIFFICULT:

DA 7   Mother is a woman. Father is a (man).
         In what way are oranges and cherries alike?

Developmental learning tasks

EASY: There are several ways that oranges and cherries are alike. For instance, they are fruits. Tell me some other ways.

MODERATE:

DIFFICULT:

Continued.

	Plus	Minus
DA 9 In what way are a dog and a lion alike? A rabbit has a tail; a train has a (caboose).		
Developmental learning tasks EASY: Close your eyes and think of what a dog looks like. Now picture a lion. They both have tails and four legs. How else are they alike?		
MODERATE:		
DIFFICULT:		
DA 11 In what way are inches, grams, and meters alike? What do these proverbs have in common? "It's an ill wind that blows no good." "Every cloud has a silver lining."		
Developmental learning tasks EASY: A proverb is a wise saying or familiar truth. Let's think about "every cloud has a silver lining" and consider what it means. You say it and then tell me what each word means, and I will then discuss it with you.		
MODERATE:		
DIFFICULT:		

▶ **Skill** 14
DIFFERENCES AND OPPOSITES   Pupil's name _____

Contrasting things according to differences and logical opposites (uses, functions, appearances, etc.)

EDUCATIONAL DOMAIN: Semantic   RLD TAXONOMY: Classification

Test criterion scores

Test	Pretest		Posttest	
	Date	Score	Date	Score
Binet—opposites				
Detroit Verbal Opposites Test				
ITPA—auditory-vocal association				
Other				

	Evaluation	
	Plus	Minus
DA 5 Cotton is soft. Stones are (hard). How are the pictures in the box different from each other? $\rightarrow$ | $\leftarrow$		
Developmental learning tasks EASY: Look at the arrows in the box. One goes one way, and the other goes in the *opposite* direction. How are they different?		
MODERATE:		
DIFFICULT:		
DA 7 The opposite of empty is (full). The opposite of open is (shut/close).		
Developmental learning tasks EASY: Look how I open this book. Now you close it for me. The opposite of close or shut is *open*. What is the opposite of open?		

Continued.

	Plus	Minus
MODERATE:		
DIFFICULT:		

DA 9   How are a submarine and a fish alike, *and how are they different?*
How is the night different from the day?

Developmental learning tasks

EASY: A submarine and a fish both move under the water. But a submarine is not alive. How else might they differ?

MODERATE:

DIFFICULT:

DA 11   The opposite of cruel is (kind).
The opposite of sharp is (dull).

Developmental learning tasks

EASY: Sharp knives can cut very easily. But some knives are not sharp and cannot cut very well; in that case we say they are (dull).

MODERATE:

DIFFICULT:

▶ **Skill** 15

SPELLING   Pupil's name _____

Correct oral and written expression of letter symbols and sound combinations (letter recognition, spelling aloud and in written form, visual recognition of correct form)

EDUCATIONAL DOMAIN: Semantic   RLD TAXONOMY: Spelling

Test criterion scores

Test	Pretest		Posttest	
	Date	Score	Date	Score
PIAT—spelling				
WRAT—spelling				
CTBS—spelling				
Other				

	Evaluation	
	Plus	Minus

DA 5 Find the letter of the alphabet in the box. Point to it.

7	d
2	5

Developmental learning tasks

EASY: Listen to me as I point to and say some letters of the alphabet. Now you do it.

c	o	m
p	a	e
s	t	d

MODERATE:

DIFFICULT:

DA 7 Listen to this word and spell it out loud for me: will . . . John will take his dog for a walk. . . . will.

Developmental learning tasks

EASY: Look at this word. It is "will." See how I trace it with my pencil and spell it. Now you trace it four times and spell it aloud.

will

Continued.

	Plus	Minus
MODERATE:		
DIFFICULT:		

DA 9   Read this box and do what it says.

> Fill in the circle by the word that is
> misspelled.
>
> ○ cat   ○ my
> ○ ar   ○ one

Developmental learning tasks

EASY: The circle has been filled
in on the misspelled word.
Fill in the circle by the word
that is misspelled.

○ boy	● boe
○ girel	○ girl

MODERATE:

DIFFICULT:

DA 11   Write the word in the box:
science . . . He likes to study
science. . . . science.

Developmental learning tasks

EASY: Copy each word below and say the letters aloud.

Science		science		*science*		SCIENCE

MODERATE:

DIFFICULT:

READING INTERPRETATION   Pupil's name _____

Meaningful understanding and application of written language (words, sentences, stories, directions, letters, newspapers)

EDUCATIONAL DOMAIN: Semantic   RLD TAXONOMY: Reading comprehension

Test criterion scores

Test	Pretest		Posttest	
	Date	Score	Date	Score
Spache—vocabulary comprehension				
PIAT—recognition				
CTBS—comprehension				
Other				

	Evaluation	
	Plus	Minus

DA 5   Look at the picture and read the word in the box. Draw a circle around the letter "t" in the box.

cat

Developmental learning tasks

EASY: The word in the box above is "cat." Tell me all you know about what a cat is and what cats do. Trace the letters in the word "cat" and say the word several times.

MODERATE:

DIFFICULT:

DA 7   Read the words in the box and *show* me what they mean.

| run | jump |

Developmental learning tasks

EASY: Tell me about this picture. Yes, a dog can run fast. Put a circle around the word "run" in the box above.

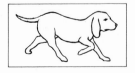

Continued.

	Plus	Minus
MODERATE:		
DIFFICULT:		

DA 9   Choose the word that means the same or about the same as the word with the line under it. Fill in the circle that goes with the word you think is right.

> Start to run.
>
> ○ catch
> ○ stop
> ○ begin
> ○ hit

Developmental learning tasks

EASY: Read each word aloud from the box above and tell me what it means. Place a plus mark (+) by each word you read and define correctly.

MODERATE:

DIFFICULT:

DA 11   Read these words silently to yourself and then underline the third word in this sentence.

Developmental learning tasks

EASY: Select a story from one of your books that you can read well. Now read it quietly to yourself. When you have finished I want you to tell me what it is all about.

MODERATE:

DIFFICULT:

▶ **Skill 17**
COMMONSENSE INFORMATION   Pupil's name _____

Factual information, knowledge, reference skills from experience and education (body parts, counting, object functions, directions, discoveries, geography)

EDUCATIONAL DOMAIN: Semantic   RLD TAXONOMY: General information

Test criterion scores

Test	Pretest		Posttest	
	Date	Score	Date	Score
WISC—information				
PIAT—information				
CTBS—study skills				
Other				

	Evaluation	
	Plus	Minus
DA 5 From what animal do we get eggs to eat?		
Developmental learning tasks		
EASY: Birds lay eggs. Chickens are birds. A hen is a chicken that lays eggs that we eat. What is a hen?		
MODERATE:		
DIFFICULT:		
DA 7 How many days make a week?		
Developmental learning tasks		
EASY: Here is a calendar showing this month. Here is the first week of the month. Put your finger here on Sunday and count the days through Saturday.		
MODERATE:		
DIFFICULT:		

Continued.

	Plus	Minus

DA 9 Look at this book. What is its name? What is the author's name? How many pages does it have?

Developmental learning tasks

EASY: Here is another book. See, it's name is _____. Here is the author's name. By looking in the back we see it has _____ pages. What is its name? Who is the author? How many pages does it have?

MODERATE:

DIFFICULT:

DA 11 In what direction does the sun rise?

Developmental learning tasks

EASY: This morning we are standing outside. Here on the ground are arrows pointing to the North, South, East, and West.

$$\begin{array}{c} N \\ W \Leftrightarrow E \\ S \end{array}$$

See, the sun is here. Every morning it rises over there and gradually ascends into the sky. What direction is that?

MODERATE:

DIFFICULT:

▶ Skill 18
EXPRESSIVE LANGUAGE

Pupil's name _____

Verbal expression and fluency of verbal concepts (coherent speech, use of proper grammar, prepositional phrases, structural language)

EDUCATIONAL DOMAIN: Semantic   RLD TAXONOMY: Fluency and encoding

Test criterion scores

Test	Pretest		Posttest	
	Date	Score	Date	Score
WISC—vocabulary				
Binet—vocabulary				
Boehm—verbal concepts				
ITPA—verbal expression				
Englemann—part II				
Other				

	Evaluation	
	Plus	Minus
DA 5 Tell me all about this thing (give the child a *pencil* to hold). What is it? How does it look? When is it used? Tell me all you can about it.		
Developmental learning tasks EASY: This is a *pen*. It is long and narrow. It is colored _____. I use it to write with. The ink comes out at this point. Now you tell me all about it.		
MODERATE:		
DIFFICULT:		
DA 7 Look at the picture and tell me what you see.  Now say, "The boy is jumping over the box."		

Continued.

	Plus	Minus
Developmental learning tasks		
EASY: Watch me jump over this pencil on the floor. See? "I am jumping *over* the pencil." Now you do it and then tell me what you did.		
MODERATE:		
DIFFICULT:		
DA 9 Tell me all you can about these two words: diamond juggler		
Developmental learning tasks		
EASY: Here is a dictionary. Together we will look up the words you did not understand. Here is the page with the definition. Let's read it together. Now you tell me what the words mean. Try and *show* me with your hands as you explain them to me.		
MODERATE:		
DIFFICULT:		
DA 11 Listen to what I say and then repeat it after me: "Measles is a highly contagious disease." Now say it again and then explain to me what it means.		
Developmental learning tasks		
EASY: Contagious means that a disease can be easily passed on or spread to other people; people can communicate or transmit a disease. We can catch a contagious disease from others. Now you tell me all about it. Have you ever had a contagious disease?		
MODERATE:		
DIFFICULT:		

VERBAL COMPREHENSION   Pupil's name _____

General verbal reasoning and practical problem solving (cause and effect, common sense regarding dangerous situations, manners, rules)

EDUCATIONAL DOMAIN: Semantic   RLD TAXONOMY: Comprehension

Test criterion scores

Test	Pretest		Posttest	
	Date	Score	Date	Score
WISC—comprehension				
Binet—problem solving				
Other				

	Evaluation	
	Plus	Minus
DA 5 What happens if you put your finger on a hot stove?		
Developmental learning tasks EASY: Here is a hot stove. When I put a drop of water on it like this, it sizzles and burns up. You put a drop of water on it and tell me what happens to it. What do you think would happen if you put your finger on it?		
MODERATE:		
DIFFICULT:		
DA 7 Here is a picture of a sailboat. What do you think makes it move? 		
Developmental learning tasks EASY: Here is a toy sailboat. We will place it in this bowl of water and blow on it. Watch it and tell me why it moves.		
MODERATE:		
DIFFICULT:		

Continued.

	Plus	Minus
DA 9 What are some of the advantages in building a house out of stone rather than wood?		
Developmental learning tasks		
EASY: Wood burns. Stone does not burn. A wood house would burn. What would fire do to a stone house?		
MODERATE:		
DIFFICULT:		
DA 11 If people chase skunks in the woods, what might happen to them?		
Developmental learning tasks		
EASY: A skunk is protected by a scent bag that can spray fluid with very disagreeable odors. What are the disadvantages of being sprayed with such a fluid?		
MODERATE:		
DIFFICULT:		

▶ **Skill** 20

RECEPTIVE CONCEPTUAL VOCABULARY

Pupil's name _____

Understanding and nonverbal interpretation of spoken language (word meanings, classification, prepositional phrases, listening, following directions)

EDUCATIONAL DOMAIN: Semantic   RLD TAXONOMY: Vocabulary

Test criterion scores

Test	Pretest		Posttest	
	Date	Score	Date	Score
PPVT				
ITPA—auditory reception				
Engleman—part I				
Other				

	Evaluation	
	Plus	Minus
DA 5 Do bees sting? Do chairs eat?		
Developmental learning tasks EASY: Bees are small brown and yellow insects that are commonly found flying in fields and gardens. They have a stinger with which to protect themselves. Bees can sting people and animals if they are angry or upset. Do bees sting?		
MODERATE:		
DIFFICULT:		
DA 7 Look at the picture and point to the girl that is standing *between* the boys. 		

Continued.

	Plus	Minus

Developmental learning tasks

EASY: See those two chairs—watch how I stand *between* them. Now you do it and tell me what you are doing. What were you just doing?

MODERATE:

DIFFICULT:

DA 9 Point to the picture of a casserole.

Developmental learning tasks

EASY: A casserole is a hot covered dish of food that is cooked or baked in an oven. Look at the pictures above and point to the casserole and tell me why it is a casserole.

MODERATE:

DIFFICULT:

DA 11 Do carpenters kneel?
Do combustibles ignite?

Developmental learning tasks

EASY: Carpenters kneel like this (demonstrate) when they are building things or nailing pieces of wood together on the floor. Now you show me how a carpenter might kneel and nail pieces of wood together on the floor.

MODERATE:

DIFFICULT:

DISCUSSION QUESTIONS AND ACTIVITIES

1. Why are these skills correlated with the taxonomy presented in *The Remediation of Learning Disabilities* (RLD)?
2. Select two test criterion tasks presented in the survey and write a behavioral objective *with minimal performance standards* for each.
3. Administer the survey to a child, write in his or her responses, and then evaluate the performance by completing the first page of the survey, including the profile.
4. What *other* forms of evaluation (including tests) do you think should be made of the child with whom you used this survey?
5. How does the survey differ from other evaluation instruments that you have seen or used?
6. How might you use the information obtained from this survey in collaboration with a psychoeducational consultant?
7. Discuss the problems that public schools might have in devoting more time and effort in teaching these critical thinking skills.

CHAPTER 10

Prescriptive use of the Stanford-Binet test

Earl is a caucasian boy in the regular second grade who has just turned 8 years old. His parents and teachers have become increasingly concerned over his poor school adjustment and very limited social participation. In first grade, concern was expressed over Earl's poor speech and language development and his difficulty in reasoning. Current school performance indicates that he knows the alphabet and consonant sounds, can count by rote to 100, and can read first grade material with poor comprehension. He cannot run, skip, or hop; he has poor handwriting and a very limited attention span; he is easily confused, and he appears emotionally insecure.

Earl's insecurity was immediately apparent when he was examined psychologically. Because of this anxiety he was first introduced to several toys and motor activities with his parents present; then he finally went with the examiner to the evaluation room. Throughout the examination, of which the Stanford-Binet was but a part (Gesell and Amatruda, 1967), he continued to require much support and reinforcement. Nevertheless, it is thought that the Binet results do give a reliable indication of Earl's functional performance at this time and that they can be used to help select objectives for prescriptive instruction (Terman and Merrill, 1962).

CLINICAL PROFILE

The overall results of Earl's evaluation are presented on the profile for the Stanford-Binet shown on p. 170. On this profile we can see that the Binet has been broken down into six major test constructs:

General comprehension	Memory and concentration
Visual-motor ability	Vocabulary and verbal fluency
Arithmetic reasoning	Judgment and reasoning

A PROFILE FOR THE STANFORD BINET (L-M)

Item Classifications by Robert E. Valett

INSTRUCTIONS: Draw a vertical line through the year for the obtained basal age. Circle all test items passed beyond this level.

SUBJECT'S NAME: **EARL** CA: **8-0** MA: **5** IQ Range: **55-65** Grade: **2nd** Date of Test: **3-11-77**

TEST CONSTRUCTS / Year:	2	2-6	3	3-6	4	4-6	5	6	7	CA 8	9	10	11	12	13	14	AA	SA I	SA II	SA III
GENERAL COMPREHENSION	3 / A	1 / 2 / 6		⑥	④ / 6	4 / ⑥ / A			2 / 4 / 5	4 / 5 / A			6	3 / 6	4	5	5 / 6 / 7	6	3	2 / 4
VISUAL-MOTOR ABILITY	1 / 4	A	1 / 3 / 5 / 6	② / ⑤			1 / 2 / ④ / 6 / A	6	③ ?		1 / 3	2	1	A	A	A	A			
ARITHMETIC REASONING						5		4			5		1 / 4	4 / A		4 / A	2 / 4	2	4	
MEMORY & CONCENTRATION	2	5	4 / A	④	② / A				6 / A	2 / 6	3 / 6	6	1 / 4	4 / A	3 / 6			4	6	6
VOCABULARY & VERBAL FLUENCY	5 / 6 / A	3 / 4	2	④	①	③	③	⑦ / A	1	1	4 / A	1 / 3 / 5	3	1 / 5 / 6	2 / 5	1	1 / 3 / 8	1 / 3 / 5	1 / 3 / A	1 / 3 / A
JUDGMENT & REASONING		1		②②③ / A	①②③	①②③ / A	⑤ / 6	2 / ③ / 5 / A	2 / 4 / 5	3 / 4	1 / 2 / 4	2 / 4 / A	2 / 5 / 6 / A	2	1 / 4 / 5 / A	2 / 3 / 4 / 5 / 6 / A	2 / 3 / 6 / 7 / A	2 / 6 / A	2 / 3 / 4 / 5 / 6 / A	2 / 3 / 4 / 5 / 6 / A

CONSULTING PSYCHOLOGISTS PRESS
577 College Avenue   Palo Alto, California 94306

STANFORD-BINET L-M ITEM CLASSIFICATIONS (Valett)

GENERAL COMPREHENSION: The ability to conceptualize and integrate components into a meaningful total relationship.

II.3.	Parts of body	VIII.4.	Similarities and differences
II.A.	Identifying objects by name	VIII.5.	Comprehension IV
II-6.1.	Identifying objects by use	XI.6.	Similarities 3
II-6.2.	Parts of body	XII.3.	Picture absurdities II
II-6.6.	Simple commands	XII.6.	Minkus completion I
III-6.6.	Comprehension I	XIII.6.	Problems of fact
IV.4.	Picture identification	XIV.5.	Direction II
IV.6.	Comprehension II	AA.5.	Proverbs I
IV.6.4.	Materials	AA.6.	Comprehension III
IV.6.6.	Picture identification	AA.7.	Essential differences
IV-6.A.	Picture identification	SA-I.6.	Essential similarities
VII.4.	Similarities 2	SA-II.2.	Proverbs II
VII.5.	Comprehension IV	SA-III.2.	Proverbs III
		SA-III.4.	Directions III

VISUAL MOTOR ABILITY: The ability to manipulate materials in problem solving situations usually requiring integration of visual and motor skills.

II.1.	Form board	V.4.	Copying square
II.4.	Block tower	V.6.	Patience: rectangles
II.6.A.	Form board	V.A.	Knot
III.1.	Stringing beads	VI.6.	Maze
III.3.	Block bridge	VII.3.	Copying diamond
III.5.	Copying circle	IX.1.	Paper cutting
III.6.	Vertical line	IX.3.	Designs I
III-6.2.	Patience: pictures	X.2.	Block counting
III-6.5.	Sorting buttons	XI.1.	Designs
V.1.	Picture completion: man	XII.A.	Designs II
V.2.	Folding triangle	XIII.A.	Paper cutting
		AA.A.	Binet paper cutting

ARITHMETIC REASONING: The ability to make appropriate numerical associations and deal with mental abstractions in problem solving situations.

VI.4.	Number concepts	AA.2.	Ingenuity I
IX.5.	Change	AA.4.	Arithmetic reasoning
XIV.4.	Ingenuity I	SA-I.2.	Enclosed boxes
XIV.A.	Ingenuity II	SA-II.4.	Ingenuity I

MEMORY & CONCENTRATION: The ability to attend and retain. Requires motivation and attention and usually measures degree of retention of various test items.

II.2.	Delayed response	VIII.2.	Wet Fall
II-6.5.	2 digits	VIII.6.	Days of week
III.4.	Picture memories	IX.3.	Designs I
III.A.	3 digits	IX.6.	4 digits reversed
IV.2.	Objects from memory	X.6.	6 digits
IV.A.	Memory for sentences I	XI.1.	Designs I
IV-6.5.	3 commissions	XI.4.	Memory for sentences II
VII.6.	5 digits	XII.6.	5 digits reversed
VII.A.	3 digits reversed	XII.A.	Designs II
XIII.3.	Memory for sentences III	SA-I.4.	6 digits reversed
XIII.6.	Copying a bead chain from memory	SA-II.6.	Passage I: Value of Life
		SA-III.6.	Repeating thought of passage: tests

VOCABULARY & VERBAL FLUENCY. The ability to use words correctly in association with concrete or abstract material; the understanding of words and verbal concepts; the quality and quantity of verbal expression.

II.5.	Picture vocabulary	XI.3.	Abstract words
II.6.	Word combinations	XII.1.	Vocabulary
II.A.	Identifying objects by name	XII.5.	Abstract words
II-6.3.	Naming of objects	XII.6.	Minkus completion I
II-6.4.	Picture vocabulary	XIII.2.	Abstract words II
III-2.	Picture vocabulary	XIII.5.	Dissected sentences
III-6.A.	Response to pictures	XIV.1.	Vocabulary
IV.1.	Vocabulary	AA.1.	Vocabulary
V.3.	Vocabulary	AA.8.	Difference between abstract words
VI.1.	Vocabulary	SA-I.1.	Abstract words III
VI.A.	Response to pictures	SA-I.3.	Vocabulary
VIII.1.	Vocabulary	SA-I.5.	Minkus Completion II
IX.4.	Rhymes: new form	SA-II.1.	Sentence building
IX.A.	Rhymes: old form	SA-III.1.	Vocabulary
X.1.	Vocabulary	SA-III.3.	Opposite analogies IV
X.3.	Abstract Words I	SA-III.A.	Opposite analogies V
X.5.	Word naming		

JUDGEMENT & REASONING: The ability to comprehend and respond appropriately in specific situations requiring discrimination, comparison, and judgement in adaptation.

II-6.1.	Identifying objects by use	VIII.3.	Verb. absurdities I	XIV.A.	Ingenuity II
III-6.1.	Comparison of balls	VIII.A.	Similarities & diff.	AA.2.	Ingenuity I
III-6.2.	Patience: pictures	IX.1.	Paper cutting	AA.3.	Dif. abs. words
III-6.3.	Discrim. of animal pictures	IX.2.	Verb. absurdities II	AA.6.	Direction II
IV-3.	Comparison of sticks	IX.4.	Rhymes: new form	AA.7.	Essential diff.
IV-4.	Opposite analogies I	X.2.	Block counting	AA.A.	Binet paper cut.
IV-5.	Pictorial identification	X.4.	Finding reasons	SA-I.2.	Enclosed boxes
IV-6.1.	Discrimination of forms	X.A.	Verbal absurdities III	SA-I.6.	Essential simil.
IV-6.2.	Aesthetic comparison	XI.2.	Verbal absurdities IV	SA-I.A.	Recon. of opp.
IV-6.3.	Opposite analogies I	XI.5.	Prob. situation II	SA-II.2.	Finding reasons
IV-6.A.	Pictorial identification	XI.A.	Similarities	SA-II.3.	Proverbs II
V.5.	Pictorial sim. & dif. I	XII.A.	Finding reasons II	SA-II.4.	Ingenuity I
V.6.	Pictorial sim. & dif. II	XII.2.	Verb. absurdities II	SA-II.5.	Essential diff.
VI.2.	Patience: rectangles	XIII.4.	Plan of search	SA-II.6.	Codes
VI.3.	Differences	XIII.A.	Dissected sentences	SA-III.2.	Proverbs III
VI.5.	Mutilated pictures	XIII.A.	Paper cutting	SA-IV.4.	Direction III
VI.A.	Opposite analogies II	XIV.2.	Induction	SA-III.5.	Reasoning II
VII.1.	Response to pictures	XIV.3.	Reasoning	SA-III.6.	Repeating thought of passage: tests
VII.2.	Pictorial absurdities I	XIV.4.	Ingenuity I	SA-III.A.	Op. anal. V
VII.4.	Similarities II	XIV.5.	Direction I		Pass. I: V of L
VII.5.	Comprehension IV	XIV.6.	Recon. of opposites		
VII.6.	Opposite analogies III				

Since Earl passed all six of the regular tests expected of children who are 3½ years of age, a dark vertical line has been drawn through the year 3-6 column, and all six subtests have been circled and darkened; this designates the basal age, or level of "perfect functioning." The letter "A" on the profile form refers to an alternate test available each year, which was not given. This has not been marked in any way.

Year 4

At the 4-year level Earl passed all subtests except No. 6, general comprehension. On the item classification sheet on p. 171 we can see that the year 4 No. 6 subtest on the Binet is comprehension II. This subtest requires the child to respond to two specific questions. These questions and Earl's answers are as follows:

> Why do we have houses? "Ships fly at home."
> Why do we have books? "Like books—it's morning."

From these answers it is immediately apparent that Earl has some difficulty in understanding the questions and also has great difficulty in expressing a suitable answer in coherent form.

Year 4½

The profile discloses that Earl missed subtests No. 4 and 5 at the 4½-year level. The item classification sheet shows that subtest No. 4 is materials; the actual questions and Earl's responses are as follows:

> What is a house made of? "A home"
> What is a window made out of? "Silver"
> What is a book made out of? "White and black"

Subtest No. 5, three commissions, requires memory, concentration, and the ability to listen and follow directions. The actual directions given are as follows:

> Here's a pencil. I want you to put it on that chair; then I want you to open that door, and then bring me the box which you see over there.

All three of these commissions or instructions must be executed in the proper order. Earl was able to place the pencil on the chair, but then he forgot the other directions and just walked around the desk and sat down.

Year 5

When he reached the 5-year level Earl missed three subtests that required visual-motor ability. The first test consists of the picture of a partial man (below) with these instructions:

> What is this? It is a man, isn't it? See, he only has one leg.
> You finish him. Make all the rest of him.

Although Earl was able to draw in a crude second leg, he failed to include any other features such as eyes, arms, and mouth, two of which are required to pass this level.

Subtest No. 2, paper folding, requires the child to "watch what I do." The examiner then takes a 6 × 6 inch sheet of paper and folds it once along the diagonal, making a triangle, and then folds it through the middle to make a triangle half as large. This task proved to be impossible for Earl, as he was unable to complete even the first simple fold and was not able to get his hands and fingers to move together as required.

The third subtest missed was No. 6, labeled patience: rectangles, which consists of two rectangular cards, each 2 × 3 inches, one of which is divided diagonally as shown here. The following directions are given:

> One of my cards has been cut in two. You put these pieces together to make a whole one just like this.

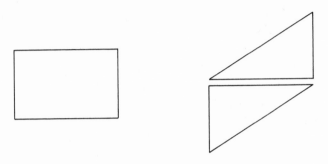

Given three tries, Earl was unable to perceive how the cards went together, and he became increasingly frustrated at his repeated failure.

Year 6

At the 6-year level, Earl passed subtest No. 1, vocabulary; the subtest was passed with difficulty, as Earl was barely able to explain what the words "orange," "envelope," "straw," "tap," "roar," and "eyelash" meant. Likewise, when shown subtest No. 3, mutilated pictures, he was hard pressed to explain that a wheel was missing from a picture of a wagon, a shoelace was missing from a shoe, an ear was missing from a rabbit, and a finger was missing from a glove.

All other subtests on this level were missed as follows:

No. 2, differences
What is the difference between a bird and a dog? <u>Dog's wing's aren't.</u>
What is the difference between a slipper and a boot? <u>You go someplace else.</u>

No. 4, number concepts
Earl, give me _____ blocks. Put them here.

When Earl was requested to give 3 blocks he responsed correctly, but when asked for 10 blocks he presented 12, for 6 blocks he gave 5, for 9 blocks he presented 12, and for 7 blocks he gave 6. From such responses it was apparent that Earl lacks understanding of basic number concepts.

No. 5, opposite analogies

A table is made of wood; a window, of "silver".
A bird flies; a fish "doesn't fly".
The point of a cane is blunt; the point of a knife is "cake".
An inch is short; a mile is "a mile".

No. 6, maze tracing

This little boy lives here, and here (pointing) is the schoolhouse. The little boy wants to go to school the shortest way without getting off the sidewalk. Here is the sidewalk. Show me the shortest way. Mark it with your pencil, but don't go off the sidewalk. Start here and take the little boy to school the shortest way.

Three similar mazes and sets of instructions were presented. Earl missed all three; his first response is presented below.

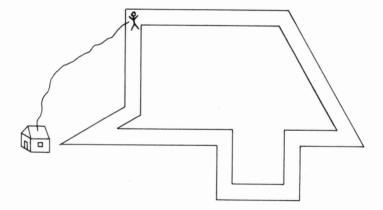

Year 7

On the 7-year level, Earl clearly failed subtests No. 1, 2, 4, 5, and 6. Subtest No. 3, copying a diamond, required him to copy a simple diamond shape with correct angulations and proportion; on this task, Earl barely passed by closely approximating one diamond in three attempts.

Most of the other tests at this level require abstract thinking and judgment such as explaining absurdities, similarities, and analogies. Test No. 6, digit span, requires repetition of three different number series (such as 3–1–8–5–9), and all of these tasks were impossible for him.

STRENGTHS

From these test results, it would appear that Earl is of extremely limited ability with few if any strengths. However, he was able to attend to all tasks, and he appeared visually aware of fine details in all pictorial matter that was presented to him. There is also evidence that his receptive vocabulary is superior to his other abilities. For instance, his response to Year 6 subtest No. 2, which asks the difference between a bird and a dog (response: "dog's wings aren't"), is typical of several of his attempts to express his understanding; he actually seems to know that dogs do not have wings, but it is almost impossible for him to express this fluently in grammatical language. This impression was further substantiated through a later conversation with his parents, who said that he knows and understands much more than he can clearly talk about but that they have learned to interpret the meaning behind his odd sentence structure.

For instructional purposes, then, it would be best to assume that Earl understands more and is actually more capable than test scores alone would indicate. Sensory-motor approaches to structural language training should include many pictures and the use of concrete manipulative materials that he can relate to in an orderly and sequential way.

LIMITATIONS

A review of the profile form helps us to consider Earl's major weaknesses and limitations. Although it does not immediately appear in the subtest scores, his major limitation is in expressive language and verbal fluency. In fact, his distorted responses are such that there is reason to suspect the existence of some kind of developmental aphasia. He also appeared to be frustrated at his inability to clearly communicate his intentions, which gives further reason to suspect a primary developmental language disability.

A secondary weakness is Earl's visual-motor abilities. The use of a pencil in drawing and doing other fine motor coordination tasks is most difficult for him. Folding, cutting, marking, sorting, and manipulating objects are all functional skills of concern here. This also relates closely to his observed awkwardness and poor gross motor performance, which would interfere in his playing games with other children and result in social rejection or isolation.

His ability to follow directions, to correctly sequence auditory information, and to perform other limited memory skills, are also of significant concern. As with other limited skills mentioned above, these should all be considered for direct prescriptive teaching and development according to teacher priorities.

DISCUSSION

An attempt has been made here to demonstrate the diagnostic-prescriptive use of the Stanford-Binet intelligence test. Although Alfred Binet called for the development of "mental orthopedic" programs to help remedy intellectual deficits and to develop mental potentialities, his test has seldom been used in such a constructive way. Instead, with children such as Earl, it has been more common to report only the derived IQ (Earl's IQ was 60, or more accurately, within the 55 to 65 range of reliability) and then to categorize him and possibly place him in a class for the "mentally retarded."

Yet we have seen that the Binet test actually consists of numerous kinds of varied tasks, both verbal and nonverbal, that can be learned through proper training and experience. To merely report a single score and categorize Earl as "mentally retarded" would probably be more harmful than helpful to him. Without detailed information concerning Earl's actual functional skills and abilities, and especially the quality and style of his responses, we do not know where or how to begin teaching him what he needs to know. How much better it is to view the IQ score as nothing but an index of current achievement that is worthless to diagnostic-prescriptive teachers without use of the actual test items and the profile of differential abilities that can be used to help him grow and learn.

There is no question, of course, that Earl is a seriously developmentally handicapped child with real limitations. But there is also no question that he can learn and gradually improve his skills and abilities and become a more integrated and wholesome person. For instance, it should be obvious that children can be taught why we have houses and books! They can be taught how houses of many kinds are made and what different windows consist of. People can learn to follow directions by starting with simple directions and gradually proceeding to more complex ones. And children can even be taught to draw, to manipulate puzzles, to figure and count, and to reason with increasing degrees of abstraction!

Such accomplishments, however, do require the formulation of highly specific and appropriate educational objectives and systematic instruction. And it is these essentials that the diagnostician and special educator must derive from their evaluations of such children. Mere labeling of children like Earl does not ensure proper special education, but the Binet and other evaluation instruments can be properly used as a rich source of tasks for developmental and remedial instruction.

DISCUSSION QUESTIONS AND ACTIVITIES

Assume that you are the diagnostic-prescriptive teacher who has been assigned to provide Earl with the special education that he needs. On the basis of the information provided in this case study, write an educational plan using the following guidelines.

1. Select three specific items from the Binet subtests that you could use for formulating priority teaching objectives. Rank them in first, second, and third priority and write out the actual test item and Earl's response to it. Now write an actual teaching or instructional objective based on each of the three items and explain how you would begin to teach them.

2. For your first priority objective as stated above, list one reference guide or remedial resource handbook with page numbers specifying possible lessons, appropriate instructional tasks, and materials that might be used to help Earl learn.

3. Write a brief home learning prescription ("homework") that Earl's parents might use to help him at home.

4. Make a vocabulary list of actual words and expressions that you might use in teaching Earl. Explain how you would organize your teaching of these concepts.

5. What other kinds of tests, evaluation, or observational data do you think would be helpful to obtain on Earl?

6. What might be a reason for not teaching just to the single item on intelligence and other achievement tests?

CHAPTER 11

A psychoeducational report

The material presented in this report is abstracted from an actual case study of a child 7 years 5 months old. The name "Terry Kohl" is, of course, fictitious, as are other names used in case reports presented in this book. Dates and other data have been modified to further protect confidentiality.

GENERAL PROBLEM DESCRIPTION

Terry has had increasing difficulty with her work in school. She struggles with her spelling and math, writes poorly, makes reversals, and is inconsistent in her performance. Her teacher reports that she has trouble with words out of context, lacks motivation, and does not know how to study. She is being considered for possible retention in the second grade.

RELEVANT INFORMATION

According to her parents, Terry is a loving and outgoing child. She memorizes song lyrics and remembers things very well. She also enjoys swimming, riding her bicycle, and playing on the monkey bars.

A recent medical examination shows Terry to be in good physical health. During her preschool years she was an awkward child who was described as hypersensitive and who avoided such things as drawing, cutting, playing with puzzles, and games requiring coordination. She showed mixed laterality, switching back and forth with both hands, and she has always been very slow in completing assignments.

Her early school history shows difficulty in coloring, cutting on lines, jumping, building with blocks, and drawing (with a tendency to write backwards). Currently, she is in a low reading group on the first grade level and much of her work is carelessly done. She feels rejected by other children in her class and needs to play with others more than she does.

EVALUATION

The following procedures and instruments were used in this evaluation with results indicated on the accompanying profile form:

INDIVIDUAL PROFILE OF LEARNING SKILLS AND ABILITIES

Name __Terry Kohl__   Grade __Low 2nd__   CA __7yr 5mo__   MA __7½-8__

GRADE:	LK	MK	HK	L1	H1	L2	H2	L3	M3	L4	M4	L5	M5	H5	M6	L7	M7	L8	M8	L9	M9	L10
AGE:	5	5½	6	6½	7	7½	(8)	8½	9	9½	10	10½	11	11½	12	12½	13	13½	14	14½	15	15½

Approximate grade expectancy

Profile (percentile/standard)

	Skills and abilities	Comments/other criterion evaluations	Very low	Below avg.	Average	Above avg.	Very high
Gross motor abilities	Balance						
	Coordination (*History /IPS*)			X			
	Strength				X		
	General physical health	*Physical exam*			X		
Sensory-motor abilities	Attention-concentration (WISC-DS)				9		
	Laterality (*History*)			X			
	Manual expression (ITPA)					45	
Auditory perception	Auditory reception (ITPA)					47	
	Auditory association (ITPA)				35		
	Auditory sequential memory (ITPA)						48
	Auditory closure (ITPA)				42		
	Sound blending (ITPA)					46	
	Consonant sounds (Spache)						
	Vowel sounds (Spache)						
	Consonant blends (Spache)						
	Common syllables (Spache)						
Visual perception	Visual form constancy (Frostig)						
	Visual position in space (Frostig)						
	Visual figure ground (Frostig)						
	Visual closure (ITPA)			27			
	Visual reception (ITPA)				34		
	Visual memory (WISC-PC)					15	
	Visual association (ITPA)					46	

Domain	Test	Notes	Score
Visual-motor perception	Eye-hand coordination (Frostig)		
	Spatial relations (Frostig)		
	Visual sequential memory (ITPA)		
	Visual motor planning (WISC mazes)	26	
	Visual motor synthesis (WISC BD)		
	Object assembly (WISC)		
	Fine motor control (WISC code)		10
	Visual motor integration (BVMG)		
	Visual-motor memory (Slingerland)	Tests 1, 2, 5, 7	X
Language abilities	Verbal expression (ITPA)		29
	Receptive vocabulary (PPVT)		114 / 17
	Expressive vocabulary (WISC/Binet)		
	Grammatic closure (ITPA)		32
	Oral reading vocabulary (WRAT/Spache)		96
	Oral reading comprehension (Spache)		X
	Silent reading comprehension (Spache)		
	Spelling (WRAT)		89
	Writing (Slingerland/IPS)	High 2nd	X
Conceptual-cognitive abilities	General information (WISC)		12
	Comprehension and reasoning (WISC)		11
	Similarities and abstractions (WISC)		
	Functional mental age (WISC/Binet)		109 / 16
	Arithmetic reasoning (WISC)		8
	Arithmetic operations (WRAT)		95
Social-personal abilities	Self identification (DAP)	7yr 3mo	97
	Social planning and anticipation (WISC PA)		12
	Social maturity (Vineland SA)		
	Self esteem (My Self Checklist)	Raw score 74	X
	Behavior ratings	Parents	X

Parent interview
Developmental task analysis (completed by parents)
Home visit and observation of Terry
An Inventory of Primary Skills (IPS)
My Self Checklist
Wechsler Intelligence Scale for Children (WISC)
Wide Range Achievement Test (WRAT)
Spache Diagnostic Reading Scales
Slingerland Screening Tests for Identifying Children with Specific Language Disability—Form A
Goodenough Draw-A-Person (DAP)
Peabody Picture Vocabulary Test—Form A
Illinois Test of Psycholinguistic Abilities (ITPA)

Terry's strengths

When presented with pictures of common objects (such as telephone, binoculars, camera, and stethoscope) Terry was quickly able to identify them and to manually demonstrate their use. She understands the common elements in her environment and is able to explain their functions by using nonverbal gestures and appropriate body language.

Terry has good auditory abilities. Her auditory memory for sequencing seven digits (4–9–6–3–5–7–1, etc.) was exceptionally good for her age. Her abilities for listening, receiving, understanding rather complex verbal questions ("Do pigeons coo?") and blending distinctive phonetic sounds together are distinctly above average.

Visually, Terry has good ability to make logical associations and to see relationships between pictures of objects and symbols that are presented to her. For instance, on the ITPA she quickly discerned and pointed out that "buttons are to sweaters as leaves are to trees." Similarly, on the WISC she realized what parts were missing from a number of increasingly complex pictures of objects (scissors, coat, fish, etc.).

Her relative language strengths are her receptive and expressive vocabulary skills. She readily understands what is being said to her, and she can define and use words well beyond what might be expected of children her age.

Terry is also able to think well using similarities and verbal abstractions. She understands the relationships between verbal concepts ("pound and yard are both mathematical measurements"). This result, together with other test findings, indicates that Terry is cognitively aware and fairly astute at dealing with concepts and ideas that she encounters.

Terry's weaknesses

Terry's awkwardness and poor coordination were demonstrated on the IPS; she had trouble in imitating body positions, correctly identifying her left and right hands, and performing several tasks requiring visual-motor organization and body control.

Visually, she was slow to provide closure to hidden and incomplete pictures on the ITPA and was just unable to find what was expected of her (such as hidden animals, tools, and clothes). It is apparent that Terry is easily confused when confronted with detailed and complex material that requires quick discrimination, manipulation, and organization.

Most of Terry's weaknesses are visual-motor perceptual ones. This was immediately apparent in her response to a request to write her birth date (February 18, 1965), as required on the IPS:

Write (or tell me) your birth date.	

Similar fine motor coordination problems were evident on the Slingerland test. In the example below Terry was attempting to copy a paragraph from a wall chart; the first sentence was "Bobby had two big fat balloons."

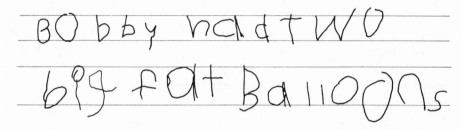

On other parts of the Slingerland that demanded visual-motor memory skills, Terry showed equally poor written form, inadequate spacing, problems in recalling and properly reproducing details, and many reversals, as in the following examples:

$$
\begin{array}{ll}
h \rightarrow d & n \rightarrow \Pi \\
d \rightarrow b & us \rightarrow su \\
g \rightarrow p & 1 \rightarrow \text{I} \\
black \rightarrow dalck & bed \rightarrow deb \\
12 \rightarrow 21 &
\end{array}
$$

However, this test also confirmed that Terry did have good *auditory*-visual memory ability in that she was able to correctly recall and discriminate initial and final sound-letter associations.

Terry's visual-motor disabilities are also apparent in several tasks that do not require writing. For instance, her visual sequential memory (ITPA) for selecting and arranging symbol chips was very poor and laboriously done; the best she could do was to arrange three symbols, such as those below, in correct order:

On the WISC block design test, Terry had great difficulty seeing the relationships of block patterns and then putting them together correctly within the time limits allowed. Even relatively simple designs, such as placing four blocks together in the design below, caused her great difficulty and resulted in her giving up the task with obvious frustration and disorientation.

Although Terry's overall social and personal skills are essentially normal, her frustration in coping with difficult tasks is easily observed in many situations at home and in school. She also has some problems in self-esteem in that she does worry that something might be wrong with her, since she perceives herself as an unusually awkward person who spills things, trips, and is generally clumsy. She would like to have more friends and to obtain some help in "math and running."

Summary

Terry is a bright and attractive little girl with many strengths. Although she is actually reading and achieving near grade level, her visual-motor memory and kinesthetic disabilities are significant ones, which do interfere with her performance and potential for learning.

Her personal history, school records, and test performance all confirm a developmental sensory-motor perceptual problem that has resulted in her specific language disability in written expression and in other tasks requiring fine motor coordination of her hands and eyes.

Although Terry has been able to compensate rather well, it is clear that she now needs some special help if more serious learning and behavior problems are to be prevented.

RECOMMENDATIONS

It is recommended that Terry remain with her regular class and not be retained in second grade. She should be encouraged to continue to develop her unique strengths and to use her good auditory and cognitive abilities.

However, it is essential to recognize that Terry's visual-motor disabilities require that her written tasks and assignments be modified so that she can work on her own level and progress at her own rate of speed. The following are some possible priority objectives:

1. To provide Terry with supplemental learning disability instruction by the resource teacher specialist. Emphasis should be placed on the development of specific visual-motor memory skills and eye-hand coordination. Direct efforts should be made to remedy the reversals specified in this report through the use of multisensory kinesthetic training techniques. Spatial orientation and organization exercises using games, puzzles, and other concrete materials should also be part of her special education.

2. Terry should be tutored on her regular writing, spelling, and arithmetic task assignments and these should be modified as much as possible using kinesthetic teaching methods.

3. A behavior modification program should be developed to reinforce Terry's concentration, attention, and time spent on assigned tasks, as well as her actual task accomplishment. Since she is aware of her problems, Terry should be involved in selecting her own rewards and privileges in joint cooperation with her regular and resource teachers.

4. Since Terry is a capable little girl and in need of more positive social involvement, she should be assigned as a peer tutor to other children; perhaps she could begin by helping with phonics or auditory training, at which she is quite good.

5. Terry's parents should supplement the resource program at home with games and related activities to help her improve her visual-motor memory (Concentration, charades, etc.). Her parents should also be included in a home backup behavior modification system that will reward Terry for attending to and completing tasks and chores such as organizing and cleaning her bedroom, simple cooking and kitchen tasks, and homework assignments.

PRESCRIPTIVE TEACHING EXCERPTS ("HALF-YEAR" REPORT)

- A behavior modification program was started at home and school. The home program is designed to strongly reinforce "positive attitudes" by awarding as much as 13 points a day.
- Our priority teaching objectives are

  1. Visual memory
  2. Visual-motor integration and coordination
  3. Arithmetic reasoning
  4. Concentration and attention

  Prescriptive instruction in these areas began with the use of Try materials, marble board designs, and chalkboard exercises. The Concentration game is also being used for developing visual memory and integration skills.
- Bead patterns, flannel board sequences, and parquetry blocks are being used to help Terry "see-talk-feel" visual patterns and reproduce them from memory.
- Jack and utility ball games are used in both gross and fine motor training. Today, much to *her* surprise, Terry picked up eight jacks!

Terry Kohl: PROGRESS EVALUATION OF PRESCRIPTIVE TEACHING

Objectives	Techniques*	Results
1. To improve her visual-motor memory, eye-hand coordination, and visual integration	Used flannel board patterns, chalkboard, marble board, toothpick designs, etc. Had her verbalize about them and touch them, in order to remember visual patterns. Some patterns were copied directly; others were total recall.	Quite a bit of improvement, especially on the marble board. She is concentrating and attending to detail.
2. To improve her ability to spell and correctly recall and reproduce relearned words	Attempted Fernald method on spelling with little or no success. Her visual memory is poor and she tends to repeat past errors. *Oral* spelling and talking about the shape, number of letters, etc. in the word seemed to help, plus repeating the word *anew* in print several times, and review and praise.	Some success, once she realized that she *could* shed the "old way" of spelling a word and relearn the "new, correct way." She was pleased with success.
3. To improve math concepts and usage in weak areas	Used manipulative materials to reinforce number combinations as families ($3 + 4 = 7$; $4 + 3 = 7$; $7 - 4 = 3$; $7 - 3 = 4$). Used toothpicks in bundles (of 10) or singly to illustrate place value system and the need for carrying in addition.	Some improvement in area that she deeply *dislikes*. Needs to move on to rationale and practice of borrowing in subtraction.
4. To encourage self-directed goals and self-responsibility	Asked her to choose a learning goal of her own. She wanted to learn cursive writing (which may, incidentally, be helpful in her spelling). We began systematically through the alphabet, using fingerpaint and then pencil and paper for each letter.	Coordination and Direction are difficult for her, but kinesthetic reinforcement helps. Should continue from "i."
5. In the area of affective education, to improve her attitude of cooperation and cheerfulness	Terry and I talked about the problem of her rejecting tasks in a negative manner and always wanting to choose what the daily program would be. We switched the "star" system to a reward for having a "good attitude," rather than for task performance.	There was great progress. She was much more willing to attempt things and to cooperate without negative comments. There was less attempt to manipulate me or the learning situation.

* Used self-checklist to help her evaluate her own progress; also, positive reinforcement for task, performance and later for "good attitude."

- Terry loves to use fingerpaint for both math and spelling exercises. The Judy 100 pegboard has also given her a kinesthetic awareness in doing her arithmetic. She resists math but does respond to movement and game approaches to arithmetic instruction.
- She is now using the self-checking chart for spelling seven words and doing simple subtraction problems. Terry will be introduced to carrying in addition and to cursive writing of the words gun, hop, mob, cat, men, dill.
- She is now spelling 8 out of 10 words recalled correctly; this is good progress for Terry.
- We are now working on improving Terry's visual-motor speed, using a stopwatch to time sorting, categorizing, and other manipulative activities.

DISCUSSION QUESTIONS AND ACTIVITIES

1. The classroom teacher reported that Terry was "in a low reading group on the first grade level, and much of her work is carelessly done." How can this information be used?
2. What are Terry's strongest learning abilities?
3. According to the test results, which is Terry's greatest single strength? To what extent is this confirmed by her personal history?
4. According to test results, what is Terry's most significant disability? Discuss how this disability affects her school achievement.
5. Select a single high or low WISC or ITPA score from Terry's test profile and interpret it relative to the standard deviation for that test.
6. Explain how Terry's mental age grade expectancy was arrived at and what validity it might have.
7. What other tests or evaluations do you think should have been given? Why?
8. Suggest some prescriptive activities that might help Terry improve her gross motor abilities.
9. Prescribe a remedial writing lesson and accompanying materials that might help Terry.
10. Design a visual-motor lesson using concrete manipulative symbolic material that would be directly relevant to Terry's disability.
11. How might Terry's regular classroom assignments and placement be modified or supplemented?
12. What realistic performance criteria might be established for Terry as conclusive evidence that she has achieved her prescriptive objectives?
13. On pp. 188 and 189 is a blank form entitled Individual Profile of Learning Skills and Abilities. Select a case file of a child you have worked with in prescriptive teaching and fill in this form using all available test scores and information. List all scores in the appropriate column and then place an X on the profile to show that score as very low, below average, average, above average, or very high. Write in any other tests used, including criterion or clinical evaluations. When completed, review the profile and explain any discrepancy that may exist between this child's general mental ability and actual achievement scores indicated.

INDIVIDUAL PROFILE OF LEARNING SKILLS AND ABILITIES

Name _____

Grade _____ CA _____ MA _____

GRADE:	LK	MK	HK	L1	H1	L2	H2	L3	M3	L4	L5	M5	H5	M6	L7	M7	L8	M8	L9	M9	L10
AGE:	5	5½	6	6½	7	7½	8	8½	9	9½	10	11	11½	12	12½	13	13½	14	14½	15	15½

Approximate grade expectancy

Profile (percentile/standard)

	Skills and abilities	Comments/other criterion evaluations	Very low	Below avg.	Average	Above avg.	Very high
Gross motor abilities	Balance						
	Coordination						
	Strength						
Sensory-motor abilities	Attention-concentration (WISC-DS)						
	Laterality						
	Manual expression (ITPA)						
Auditory perception	Auditory reception (ITPA)						
	Auditory association (ITPA)						
	Auditory sequential memory (ITPA)						
	Auditory closure (ITPA)						
	Sound blending (ITPA)						
	Consonant sounds (Spache)						
	Vowel sounds (Spache)						
	Consonant blends (Spache)						
	Common syllables (Spache)						
Visual perception	Visual form constancy (Frostig)						
	Visual position in space (Frostig)						
	Visual figure ground (Frostig)						
	Visual closure (ITPA)						
	Visual reception (ITPA)						
	Visual memory (WISC-PC)						
	Visual association (ITPA)						

Category	Test item													
Visual-motor perception	Eye-hand coordination (Frostig)													
	Spatial relations (Frostig)													
	Visual sequential memory (ITPA)													
	Visual motor planning (WISC mazes)													
	Visual motor synthesis (WISC BD)													
	Object assembly (WISC)													
	Fine motor control (WISC code)													
	Visual motor integration (BVMG)													
Language abilities	Verbal expression (ITPA)													
	Receptive vocabulary (PPVT)													
	Expressive vocabulary (WISC/Binet)													
	Grammatic closure (ITPA)													
	Oral reading vocabulary (WRAT/Spache)													
	Oral reading comprehension (Spache)													
	Silent reading comprehension (Spache)													
	Spelling (WRAT)													
Conceptual-cognitive abilities	General information (WISC)													
	Comprehension and reasoning (WISC)													
	Similarities and abstractions (WISC)													
	Functional mental age (WISC/Binet)													
	Arithmetic reasoning (WISC)													
	Arithmetic operations (WRAT)													
Social-personal abilities	Self identification (DAP)													
	Social planning and anticipation (WISC PA)													
	Social maturity (Vineland SA)													
	Self esteem													
	Behavior ratings													

CHAPTER 12

Programming figural operations

Almost all of the many models of cognitive development stress the importance of sensory and perceptual experience and integration. Inhelder and Piaget (1958) have demonstrated that it is in the course of early concrete experimental manipulation of things that the child begins to organize his perceptions into simple groups and classes. William James (1890) explained in some detail how higher order reasoning is actually the ability to perceive the essence of things through the discrimination and association of their similarities and differences. Gestalt psychologists such as Werner (1961), have experimentally shown how similar perceptual associations and groupings are developed and begin to be organized as symbols, signs, and abstract ideas.

Most applied psychologists have also recognized that perceptual association and organization are the essential elements in cognitive operations, and they have attempted to measure and evaluate them through tests of all kinds. These tests have usually included a combination of visual and visual-motor tasks that require discrimination, organization, association, and other figural operations culminating in the recognition of basic similarities and their application as "ideas." For example, the widely used Stanford-Binet test* relies heavily on such tasks on the preschool level; abilities to see similarities and differences in pictures and abstract designs, to order one's perceptions, to detect absurdities and construct analogies, and to make other transpositions of figural data are frequently required. The performance scale of the Wechsler Intelligence Scale for Children† also contains several subtests such as picture completion, block design, and object assembly, which require figural operations to be evaluated through concrete visual-motor activities.

The work of Guilford (1967, p. 227) on the structure of intellect presented us with a new appreciation of the importance of perceptual organization. Guilford's research shows that "figural content" is one of the four major kinds of

---

*Terman, L., and Merrill, M. Stanford-Binet Intelligence Scale, Third Revision, Form L-M, Houghton Mifflin Co., Boston, 1962.
†Wechsler, D. Wechsler Intelligence Scale for Children—Revised, The Psychological Corp., New York, 1974.

intellectual expression and that visual, auditory, and kinesthetic modalities are all involved in attributing meaning to the internal structural relations of figural perceptual information. Some tests, such as the Illinois Test of Psycholinguistic Abilities,* attempt to measure such skills as visual memory and visual picture association and to relate them directly to higher order linguistic development. Other tests such as the Columbia Mental Maturity Scale† and the Raven Progressive Matrices† have focused exclusively on visual figural tasks and operations. In his manual on the use of the Coloured Progressive Matrices, Raven has summarized his experimental work, which shows the qualitative development in these figural operations, beginning with simple form discrimination and slowly proceeding to increasingly more difficult levels of organization, integration, and analogous reasoning.

Considerable work has also been done on the application of research findings to developmental education and therapy. Figural operations can be evaluated, specified, ordered, prescribed for, and then programmed. Children can be helped to make and develop figural discriminations and operations of all kinds. In this chapter we will examine some of the more basic figural operations with visual content that are frequently utilized in psychoeducational programs. The material to be presented here has been divided into four developmental levels:

- FUNDAMENTAL SKILLS: Preschool to about age 5 years
- PRIMARY SKILLS: Kindergarten to second grade (5 to 8 years)
- ELEMENTARY SKILLS: Third and fourth grades (8 to 11 years)
- ADVANCED SKILLS: Fifth and sixth grades (11 to 12 years and older)

Each of these levels will be illustrated with different figural exercises that can be used with children. All of the figural material presented has been based on the earlier developmental research cited, although they are unique in their actual design and composition.

FUNDAMENTAL SKILLS

The fundamental figural operations are those that are usually acquired by the time that a child enters school. They are most often learned in the informal environment of the home where the child naturally explores, contacts, manipulates, and refines his early experiences.

Concrete sensory-motor exploration and feedback are the most important aspects of this educational process. Developing personal awareness and perceptions of things such as clothes, furniture, household objects, and toys is the meaningful work of the child at this early age. Gradually, the understanding of how objects and things function and relate to each other begins to develop, and the resulting mental pictures and images can then be used to solve more difficult problems.

---

*Visual reception and visual association subtests, University of Illinois Press, Urbana, Ill.
†The Psychological Corp., New York.

Infant stimulation, preschool programs, and other forms of early intervention and prescriptive education have all been used successfully to help very young children acquire these beginning figural operations and cognitive abilities. Among the more important of these is the recognition of similarities and differences in color, size, design, shape, and function and in the identification of essential parts and the pairing of objects.

The following material is merely illustrative of *teaching* (not testing) material and procedures that can be used at each level. Of course, all such material should be supplemented and modified by the teacher to ensure that the child understands what is expected and that he or she actually learns the basic concepts and operations involved.

▶ **Objective:** Recognizing similarities and differences of color

1. Put your finger on the shapes that look alike. They are the same.
2. Say, "These shapes are the same," as you touch each one again.
3. Trace the shape that is different with your finger. It is different because it is black.
4. Use a pencil to trace around the shape that is different.
5. Tell me why the shape that you traced is different.

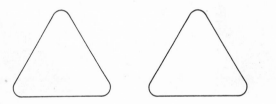

▶ **Objective:** Recognizing similarities and differences of size

1. Put your finger on the shape that is different. Trace it with your finger.
2. The shape that is different is small. The shapes that are alike are large.
3. Mark the one that is different.
4. Tell me why the one you marked is different.

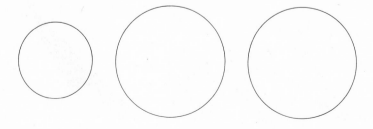

▶ **Objective:** Recognizing similarities and differences of shapes

1. Put your finger on the shapes that look alike. They are the same.
2. Put your finger on the shape that is different in that it does not look like the other two shapes.
3. The shape that is different is square. The shapes that are alike are round.
4. Use a pencil to trace the shape that is different. Now tell me why it is different.

▶ **Objective:** Recognizing similarities and differences of designs

1. Put your finger on the designs that look alike. They are the same.
2. Put your finger on the design that is different and mark it with your pencil.
3. The design that is different has lines going through one side instead of being colored black.
4. Trace the design that is different with your finger and tell me why it is different as you trace it.

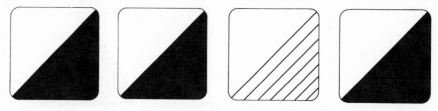

▶ **Objective:** Recognizing similarities and differences of objects by color

1. Put your finger on all of the objects that look alike. They are the same.
2. Touch each object that looks alike again and tell me why they look alike and are the same.
3. Yes, these objects are knives and one is different. Mark the one that is different.
4. Tell me why the one you marked is different.

▶ **Objective:** Recognizing similarities and differences in objects by size

1. Put your finger on the objects that look alike. They are the same.
2. These objects are glasses. Touch those that look alike and say, "These glasses are the same."
3. Touch the glass that is different. Color it red.
4. The glass you colored is larger than the others. It is large and the others are small.
5. Tell me why the one you colored is different.

▶ **Objective:** Recognizing similarities and differences in objects by shape and function

1. Put your fingers on the objects that are the same. They are houses and they look alike. People live in houses.
2. Mark the object that is different from the others. It is a tree. Trees grow in the ground and have limbs and leaves.
3. Tell me why the ones that look alike are the same. Tell me as many things as you can.
4. Explain to me why and how the one you marked is different.

▶ **Objective:** Recognizing missing parts in similar objects

1. Put your finger on the objects that look alike. They are the same.
2. Color in the object that is different.
3. All of these objects are called cups. The cup that is different does not have a handle.
4. Trace the cup that is different and tell me why it is different.

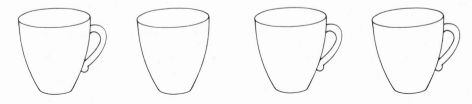

▶ **Objective:** Recognizing similarities and differences in object pairs

1. Put your finger on the objects that look alike. They are the same and they belong together if they look exactly alike.
2. There are two circles that go together and are alike; touch them. There are two triangles that go together; color them and tell me why they are alike.
3. Put your finger on the object that is different because it does not look like any of the others.
4. Trace it with your pencil and tell me why the object is different from the others.

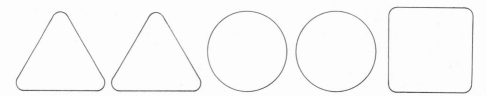

PRIMARY SKILLS

Most kindergarten programs attempt to help children acquire and develop specific figural skills that will relate to academic functions. Much emphasis continues to be placed on the acquisition of these skills during the first and second grades.

Among the more important visual figural skills to be learned are those of identifying position in space, recognizing missing parts, organizing symbol pairs, completing visual patterns, making directional orientations, integrating designs, and understanding simple class and functional differences.

Numerous educational programs and materials have been created for use on this level. Among the better known ones is the Frostig Program for the Development of Visual Perception,* which includes such training exercises as "position in space" and "spatial relationships." The Continental Press materials† include a series on visual discrimination, seeing likenesses and differences, and others that have proved to be of special value with exceptional children.

Primary figural shapes and relationships, and letter and number symbols, have been structured for independent use with programmed learning machines such as the Cyclo-Teacher.‡ A number of school systems, such as the Fresno City Unified School District, have also designed special programs like POINT (Patterned Observation and *Int*ervention),§ which provides numerous visual-integration skills for use in the regular primary classroom.

---

* Frostig, M., and Horne, D. The Frostig Program for the Development of Visual Perception, Follett Corp., Chicago.

† See catalog, Instructional Material for Exceptional Children, The Continental Press, Inc., Elizabethtown, Pa., 1975.

‡ Programs P205, P214, P223, and M60, Dept. C-T, Field Enterprises Educational Corp., 510 Merchandise Mart Plaza, Chicago, Ill.

§ Department of Curriculum, Fresno City Unified School District, 1766 North Helm Ave., Fresno, Calif.

▶ **Objective:** Identifying position in space sequence

1. Look carefully at all of the shapes in the long box. Trace them with your finger.
2. Notice how each shape begins to fall a bit to the right. Color in all of the shapes in the box with a blue crayon.
3. If the shapes continue to fall, what position will the next one be in? Mark the shape below the box that would come next.
4. Color in the shape you marked and explain to me again why you marked that shape.

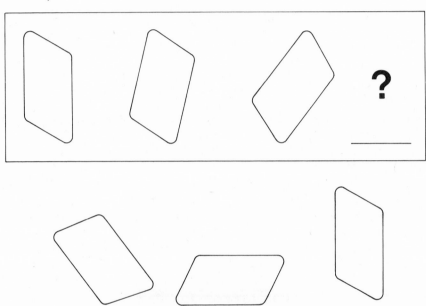

▶ **Objective:** Recognizing missing parts in similar objects

1. Look at all of the objects above. Put your finger on the ones that look alike. They are the same.
2. Put your finger on the object that is different. Mark it with your pencil.
3. These objects are called forks. Tell me why the forks you touched are alike.
4. What makes the fork that you marked with your pencil different?

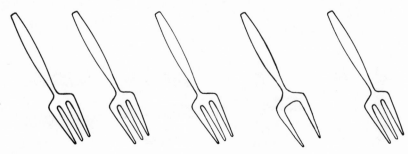

▶ **Objective:** Recognizing similarities and differences in symbol pairs

1. Put your finger on the symbols that look alike. They are the same and they look alike because of their shape. The shapes that look alike go together and are pairs.
2. Now you explain to me why these pairs go together.
3. Put your finger on the one that is different. It is not like or similar to any of the other symbols.
4. Trace the symbol that is different with a colored pencil or crayon. Explain how it is different from the others.

▶ **Objective:** Completing a simple visual pattern

1. Look carefully at the big circle below. Notice how dark lines go across the circle. Some of the lines are missing from the small white circle.
2. Touch each of the small circles with lines in them. Trace the lines with your fingers.
3. Now trace the lines in the big circle with your pencil. Draw in the lines that complete the design in the small white circle.
4. Which of the small circles match or look like the lines you drew in to complete the big circle? Mark the small circle with a big X.

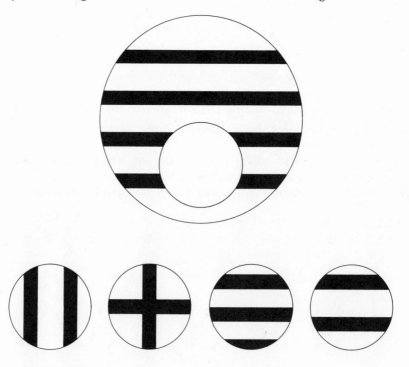

▶ **Objective:** Recognizing missing parts in symbols

1. Touch all of the symbols that look alike.
2. Touch the one that is different. Trace it with your finger. Tell me how it is different from the others.
3. Use your pencil to make the symbol that is different look just like the others.

▶ **Objective:** Recognizing visual pattern sequences

1. Look at all the small dark circles in the long box. Start at the left and put your fingers on the dots in each small box.
2. Look at the last small box with a question mark in it. Think quietly about what small dark circles would best fit there.
3. Put your finger on all the small circles in the boxes. Mark the box that best completes the pattern above.

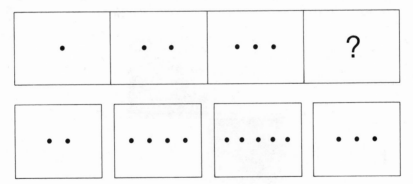

▶ **Objective:** Recognizing directional similarities and differences

1. Trace each of the designs with your fingers.
2. Put to each design that is alike. Tell me why they are alike.
3. Point to the design that is different. Trace it with a crayon and tell me why it is different.
4. Go to the chalkboard and draw six other designs similar to these but slightly different. Make five of them alike. Make one design different *in the same way that the design below is different.*

▶ **Objective:** Recognizing differences in symbol pairs

1. Look carefully at all of the designs in the boxes.
2. Put your finger on the boxes that go together. Tell me why they go together.
3. Mark the designs in the box that do not go with the others. Tell me why they do not belong with the others.
4. Go to the chalkboard and make some similar pairs of designs. Mark the one that is different and tell me why it is different.

▶ **Objective:** Integrating simple visual designs

1. Put your finger on the big box. Touch each of the four small blocks in the design that make up the big box.
2. Touch each of the blocks below. Mark the three block designs that can be put together to make one like the big box.
3. Tell me how these three blocks must be put together to make the big box.

▶ **Objective:** Recognizing simple class differences

1. Put your finger on each of the symbols below and tell me what they are.
2. Put your finger on two of the symbols that go together. Explain to me why they go together.
3. Put your fingers on two more figures that go together. Why do they go together?
4. One figure does not go with the other four. Why? Put a large circle around the one that does not belong.

▶ **Objective:** Recognizing directional similarities and differences

1. Use a black crayon to color over the dark area in each of the circles below.
2. Three of the circles go together. Touch the three that belong together. Why do they go together?
3. Mark the circle that does not belong with the others. Tell me why it does not belong.
4. Copy these circles on the chalkboard and put a large X across the one that does not belong.

► **Objective:** Completing a simple visual pattern

1. Look carefully at the design in the big circle. Notice the small boxes in the circle with dark lines in them. Trace the dark lines with your finger.
2. Look again at the design in the large circle. Now think what the dark lines would look like if lines were drawn in the empty white box.
3. Slowly trace the lines in each box with your finger. Which box do you think would best complete the design in the big circle? Mark it with your pencil.
4. Use a black crayon and draw in the missing lines in the white box to complete the design.

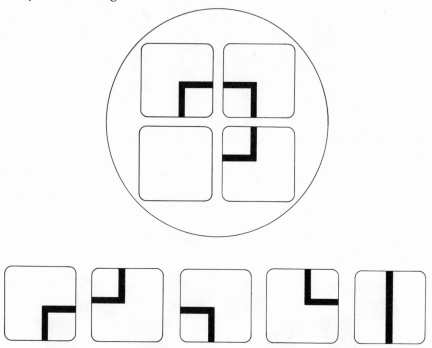

► **Objective:** Integrating visual symbols

1. Mark the two parts that could be put together to make the circle.
2. Cut the parts out and put them together to see if they are correct.

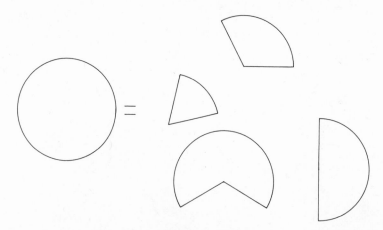

▶ **Objective:** Integrating visual symbols

1. Mark the two parts that could be put together to make the triangle.
2. Cut the parts out and put them together to see if they are correct.

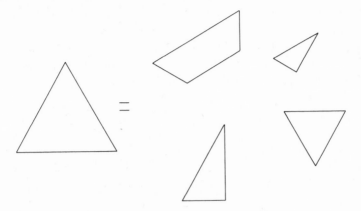

▶ **Objective:** Recognizing figural relationships

Mark the one that completes the design. Explain your choice.

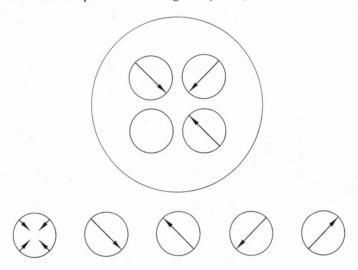

▶ **Objective:** Recognizing figural relationships

Mark the one that completes the design. Explain your choice.

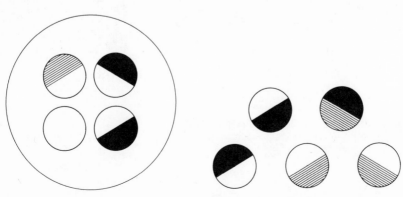

ELEMENTARY SKILLS

The elementary figural operations presented here are those that are usually acquired between the ages of 8 and 10 years or during the time most children are in the third and fourth grades. These operations are not nearly as concrete as those learned earlier. Increasingly, they deal with more abstract figural relationships. However, they continue to rely on such basic sensory and kinesthetic experiences as manipulating, marking, tracing, and drawing to enable learning to occur.

At this level, language becomes a more important factor in understanding the figural relationships presented. The child must begin to "converse with himself" about the functional differences of objects perceived, how visual symbols might be integrated, what figures might look like if analyzed and synthesized in certain ways, what the common properties of things might be, and the nature and meaning of signs and symbols.

Some educational materials on this level, such as the Visual Perception Skills Filmstrips,* teach "visualization" as the ability to integrate complex and overlapping visual stimuli with demanding auditory and verbal concepts. A A number of years ago, David Engler (1958) developed a program for parents that included picture classification tasks and related language tasks that could be used to help develop total cognitive ability in children. In prescriptive teaching, Aurelia Levi (1965) has demonstrated the importance of having children verbalize possible figural operations as part of their therapy program.

▶ **Objective:** Identifying functional differences

1. Look at each of these objects. They are all musical instruments. Touch each one and tell me how they are played.
2. Three of them are similar in some way. Point to them and tell me how they are similar.
3. Mark the one that is different and tell me why it is different.

---

*Educational Activities, Inc., Box 392, Freeport, N.Y.

▶ **Objective:** Identifying functional differences

1. Look at each of these animals. Touch each one and tell me their names.
2. Touch them again and tell me what kind of animals they are. Explain what they do and how they are used.
3. Three of these animals belong together. Which ones? Why?
4. One animal does not belong with the others. Mark it and tell me why it does not belong.

▶ **Objective:** Integrating visual symbols

1. Mark the three parts that can be put together to make the square.
2. Cut the parts out and put them together to see if they are correct.

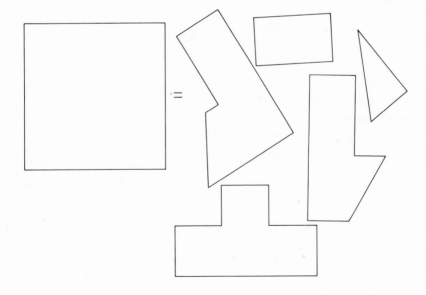

▶ **Objective:** Integrating visual symbols

1. Mark the two parts that can be put together to make the design.
2. Cut the parts out and put them together to see if they are correct.

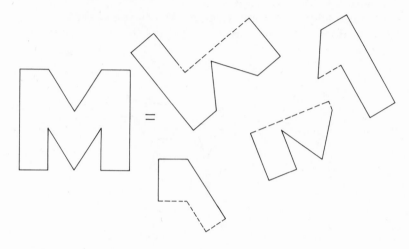

▶ **Objective:** Identifying functional differences

1. Touch each object below and tell me its name.
2. Touch them again and tell me what they do or how they are used.
3. Three of them belong together. Which ones? Why?
4. Which one does not belong? Why?
5. Cut out four pictures of things you can find in magazines—three that go together and one that does not belong. Mark it and tell me why the one does not belong.
6. Put a circle around the object below that does not belong.
7. Tell me another object that you could put with the three that go together.

▶ **Objective:** Identifying functional differences

1. Touch each object below and tell me its name.
2. Touch them again and explain what they do, how they are used, or what their purpose is.
3. Show me those objects that go together because of what they do. Tell me what they do—what they have in common.
4. Mark the one that does not go with the others. Explain to me why it does not go with the others.
5. Write a brief sentence explaining what the three similar objects have in common.

▶ **Objective:** Analyzing and synthesizing designs

1. Look carefully at the design in the box above the line. Trace the design with your pencil.
2. Look at all four of the designs below the line. Trace them with your finger.
3. If you select two of the designs below the line and put them together, they will look like the design in the box. Mark the two designs that go together.
4. Explain to me why you marked those two designs. Describe how and why they go together.

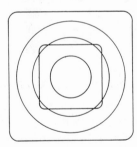

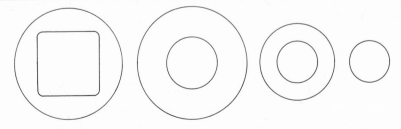

▶ **Objective:** Recognizing figural relationships

1. Look at the large box design. Touch each of the four parts that make it up.
2. Use a black crayon to trace each of the dark parts of the blocks in the design.
3. Touch each of the small blocks. Mark the one that best completes the pattern. Tell me why it best completes the pattern.

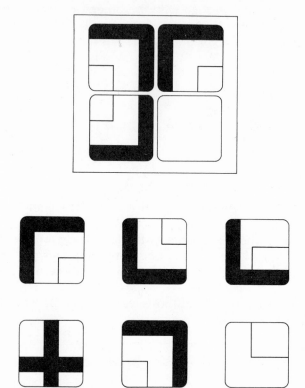

▶ **Objective:** Identifying similar abstract symbols

1. Put your finger on the numeral in each box and tell me what it is. All of the figures in the box are numerals that we use in counting.
2. Put your finger on each figure below the box and tell me what it is.
3. Which figure or symbol best goes where the question mark is? Why? Mark it with a big X.

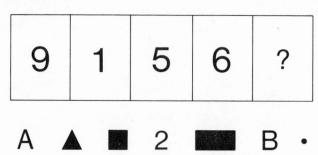

▶ **Objective:** Recognizing abstract series

1. Put your finger on each symbol in the box and tell me its name.
2. The first symbol is a letter, the second symbol is a numeral, the next is a letter, and the next is a numeral.
3. What would the next symbol be in the series? Why? Find it and trace it with a red crayon.

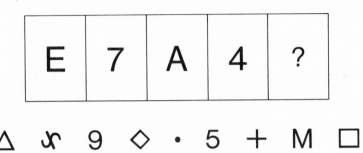

△ ⌓ 9 ◇ • 5 + M □

▶ **Objective:** Identifying similar functions

1. Put your finger on each object and tell me what it is.
2. Explain to me what each object is used for or what it does.
3. Put your finger on two objects that have identical purposes.
4. Put your finger on two other objects that have similar purposes. What is that purpose.
5. Which object above does not belong with the others? Why? Mark it with your pencil.
6. Tell me another object that would go with the one that you marked. In what way is it similar?

 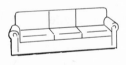

▶ **Objective:** Identifying similar functions

1. Put your finger on each object and tell me what it is called.
2. Touch them again and explain what they are used for.
3. Put your finger on two of them that are similar. Tell me how they are similar.
4. Touch two more that have a similar purpose. What is that purpose?
5. Put a circle around one object that is quite different from the others. Explain to me how it is different.

▶ **Objective:** Recognizing abstract similarities and differences

1. Touch each of the figures below and tell me their names.
2. Some of these are numerals. Touch the numerals and tell me their names.
3. Some of these are letters. Touch the letters and tell me their names.
4. Show and tell me the symbols that go together. Tell me why they go together.
5. One symbol does not belong with the others. Mark it and tell me why it does not belong. What is this symbol called? Tell me some other kinds of symbols that would go with this one. Draw one on the board.

5 A 9 7 F ◇ M

▶ **Objective:** Recognizing directional differences in abstract figures

1. Touch each of the figures below and describe them to me in some detail.
2. Touch the ones that go together. Tell me why they go together.
3. Mark the one that is different, that does not belong with the others. Tell me why it does not belong.
4. Write in the box another figure that would go with the figure below that is different.

ᘔ ⅃ Γ 3 5 4 ▭

▶ **Objective:** Recognizing figural relationships

1. Study the design in the circle. Touch each part with your finger and describe each part in detail.
2. Look at the design and determine which part is needed to best complete the total figure.
3. Look carefully at each part below. Mark the part that best completes the design.
4. Explain why that part best completes the design.

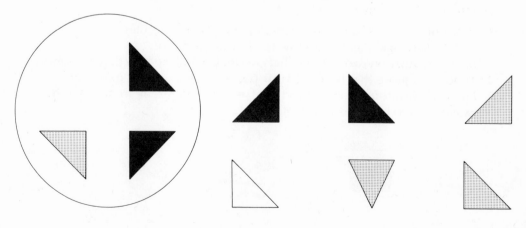

ADVANCED SKILLS

Most advanced figural and other cognitive operations are not acquired by children until they are about 11 years of age or older. Much of the fifth and sixth grade curriculum is predicated on the acquisition of these skills and operations, although they are seldom directly taught in the curriculum itself.

It is at this level that the child begins to understand abstractions and develop more formal mental manipulations. Some of the visual figural operations of importance here are recognizing abstract similarities and differences, understanding complex figural relationships, synthesizing detailed figural patterns, manipulating proportions, and transposing and projecting figural designs.

Many of these operations are called for in the more subject-oriented courses on the upper elementary and secondary school levels. Science courses and units use figural operations in laboratory experiments, music and art courses require complex figural integration, and even games such as checkers and chess require figural cognitive operations.

On the advanced level it is of increasing importance that a task analysis be made of the pupil's subject matter itself to determine the actual mental operations involved. Most of these require the integration of figural with symbolic and semantic operations.

▶ **Objective:** Recognizing figural relationships

1. Touch each of the circles and describe them in detail.
2. Point to the ones that are similar. Explain how they are similar. Explain how they are different.
3. Mark the one that is different in that it does not belong with the others. Explain why it does not belong.
4. Draw similar designs on the chalkboard. Mark the one that is different. Explain why it does not belong.

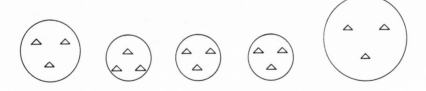

▶ **Objective:** Synthesizing figural patterns

1. Look carefully at the pattern to the left. Trace each part with your finger.
2. Trace each of the other patterns with your finger.
3. Mark *two* patterns that could be put together to make one like that on the left. Tell me why the ones you did *not* mark are inappropriate.

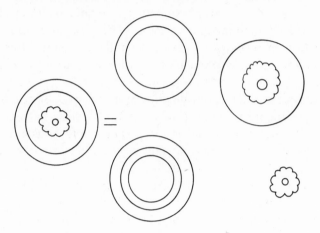

▶ **Objective:** Recognizing proportional relationships

1. Use a ruler to measure the large F.
2. Use a ruler to measure the parts. Place an X on the parts that go together to make a large F exactly like the one above.
3. Make another F on the chalkboard exactly like this one.

▶ **Objective:** Recognizing proportional figural relationships

1. Trace the design to the left with your pencil.
2. Mark the two parts that if placed together would look like the design.
3. Explain why the parts you *did not mark* do not fit together.
4. Copy each of the designs below on the chalkboard and then mark those that go together.

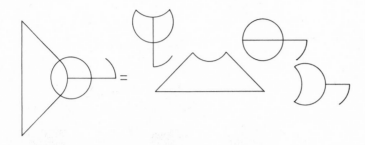

▶ **Objective:** Synthesizing abstract designs

1. Use a black crayon to color in the dark parts of all the blocks.
2. Check the three blocks that will make the large design if put together. Describe how they must be placed.

▶ **Objective:** Recognizing figural relationships

1. Trace each design with your pencil.
2. Touch those designs that are similar. Explain how they are similar.
3. Put a circle around the design that is different. Describe how it is different.
4. Draw another design in the box below that is similar to, but different from, the one that you have circled.

▶ **Objective:** Transposing figural relations

1. Touch each design in the box and describe it in detail.
2. Mark the design below that best completes the box. Explain your choice.

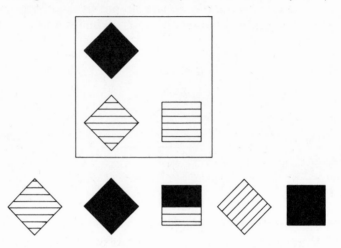

▶ **Objective:** Projecting figural relationships

1. Trace the design in the box with your finger and describe it in detail as you do so.
2. Mark the circle that best completes the design. Tell me why you marked that circle.
3. Use a ruler and pencil to draw in the missing design by connecting the lines and shading the intersections.
4. Create another similar design and parts of your own. Explain it to me.

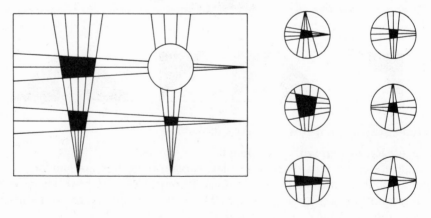

A series of increasingly difficult figural learning tasks has been presented in this chapter. All of the operations involved can be acquired through maturation and appropriate education. For cognitively handicapped children, the learning process must be an intensely prescriptive one with numerous multisensory supplemental experiences emphasizing kinesthetic involvement and mediational language. Similar lessons and methods can be used to teach other kinds of cognitive operations as needed.

DISCUSSION QUESTIONS AND ACTIVITIES

1. Select a single test item from the Stanford-Binet or WISC, demonstrate it, and point out the specific figural operations involved.
2. Present the Illinois Test of Psycholinguistic Abilities to your discussion group and critique the figural operations involved.
3. Administer the Columbia Mental Maturity Scale and make a task analysis of the errors on cards missed. Design a program to remedy these deficiencies. Conduct the remedial program, recording your lessons and activities. Readminister the Columbia Mental Maturity Scale and describe changes observed from the pretest to the posttest.
4. Conduct and report on a similar program using the Raven Progressive Matrices as the criterion instrument.
5. Use the lesson material presented in this chapter with a handicapped child. Present and discuss your findings to your discussion group.
6. Explain how you might have supplemented your lessons with multisensory activities more than you actually did.
7. Make a task analysis of your pupil's erros on these lessons. Design three additional lessons and worksheets that could be used to help remedy these kinds of cognitive errors.
8. Demonstrate and critique one of the commercially available learning programs referred to in this chapter.
9. Carefully review a current research article selected from a professional journal that has to do with the remediation of cognitive figural operations. Write a report on the article explaining how you might use or modify the techniques or method involved.

CHAPTER 13

Creative thinking

One of the most important cognitive functions is creative thinking, but, since it is a dynamic and multifaceted function, it is seldom specified in cognitive models or taxonomies. However, the various mental processes involved in creative thinking have been recognized for some time.

COMPOSITION

The father of modern intelligence testing, Alfred Binet, recognized that imagination and autocriticism were important elements in human behavior and required careful evaluation. Unfortunately, most psychometric tests of intelligence have overemphasized convergent thinking abilities such as verbal comprehension, computation, and classification, since these are the ones most often called for in school and academic learning situations. The developmental psychologist Jean Piaget has also demonstrated how the more advanced cognitive operations, such as hypothetical-deductive logic, gradually evolve from the more intuitive and concrete experiences of early childhood; the unique combinational symbolic elements in propositional thinking are acquired through experience and training and include certain qualitative aspects, such as personal style and attitude, which are also among those skills and abilities infrequently considered in traditional intelligence testing.

We have also seen that Guilford's structure of intellect (SOI) model contained several components related to creative thinking. For instance, Guilford's SOI "behavioral content" recognizes personal moods and intentions; he also considered "divergent production" to include originality, and many of his experimental tests and efforts were devoted to exploring how this ability could be adequately measured. The SOI model also specifies "transformation" as a mental product or expression that evolves from the unique combination of units by which other possible relations are perceived, changes are sought, and new products are finally created.

All of these investigators recognized that creative thought was a rather unique expression and utilization of acquired facts and knowledge. The development of creative thought and expression is highly valued because its end product,

217

whether it be in scientific, artistic, or industrial form, usually contributes to cultural evolution, human betterment, and enjoyment. Considerable research has shown that the unique aspects of creative thinking do involve cognitive processes and operations but are also dependent on the concomitant development and utilization of related personality functions such as feeling and affect.

For example, Block and Dworkin (1976, p. 389) have reviewed most of the psychometric research and concluded that "there is only a very low relationship between creative abilities and intelligence *as ordinarily measured*" (emphasis mine). Furthermore, the classic study of Getzels and Jackson (1962) concluded that creative thought develops from the elaboration of various fantasies that are closely related to daydreaming and childlike play with ideas; the creative person tends to be one who is open to and accepting of freely rising ideas, whereas the noncreative individual tends to suppress them. It is also important to note that although divergent thought processes such as fantasy may result in originality of ideas, the essential criterion for creative thinking is one that demands both original and relevant problem-solving responses that eventually result in the development of new or unique products and ideas.

CREATIVE PROCESSES

The mental processes involved in creative thinking are becoming more clearly understood. Recently, we have discovered that mental processes and thinking vary according to brain hemispheric function, development, and use. It has been demonstrated, for instance, that each person actually has two brain systems, which drastically affect the way he or she thinks and acts. Bogen (1969) has summarized the research showing that the left side of the brain is largely concerned with propositional-logical thought processes such as language and mathematics, while the other side of the brain is given to appositional, imaginative, visual-spatial-perceptual processes. Related studies by Deikman (1971) also conclude that there are two major modes of human consciousness: the active muscular-manipulative mode and another "receptive" mode of equal importance. Whereas the left brain functions and the active muscle system are usually concerned with comparing, relating, and manipulating the environment, the "receptive" system is a far more open one, with diffuse attention, decreased boundary perception, sensory impressionism, and paralogical thought processes in operation.

It appears that creative thinking demands the development and fullest integration of both sides of our brain. Many psychologists have also pointed out that creative thinking is a uniquely human function to be treasured and developed to the fullest possible extent. William James (1890) recognized creative constructiveness as a human instinct rooted in our biological nature. More recently, Maslow (1962) argued that the essential inner nature of human beings is instinctoid and shows itself in creative inclinations, propensities, tendencies, and potentialities that are shaped by life and education. Maslow described a different form of human cognitive functioning, which he named B-cognition. In this form of cognition, experience and objects tend to be perceived as whole and complete units; some of the creative processes involved include spontaneity, courage, perspicuity, integration, and self-acceptance.

A summarization of the major creative thinking processes would include the following operations:

- IMAGINATION: Ability to form new or different mental images and concepts
- FANTASY: Ability to create wishful, ingenious, visionary thoughts and images
- ORIGINALITY: Ability to think in novel, independent, divergent, flexible, or transformational ways
- REVERIE: Ability to enter a state of dreamy, intuitive, inspirational reflection or meditation
- PLAYFULNESS: Ability to move and act in an open, frolicking, delightful, or humorous way
- CREATIVE LANGUAGE: Ability to use language forms to express associative, symbolic, or allegorical-metaphorical ideas and relationships

It can be readily seen that these kinds of mental abilities are ones that are generally found in young children before they are unduly conditioned by their culture. With time and experience, thought control and shaping begin and the person may actually be punished as he or she grows older and fails to conform to the prevailing conventional ways of thinking and acting. In this way, our natural creative instincts and intuitions are frequently inhibited and thwarted— if not actually destroyed.

Many educators and psychologists, such as Maslow (1971), have reminded us that we should become more interested in the creative process itself than in the product alone. Therefore it has been suggested that the schools give more attention to the inspirational phase of creativity, helping children to look within themselves to develop their unconscious processes such as fantasy and imagination.

SOURCES OF CREATIVE THINKING

How do creative thoughts arise in the mind and finally take form and shape in some product? Can anything be done to influence the development and frequency of creative thinking? Can the quality of creative thinking be improved through special forms of education? These are a few of the crucial questions of concern to educators and parents alike.

Extensive studies of the creative process indicate that there are several sources or determinants involved (Kretch and Crutchfield, 1958). The first of these is the nature of the stimulus pattern, with its unique spatial and organizational qualities; thus a person may view a stained glass window and make associations about it according to its design and structure. The second determining factor is the specific fund of acquired knowledge (such as facts and information about stained glass windows) that the perceiver brings to the situation. The third and most important factor appears to be the personality structure of the person involved; the open-minded and flexible person will more readily play with and combine the various possible components of stained glass windows (or whatever else might be perceived and experienced) and therefore be more likely to come up with a new and unique production than a person who is closed minded or narrow in perceptual approach.

Of course, facts, knowledge, and technical skill are important in creative thinking, and no amount of flexibility or open-mindedness can substitute for these basic requisites. But too many facts can actually constrict and narrow one's creative approach to thinking and problem solving. Most persons have a substantial fund of factual information on which to build but lack the flexible personality attributes and receptive attitude necessary to allow their creative processes to be exercised. Jung (1960, pp. 402 to 403) has reminded us that although much of our thinking results from the facts and data that we have actually put into our intellect, there is another more symbolic form of thinking that consists of images and inspirations that spring from within the unconscious human psyche itself. It is Jung's contention that it is only possible to live the fullest life when we are in harmony with these symbols and images that spring from our deepest self.

Analytic psychology presumes that a source of creative energy and intelligence is to be found within the psyche or central self of each person. Occasionally this source of energy expresses itself in dreams, images, intuitive inclinations, and even inspirational productions such as song, dance, and other artistic endeavors. However, in most persons the creative psyche lies dormant and may even atrophy through ignorant neglect. This concept has been expressed in many other different ways. In their discussion of the psychology of creative intelligence, Bloomfield et al. (1975) conclude that creative thought actually arises spontaneously from a center deep within us—and the closer a person comes to opening and experiencing the most quiet aspects of the thinking process, the more energy and intelligence will be produced and expressed. In this context creative intelligence is defined as the human energy empowering and directing activity and the innate human capacity for progress and evolution.

In one of his most famous works, William James (1901/1958, p. 72) wrote that human intuitions spring from the deeper levels of our subconscious life and finally culminate in our faith, impulses, and rational actions of everyday life. Jung further substantiated this point of view by stating that

> whenever the collective unconscious becomes a living experience and is brought to bear upon the conscious outlook of an age, this event is a creative act which is of importance for a whole epoch.*

Some of the epochal acts that were attributed by their originators to unconscious creative forces include Dante's *Divine Comedy*, Goethe's *Faust*, and the

---

*From Jung C. The spirit in man, art, and literature. Vol. 15 of *The collected works of C. G. Jung* (Bollingen Series). Princeton, N.J.: Princeton University Press, 1966, p. 99.

products of many musicians and artists. Shakespeare (Sonnet 86) referred to his own unconscious creative source as an "affable familiar ghost which nightly gulls him with intelligence." Another psychiatrist-researcher, Bucke (1901), posited that these ghostly intuitions and creative thoughts stem from a broader cosmic consciousness, which works through the human psyche to further human development and evolution.

Accordingly, these proponents insist that the primary source of creative thought lies within the unconscious personality itself and not in the self-conscious logical mind and rational efforts of the individual person. Education for creative thinking must therefore be a balanced one that involves and attempts to develop one's unconscious processes and potentialities. It is to be hoped that through such a new and total education each person will also learn that he "himself is the source of the best and most a man can be or achieve; the more this is so—the more a man finds his source of pleasure in himself—the happier he will be" (Schopenhauer, 1901, p. 22).

EDUCATIONAL APPROACHES

It is generally acknowledged that creative thinking and problem solving involve four stages. These are usually referred to as preparation, incubation, illumination, and verification. Preparation requires the acquisition of relevant knowledge and its experience through such means as playful manipulation and other creative operations previously discussed. Incubation is a period of "internalization" of knowledge and experience and the giving of one's self adequate time to assimilate and integrate data without undue interference or distraction. After a period of flexible openness the third stage of insight occurs and the person is said to be "illuminated" with the new idea or thought necessary for solving the problem of concern. Verification is the final step and requires functional application of the creative thought or product and self-feedback for further refinement.

Formal education should provide opportunities for each of these four stages in creative thinking to occur. This would include actually teaching the stages to children and providing them with numerous opportunities and learning experiences that would actively promote and encourage incubation, insight, and verification. Currently, most schools stress convergent thinking and the acquisition of lower level cognitive skills and facts that contribute to the initial preparation for creative thinking. But this is inadequate since we have seen that the unconscious processes must themselves be prepared and actualized for the more advanced stages of creative thinking to be activated. Most experts in this field have advocated the increased use of discovery methods, the exploration of intuitive ideas, the encouragement of novel, imaginative, and self-evaluated projects, and greater experimentation.

There are many ways that can be used to teach children to think, imagine, reason, and comprehend themselves more fully. The human potentiality for learning, thinking, feeling, and imagining new and better ways of doing, acting, and living can always be more fully actualized. Children must be taught that through study, reflection, and creative experience they can come to know and understand themselves more fully and gradually become more capable of functioning in everyday life. We must actually teach our pupils that they do have within their basic selves the potentiality and the power to become more than they now are, and it is this creative evolutionary striving in humankind that moves us on toward a greater personal and human destiny. Children also need to be taught how to open themselves in such a way that their creative inclinations and potentialities can be manifested.

The basic requisite in designing such an educational program is, of course, the personality, attitude, and goals of the teachers immediately involved. Above all, teachers must value the development of creative thinking in their own selves and treasure and promote it in the children they work with. Also, teachers must not be threatened by divergent, imaginative thinking and other expressions of creative intelligence in their pupils. And they must become more willing to provide their students with open, flexible, individualized opportunities for developing creative thought and action. A few of the ways that this might be done are presented here.

In a current report on research and development in training creative thinking, Davis (1976) states that creative problem solving is in part a voluntary act that can be promoted by the schools striving to develop a creative awareness in children. This can be accomplished through the use of such educational techniques as brainstorming (generating a long list of fanciful problem solutions), attribute listing (mentally changing parts of objects and ideas to create new ones), and various idea checklists. An example of a good idea checklist is to present the learner with a sheet containing the following aids for helping a person think of physical changes that might be made in an object (such as an automobile, bicycle, or house).

An idea checklist
- Change the design or style.
- Change the color.
- Change the materials.
- Change the shape and/or size.
- Change by rearranging parts of the object.
- Add something to or subtract something from the object.

A number of these creative thinking techniques have been published by Davis and Houtmann (1968) in a guide for training the imagination of school children. A similar book, but one that stresses the use of fanciful story telling to develop creative thinking in children, has been written by DiPego (1973). Several models for developing fantasy in children as part of a creative thinking program have been critiqued by Jones (1970). Other creative problem-solving strategies have been developed by Sherry (1977) and by Covington et al. (1972).

Most of the commonly used creative learning teaching programs and methods have been summarized by Torrance and Myers (1970) in their major text on this subject.

The following are a few examples of commonly used learning tasks that require children to organize and synthesize facts and information in new and creative ways:

- Select a series of common objects and ask the child to suggest how many different ways they might be used (brick, roasting pan, cardboard box, spoon, can, etc.).
- Present several pictures (park, moon, ocean, etc.) and have the child free-associate what might go with each one.
- Present a problem: If you came to a river and there was no way to get across since there was no bridge, how might you cross the river?
- Have children listen carefully as you read a paragraph of a current news article and then respond to questions (what, where, how, etc.) and speculate about what other endings might be possible under different conditions.
- Present a problem: Suppose your best friend's dog just had the most wonderful puppies in the world. You really want one, but your mother says that you are not old enough to take care of it. How do you think you could convince her?
- Present a problem: Here are some materials to work with (clay, paper, glue, rock, crayons, etc.). Pretend that you are living in the future and you are going to take a trip to Mars. From these things, imagine and create something that you might need on Mars and then show me and tell me how you would use it.
- Present a problem: Pretend you are a Christmas tree that can talk. Describe your feelings and experiences to me.
- Have the child use fingerpaint to make a picture of a dream that he or she can remember and then tell all about it.

Many tasks similar to those presented above are also used in tests of creative thinking. The Torrance Tests of Creative Thinking* are among the most widely used to evaluate creative thinking with words, pictures, sounds, and images; these tests are scored for fluency, flexibility, originality, and elaboration. Other practical approaches to evaluating creative thinking have been presented by Guilford and adapted by Getzels and Jackson (1962). The major kinds of items found in most of these tests include the following:

- IDEATIONAL FLUENCY: Writing or saying words with similar functions, sounds, letters, etc.
- UTILITY: Listing many different uses for common objects such as a shoe
- DECORATIONS: Decorating pictures of actual objects as innovatively as possible
- WORD ASSOCIATION: Using and defining words in as many different ways as possible
- HIDDEN SHAPES: Finding hidden pictures, shapes, or objects in varied figure-ground cards such as wallpaper books, ink blots, cloud pictures, and photographs
- FABLES: Providing different innovative endings (humorous, moralistic, sad, etc.) to incomplete fables or myths presented in short story form

---

*Torrance, E., Torrance Tests of Creative Thinking, Personnel Press, 191 Spring St., Lexington, Mass. 02173

- MAKE-UP PROBLEMS: Developing a set of questions logically derived from a brief paragraph of given information (such as advertisements and news stories)
- EXPRESSIVE LANGUAGE: Telling or writing a short story, joke, or poem from incomplete sentences (For example, "The man from Mars was _____.")
- IMAGINATIVE PROJECTS: Composing, painting, drawing, acting, building, or constructing symbolic fantasy-like products arising from personal reverie and unconscious spontaneous creations

Most of the criterion test items used to evaluate creative thinking can also be used as a source of teaching tasks, activities, and objectives. In addition, it is necessary for the teacher to provide other activities that will help to develop the open and receptive-reflective state of mind that we now know is essential to creative thinking. It is helpful to recall that Binet, Thurstone, and other psychometrists have continually reminded us of the temperamental factors in creative activity and that creativity is encouraged by a receptive rather than a critical attitude. Since creative solutions are more likely to occur during "periods of relaxed dispersed attention than during periods of active concentration on a problem" (Anastasi, 1976, p. 389), the educational program must be sure to include periods for relaxed, dispersed, and receptive awareness to take place.

Several educational approaches have been successfully used to develop creative receptive awareness. Greene, Greene, and Walters (1971) devised a psychophysiological training program for creativity using biofeedback to produce a reverie-imagery state that permits both the conscious and the unconscious mind to propose creative solutions to problems. Similarly, several meditation programs have been used in educational settings and have been found to significantly improve attention and concentration, auditory discrimination, associative memory, perceptual-motor coordination, and grade point averages; considerable evidence exists that brain wave patterns during reflective meditation are synchronized between both hemispheres and that this increased psychoneurological integration might explain the noted improvement in behavior (Bloomfield et al., 1975).

Other methods of self-actualization of creative potentialities, including a number of educational programs and exercises, have been presented (Valett, 1974, 1977). Another approach now being used in the schools is Psychosynthesis (Assagioli, 1965), which includes specific instructional techniques for developing imagination, visualization, symbolization, and the will to act creatively. Two illustrations of receptive-reflective training techniques are presented here. The first one, The Unconscious Self, is a simple and direct attempt to consciously consider the meaning of information obtained from the unconscious. The second example is a commonly used meditative lesson for developing visualization, openness, and reflection.

THE UNCONSCIOUS SELF
Attempt to describe these in detail:
1. Your most important wishes and aspirations.
2. A vivid dream that you have experienced.

3. Some recurring thoughts or ideas that have appeared to you.
4. The most unusual experience you have ever had.
5. Some feelings or sensations that you have had that seemed to be beyond your control.
6. The visual images or impressions that occur to you during a 3-minute period of quiet reflection and meditation.
7. Sit quietly with your eyes closed and listen to a classical record (such as Bach's Concerto for Two Violins in D minor) for a few minutes. Then open your eyes and use fingerpaint to create a picture reflecting the mood of the music.
8. A time when you said something or acted in some way that surprised you in that it "slipped out" of your unconscious.

BUTTERFLY

Purpose: The purpose of this exercise is to help you learn to increase your ability to relax, to attend, and to visualize pictures in your mind by using your imagination.

Posture: Sit or lie down in a quiet and relaxed position with your eyes closed.

Meditation: As you remain very quiet, you find that you will begin to relax all over. Just let yourself go and remain very still and let all the tenseness drain from your body. As you do so, you will begin to breathe deeply, which will help you to relax even more. You are already feeling very good throughout your entire body and you are increasingly aware of your breathing. Now concentrate on your exhalations and focus on the deep sense of relaxation that you experience with each breath that leaves your body. Very good, just let yourself go and relax even more.

Gradually you are becoming aware of and getting in touch with your center of self-energy. You feel relaxed and invigorated as you focus on the center of energy that is moving up through your body and slowly coming to rest at the point between your eyes. You are feeling very good and relaxed as your center of energy now begins to brighten and form a picture. Just give yourself up to your creative imagination. Your imagination will now begin to create a picture from this center of energy which is focused in your mind.

The scene is of a beautiful sunny day with a slight breeze. You are in a park sitting quietly and looking at a chrysalis of a butterfly that has been attached to a stalk of a green bush. It is just about time for the pupa to begin to open. As you watch you see it begin to happen. Watch the pupa quiver and move. Now it is moving again. The transformation is taking place and slowly the hard cover is splitting, and now the chrysalis is opening and the new butterfly is struggling to emerge.

It is a fascinating scene as slowly, so very slowly, the butterfly pulls itself out of the stalk and moves itself about. Watch how it rests and then very slowly begins to move about in the sun. Gradually it is drying in the sunlight. Much time has gone by, and now the butterfly is stretching its legs and expanding its wings. Now you can see the beautiful colors and patterns in its wings and body as it spreads itself and reflects the sunlight.

It is becoming more active now and is moving out on a leaf. You enjoy watching the beautiful creature as its wings begin to move. The colors on the wings are glowing in the light of the sun. It seems to be waiting for the breeze. There it comes—and the butterfly rises gently, catches the breeze, and flutters for an instant above the leaf. Now it is fluttering and circling higher and higher in the air and moving up toward the warm sun. As it flutters and flys away, you feel its joy of transformation and freedom. You feel light and breezy and very good inside as you watch the butterfly slowly drift away in the rays of the sun.

Now quietly watch the butterfly and imagine what it will do next—how it moves and where it will go. In a minute you will open your eyes and use the crayons on your desk to draw a picture of the butterfly as you imagined it to be. Then share your picture with someone as you explain what you imagined it to be and what it would do next.

Most of the creative thinking exercises presented here have been directive ones. As with other kinds of learning, children need guidance and structure about what they are expected to do and just how they are to proceed to begin to think creatively. However, once a creative thinking program has been established, children quickly become adept at the techniques involved and require less direction and supervision. It is at this point that regular 4- or 5-minute periods should be set aside for reflective imagination or meditation. This "imagination time" is necessary for children to learn the values of silence and reflection for developing imaginative thoughts and ideas from their own intrinsic sources rather than from continual reliance on external stimulation and direction from others.

DISCUSSION QUESTIONS AND ACTIVITIES

1. Share and discuss the most creative learning experience you had during your elementary or secondary school years.
2. What are some of the natural play experiences by which children think divergently and attempt to transform objective thoughts and reality?
3. How might you explain the low correlation between creativity and IQ test scores?
4. Discuss some of the recurring daydreams you have experienced. In what way might they have been of some help to you?
5. What does the receptive mode of consciousness have to do with B-cognition?
6. Critique the premise of analytic psychology regarding the source of creative thinking.
7. List several of your own latent potentialities that are yet to be developed.
8. Which of the four stages of creative thinking do you believe the schools might have the greatest difficulty with? Why?
9. Demonstrate a lesson from a creative thinking program that could be used in an elementary school class.
10. What place do meditation or "imagination time" periods have in creative thinking programs?
11. To what extent should creative thinking be taught to slow-learning or educationally handicapped children?
12. How might pupil progress in creative thinking be reported to parents, school boards, and others concerned?

CHAPTER 14

Teaching strategies

Critical thinking skills are learned and acquired through the process of experience and education. We know that cognitive growth occurs in developmental stages from birth through adulthood but that most of this growth takes place in the preschool and primary years. The personal interactions between child and parents, and between child and teacher, are major determinants of what the child will learn. It is important that the nature of such interactions be clearly analyzed and understood, as they form the basis for all successful teaching.

In an early article on how children develop intellectually, Hunt (1964) concluded that it was possible to substantially increase children's mental capacities through such means as early perceptual and cognitive experience, responsive and realistic parental involvement, social-environmental changes, and good teaching. What is known as good teaching is essentially a series of teacher-designed cues and verbal interactions that provide children with an understanding of what they are doing, answers their questions, and stimulates their further interest and self-direction. The effective teacher, then, is one who is successful in designing and executing these interactions in such a way that desired pupil learning occurs.

SOME VARIED STRATEGIES

Considerable research has been done on effective teaching strategies. The main concern has been to identify those methodological factors that lead to the pupil learning what he or she has set out to learn. It is hoped that sound instructional procedures will result in mastery or near mastery of the concepts or skills being taught. This presumes, of course, that the concepts or skills to be taught have been clearly identified and that both teacher and pupil are working cooperatively to ensure their acquisition and mastery.

The research of Benjamin Bloom (1971) on mastery learning shows the importance of breaking the learning task down into fundamental cognitive, psychomotor, or affective instructional units that can be analyzed, evaluated, taught, and learned. These learning tasks then need to be considered in terms of the entry behaviors required—the "prerequisite skills," which account for as much as 50% of the variation in task achievement. Research also indicates that the affective entry components such as pupil motivation, set, and willingness to learn account for as much as 25% of variation in task achievement. The remaining 25% of variation in pupil achievement is determined by the quality of instruction.

The quality of instruction includes three important factors:

1. CUES: The structure and discriminations in the ordering of learning tasks and in their presentation and explanation to the student
2. RESPONSE AND PRACTICE: The amount and intensity of pupil participation in learning
3. REINFORCEMENT: The kind, amount, and scheduling of rewards and consequences for task performance

Teachers, then, must be concerned with clearly identifying learning objectives and instructional tasks, enhancing set or motivation for learning, structuring task cues, and reinforcing pupil participation and appropriate response. Other research by Bloom (1974) shows that when learning tasks are appropriately structured with feedback and correction, and as pupils are given additional time and help in task correction, 90% or more of the students can achieve mastery learning of most curricular expectations.

The two major problems in improving instructional quality appear to be how to systematically cue and structure pupil task learning and how to provide the time necessary for slower students to learn, which may be more than five times the amount of time required for average or fast-learning students.

Additional time devoted to teaching cognitive skills can be provided in a number of ways. Most schools are now beginning to reorganize classes and learning groups to allow more individual and independent instruction to take place. Varied achievement groups (including children of different ages), classroom learning centers, school resource rooms and laboratories, peer tutors, parent and community volunteer aides, and many programmed learning kits are but some of the major approaches being used. The provision of specialist teachers to provide supplemental prescriptive education is increasingly being provided in the schools and appears to be most effective in the primary years (Lambert, 1976). Our immediate concern here is with strategies than can be used to improve the quality of this supplemental diagnostic-prescriptive education for children with cognitive deficits.

Considerable research has been done on how to teach problem solving to young children and to those with special difficulties in thinking and cognition. Most of this research centers on reducing the abstractness of visual and verbal cues to increase correct pupil response and the subsequent transfer of acquired skill to other similar learning tasks and situations. Several major experimental approaches to concept learning in children have been summarized by Wittrock (1966). Much of this research has been translated into practical forms for direct use in the classroom. For example, some studies by Sternberg (1975) have implications for special educators, illustrating how "pattern recognition" is a necessary component of reasoning in mathematics and language development and then demonstrating how such learning can be structured with appropriate cues and pupil response. The actual conditions and fundamental components of the learning process, including a pragmatic structure for programming reasoning and problem-solving skills, has been outlined in detail by Gagné (1970).

Although most research in cognitive development continues to focus on instructional design and programming strategies, increasing attention is being given to the affective and motivational components of reluctant and slow learners. It has been recognized, for instance, that without proper attention or "set" on the part of the learner, even the most well-designed instructional system and the best teacher cannot ensure pupil learning. The problem here is how to initially increase pupil attention, openness, concentration, and commitment to the learning process itself. A recent monograph has summarized some intensive research in this area and concludes that cognitive and intellectual development programs have been most effective when intensive tutoring has included relaxation, biofeedback, and autosuggestive training (Sexton and Poling, 1973). Similar studies on reducing cognitive impulsivity through self-reflection training, peer modeling, and self-reinforcement programs have demonstrated the importance of the affective component in thinking and learning (Glenwick, 1976).

Young children and others with specific learning and behavioral disabilities seem to learn best when sensory-motor involvement and response are programmed as part of the cognitive lesson. The uses of movement in eliciting high-level cognitive activity in children and youth has been well studied. The research of Cratty (1973), among others, has resulted in a number of teaching strategies using active movement and games to improve such cognitive skills as memorization, categorization, language communication, evaluation, and problem solving.

Considerable effort has also been expended in designing reinforcement strategies and programs to increase pupil motivation and achievement. In fact, behavior modification and reinforcement programs of all kinds have proliferated in education. The practical application of these strategies to academic achievement has been demonstrated through the works of Becker (1971), Valett (1969, 1970, 1974), and many others. A recent study on the use of various prescriptive teaching strategies in the individualized instruction and mainstreaming of exceptional children stresses the importance of using alternative programs and treatment strategies that match pupil learning style and needs (Snow, 1976). It must always be remembered that reinforcement strategies and techniques must be adapted and used with sound and appropriate learning tasks and lessons. Both task and reinforcement strategies are necessary for effective learning to occur.

INDIVIDUALIZED INSTRUCTION

Most of the principles discussed in the first part of this chapter have been implemented in several different individualized instruction programs. One of the most advanced is the Individually Prescribed Instruction (IPI)* system which was created and researched in the 1960s through the Learning Research and Development Center at the University of Pittsburgh. The IPI objectives are as follows:

1. To enable each pupil to work at his own rate through units of study in a learning sequence
2. To develop in each pupil a demonstrable degree of mastery
3. To develop self-initiation and self-direction of learning
4. To foster the development of problem-solving thought processes
5. To encourage self-evaluation and motivation for learning

The IPI system has been widely tested in the field and now consists of an extensive bank of individualized learning programs that include reading, mathematics, science, spelling, and social studies. Clearly stated behavioral objectives, pretests and posttests, sequential learning tasks, and immediate feedback and correction allow continuous progress in learning to occur. Research results indicate that IPI students like school better than non-IPI students and that more of them enjoy mathematics than regular students, although there are no significant achievement differences in favor of IPI pupils.

Many school systems have devised their own systems of individualized instruction. The Duluth, Minnesota, school system experimented with a number of different approaches to individualized instruction for both regular and special students; one of these, the Franklin-Nettleton Project, has become a model for use with educationally deprived and special education pupils (Esbensen, 1968).

The Los Angeles Unified School District has created another approach, called system FORE,† which consists of the following components:

FUNDAMENTALS: Basic skills in reading, mathematics, and language
OPERATIONS: Assessment procedures, determining objectives, and special grouping of pupils
RESOURCES: Instructional materials and special resource teachers
ENVIRONMENT: Establishment and use of special learning centers

System FORE must be used in an entire school and comes complete with in-service training films and materials. Although it has been used with regular pupils, it has been particularly successful with exceptional students of all kinds.

Numerous other school districts have also developed rather unique approaches to individualized instruction. The Bakersfield City School District is typical of those with individualized reading programs in the elementary schools (Shannon and Blaylock, 1975). However, the Bakersfield program goes further

---

*Research for Better Schools, Inc., 1700 Market St., Philadelphia, Pa. 19103, 1973.
†Special Education Div., Los Angeles Unified School District, Room H-104, 450 North Grand Ave., Los Angeles, Calif. 90012, 1972.

in that it has designed special materials for informing parents of the specific reading objectives their children are being taught and how the parents might help children in the accomplishment of these objectives.

Educational technology is also contributing to the rapid growth and implementation of individualized instructional strategies. Special apparatus such as the Language Master Systems* and other sophisticated recording and audiovisual equipment now make it possible to program even the most primary language and conceptual skills. Simple programmed learning machines such as the Grolier Min-max Teaching Machine† and the Cyclo-Teacher‡ provide structural and systematic learning tasks and materials for use with all kinds and levels of pupils.

American corporations are also entering the field to provide systems for individualized instruction. The Westinghouse Learning Corporation has devised PLAN,§ a comprehensive approach to individualized learning that contains specific behavioral objectives and sequential teaching units and materials. The Random House Educational Systems Division has designed the High Intensity Learning Systems,‖ which provide complete instructional management, criterion-referenced objectives, and correlated learning materials. Other companies are currently developing similar systems.

There are also many other ways of individualizing instruction that can be utilized by teachers who are so inclined. The common element in all of these approaches is the use of an entry kind of achievement pretest to determine current pupil performance; students are then divided into several different learning groups, and pupils are exchanged with other teachers and sent to a variety of learning centers and resource rooms where they progress through study units or cycles of learning materials and objectives at their own rate of speed. Throughout the school year, learning groups are reorganized with pupils continually cycled to the most appropriate and flexible class or subgroup. Programmed materials, cross-age tutors, and parent volunteers are almost always involved in successful programs.

The checklist on pp. 234 and 235 has been designed¶ for use by concerned citizens, teachers, administrators, and parents who are interested in determining the degree to which individualized instructional strategies have been implemented in a classroom. By visiting the classroom and carefully observing pupil-teacher behavior it is possible for psychoeducational consultants to help teachers to understand what they may actually do to further improve the extent of individualization in their particular program.

---

*Bell & Howell, 2201 W. Howard, Evanston, Ill. 60202.
†Instructional Systems Div., Grolier Educational Corp., 845 Third Ave., New York, N.Y. 10022.
‡Dept. C-T, Field Enterprises Educational Corp., 510 Merchandise Mart Plaza, Chicago, Ill. 60654.
§Westinghouse Learning Corp., Tenth Ave., New York, N.Y. 10017, 1973.
‖Random House Educational Systems Div., New York, 1975.
¶By combined education committees, League of Women Voters and American Association of University Women, Fresno, Calif.

INDIVIDUALIZED INSTRUCTIONAL STRATEGIES CHECKLIST
(CLASSROOM OBSERVATION)

School _____ Subject _____ Grade _____

No. teachers _____ No. students _____ No. aides _____ No. volunteers _____

Name of observer _____ No. minutes observed _____

	Very much	Some	Very little	None	Unable to observe
1. Does physical environment (arrangement, displays) enhance learning?					
2. Is there freedom of movement? (How many students left seats? _____)					
3. Is teacher primarily lecturing? (How many minutes lecturing? _____)					
4. Is everyone working on the same thing at the same time?					
5. If students are working individually, are worksheets standardized?					
6. Did you see students involved in selecting their own objectives?					
7. Were students involved in evaluating their own progress?					
8. Was there verbal interaction between teacher and students?					
9. Was there verbal interaction among students?					
10. Did the teacher move about and help students individually?					
11. If teacher aides were present, were they assisting in *instruction*?					
12. Were audiovisual and manipulative materials actually in use?					

	Very much	Some	Very little	None	Unable to observe
13. Is there evidence of an evaluation procedure to measure individual progress?					
14. Are provisions made for different rates of learning?					
15. When students perform successfully, are praise and approval shown?					
16. When students are not successful, is ridicule or derision used?					
17. Did you feel an air of excitement, student-teacher rapport, etc.?					

18. Did you personally read and inspect an individualized study unit or lesson plan actually being used by a student? _____ *Describe* it:

19. How many different study or work groups did you observe *simultaneously* in action during your visit? _____ *Describe* them:

20. How many students are you *certain* were working on a lesson individually prescribed for them (*different* from others in class)? _____ *Explain:*

PRESCRIPTIVE TEACHING PLANS

In this section we will consider the components of prescriptive teaching plans or "lessons" as strategies for cognitive development. Children with thinking and cognitive deficits certainly require a diagnostic-prescriptive plan that will logically ensure that they be taught the skills and concepts that they need to know. The plan must be carefully devised in such a way that the pupil clearly *understands* just what it is that he or she is trying to learn. It must also provide sequential teaching tasks so that the child is actually introduced to, shown, enlightened, taught, and enabled to perform the skills or operations with increasing success.

The dynamics of prescriptive instruction have long been known and researched. One of the earliest detailed (and dramatic) descriptions of this process was written by Jean Itard in a diary he maintained while attempting to teach Victor, a 10-year-old severely handicapped retarded boy. In considerable detail, Itard recorded his efforts to develop sensory, social, and intellectual functions in Victor. For example, after considerable instruction in the acquisition of prerequisite sensory and perceptual skills, Itard set out to teach the basic language concepts and finally came to verbs. An excerpt from his prescriptive lesson plan follows:

> After the explanation of the adjective, came the verb. To make this understood by the pupil I had only to submit to several kinds of action an object of which he knew the name. These actions I designated as soon as executed, by the infinitive of the verb in question. For example, I took a key and wrote its name upon the blackboard. Then *touching* it, *throwing* it, *picking* it up, *kissing* it, *putting* it back in its place, and so on, I simultaneously wrote in a column at the side of the word key, the verbs to touch, to throw, to pick up, to kiss, to replace, etc. For the word key I then substituted the name of another object which I submitted to the same functions . . .*

Through such sensory-motor demonstrations as this, Itard introduced the concepts he wanted Victor to learn. By subsequently requiring the boy to imitate his actions and to use the appropriate language required, he ensured that Victor "understood" what was demanded of him. Then the teaching plan was gradually modified according to the kinds of errors that Victor made in actual practice and use of the concepts being taught; but the systematic instructional strategies remained highly structured and consistent throughout.

Maria Montessori further refined teaching strategies and methods for use with children who have cognitive difficulties. Although Montessori's system and sensory-motor instructional materials stimulated spontaneous exploratory learning, she also insisted on the use of exact teaching procedures to be sure that concepts were acquired. For example, in teaching certain basic language con-

---

*From Itard, J. *The wild boy of Aveyrnon* (G. Humphrey and M. Humphrey, Trans.). New York: Appleton-Century-Crofts, 1962 (Originally published, 1894), p. 82. Reprinted by permission of Prentice-Hall, Inc.

cepts such as large and small, the teacher would first use sensory-motor exercises to ensure that the child recognized the differences between the qualities of objects being presented. Then the teacher would *fix the idea* of the quality with structured words and language. For instance, after a child had played many times with pink cubes and built and rebuilt cube towers of all kinds, the teacher would encounter him with the two most extreme cubes (the largest and the smallest) and, showing them to him, say:

> This is large. This is small. This is *large,* large, large. Give me the *large* one. . . . This is *small,* small, small. Give me the *small* one. . . .
> Again—give me the large one. Now give me the small one.
> Now—what is this? (large) . . . And what is this? (small) . . . and so on.*

These and several other methods were further structured and systematically integrated into conceptual learning programs by instructional designers. One of the most notable examples of such programmed instruction is the DISTAR language and reading program† developed by Carl Bereiter and Siegfried Engelmann. As a result of extensive research in conceptual learning, Engelmann (1969) writes of the necessity to teach children the *rules* of the thinking and learning process. The prescriptive teaching lesson must be structured in such a way that children understand they must follow certain rules and that they will be immediately reinforced when they do so. Systematic concrete instruction followed by rote drill and practice are essential aspects of prescriptive instruction. For example, a lesson on verbal blending is described in part as follows:

> O.K., John say *at.* When I tap you like this, say *at.* Don't worry about what I say; you're going to say—what? . . . Yes, *at.* (The teacher now says *mmmm*—one long humming sound—and then taps the child.) Let's do it again and see what word we have: *mmmm-at.* Say it fast and you'll see what word it is: *mat.* Let's hear it again: *mmmm–at.* etc, etc.‡

The actual steps in prescriptive concept learning have been studied in some detail. The major steps include concept specification, analysis, constructing appropriate learning tasks, systematic programming of pupil response, and reinforcement. Most prescriptive concept learning lessons must also include tasks to teach what the concept "is not"; Barbara Bateman (1969) calls this teaching both the applicable instances and the "not-instances." That is, the teaching routine must be consistent with the concept being taught and *only* with that concept and the critical discriminations the child must make. For example, in teaching a concept such as heavy, several pairs of objects that are alike in every respect (size, color, shape, etc.) *except weight* should be used, and the "*not-heavy*" attribute should also be taught.

These critical steps in concept learning can all be summarized in a prescrip-

---

*From Montessori, M. *Dr. Montessori's own handbook.* New York: Shocken Books, Inc., 1965, pp. 124 to 125.
†Science Research Associates, Inc., 259 E. Erie St., Chicago, Ill. 60611.
‡From Engelmann, S. *Preventing failure in the primary grades.* New York: Simon & Schuster, Inc., 1969, p. 92.

tive lesson outline for practical application. It is suggested that special educators and other therapists use the following outline as a guide to ensure that all necessary instructional-teaching steps have been planned.

PRESCRIPTIVE LESSON PLAN

1 Pupil's name _____ Age _____ Program _____
2 Date of lesson _____ Place _____
3 SPECIFIC COGNITIVE SKILL OR ABILITY: What skill or ability is being taught?
4 PRETEST TASKS AND RESULTS: How were the present performance and entry skills and abilities determined? What were the results of tests and measurements?
5 TEACHING OBJECTIVE: What is the pupil to learn, do, or achieve during this lesson? What is the desired performance standard or expectation?
6 RATIONALE: Why did you select this objective at this time? Why is it of priority importance for this pupil?
7 INSTRUCTIONAL MATERIALS REQUIRED: What lesson and task materials, programs, equipment, etc. will be needed to teach these skills? How do the materials provide pupil feedback and permit self-correction?

---

8 SPECIFIC TEACHING PROCEDURES
    8.1 Teacher explanation of objectives and learning tasks
    8.2 Pupil exploration, survey, and paraphrasing of objectives and tasks
    8.3 Teacher demonstration and verbalization of initial learning task
    8.4 Pupil verbal interpretation of initial task
    8.5 Pupil imitation and overt verbalization of initial task
    8.6 Sequential learning tasks (Teacher lists and presents several tasks of increasing difficulty for pupil practice, *including pupil verbalization and self-direction.*)
    8.7 Teacher or program reinforcement of pupil (type and schedule of reinforcement)

---

9 POSTTEST AND RESULTS: How was the final task performance determined? To what extent was the original teaching objective realized?
10 LESSON EVALUATION AND CRITIQUE: How appropriate were the learning tasks in this lesson? How was pupil interest and motivation? How could the lesson have been improved or changed for additional prescriptive teaching in the future?

The most important part of the prescriptive lesson plan is the list of the specific teaching procedures (No. 8) to be followed. It is here that the learning cues, serial tasks, and pupil responses must be carefully designed and presented. For concept learning, it is essential that pupil verbalization (both overt and covert) be deliberately programmed into the teaching procedures. Without adequate pupil verbalization and clarification it is not possible for cognitive mediation and concept understanding to take place and develop.

Of course, it is not always possible or necessary for teachers or therapists to always write such detailed prescriptive lesson plans. However, it is very important for new or inexperienced teachers to develop several such detailed plans until they become thoroughly acquainted with the principles and procedures of individualized *prescriptive* instruction. To this end it is also important that teachers learn to evaluate the effectiveness of their own prescriptive instruction. The Prescriptive Teaching Analysis Record on p. 239 can be used for this purpose

PRESCRIPTIVE TEACHING ANALYSIS

Pupil's name _____   Date _____   Prescriptive teacher _____

Learning objective (minimal performance expectations)	Objective domain			Objective selected by			Teaching materials used by student	Learning situation				Performance evaluation					Attitude evaluation				Task evaluation		
	Psychomotor	Cognitive	Affective	Prescriptive teacher	Regular teacher	Self		Individual instruction	Special group instruction	Regular classroom instruction	Home-community instruction	Poor (0%-10%)	Fair (10%-25%)	Average (25%-75%)	Good (75%-90%)	Excellent (90%-100%)	Began task	Worked hard	Completed task	Other:	Inappropriate	Appropriate	Very appropriate (85%)
												Points 1	2	3	4	5							
Task #1:																							
Task #2:																							
Task #3:																							

On the back of this form critique your objectives and tasks and describe what you might do to improve pupil performance in future prescriptive lessons.

PRESCRIPTIVE LESSON PLAN
FOR LEARNING-HANDICAPPED PUPILS

Lesson topic _____ Date of presentation _____

Place _____ Time _____ Lesson No. _____

Developmental age level of pupil(s) _____ Program _____

Objective and performance expectations:

Learning tasks and activities:

Materials required:

Sequential teaching procedures:

Results and evaluation:

Teacher/therapist signature _____

Type any supplementary information or comments on the back of this form.

and will help the inexperienced teacher or therapist evaluate the priority learning objectives and tasks in some detail; objectives and task can be written on this form and quickly checked in appropriate columns with notes that can be used in future lesson revision and prescriptive planning.

As soon as the teacher has gained sufficient experience in actually applying the principles of prescriptive instruction, lesson plans can be considerably shortened. A simple prescriptive lesson plan outline for use with learning-handicapped pupils is presented on p. 240; this form is usually sufficient as a guide for most experienced professionals and should be adapted or supplemented to meet whatever special needs may exist.

SAMPLE LESSONS

Excerpts from several concept lessons are presented here to illustrate the importance of task seriation and pupil verbalization. These are only brief examples, and it should be realized that the actual teaching procedures in each case involved significantly more verbalization, clarification, and practice than may be indicated by the examples given.

Similarities and differences

Rosa is a 9-year-old educationally handicapped girl with many problems in thinking. She is being seen once a day in a learning resource room by a special educator who is supplementing her regular classwork and tutoring her in specific cognitive skills and problem-solving techniques. Several of the lessons have had to do with teaching Rosa to recognize similarities and differences as follows (T = teacher; P = pupil):

T: Rosa, look at the pictures below and think about how they are similar, or alike.

If you are thinking that they are all circles or balls you are right. They are also round and all of them are on the line. Now think how they are all different, or not alike. For example, one way that they are different is that they are of different sizes— this one (pointing) is very small and this one is the largest. What other way are they different?

P: Some are black and some are white.

T: Good—that's right. Now tell me how they are similar again.

P: They are all round. . . . They are all on the line.

T: That's right, Rosa. Now I want you to write on this sheet of paper two ways that they are similar and two ways that they are different, OK?

P: OK.

Similar: Round, circles

Different: Size, color

T: Fine, Rosa. This time look at the pictures below. See where it says "name"? Since both boxes have letters in them, I will write "letters" in the box like this.

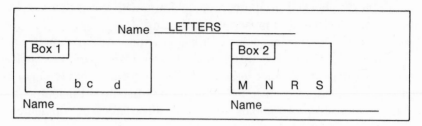

One way that all of the letters in box 1 are similar is that they are small, or lowercase. Tell me another way that they are similar.

P: They follow each other.

T: Right—they follow each other, and we call that alphabetical. How are the letters in box 2 similar?

P: They are all big capital letters.

T: OK. Let us see now how they are different. In box 1 they are spaced differently. How are they different in box 2?

P: I don't know—they are bigger?

T: Look carefully and tell me what letters you see as I point to them.

P: M, N.

T: What letter *usually* comes after N?

P: O, then P. Oh, I see, they are not in order!

T: Very good, Rosa. Now write in a name for the letters in each box above and then write on your worksheet how the letters in each box are similar and how they are different.

Box 1	**Box 2**
Name: Small	Name: Capitals
Similar: In order	Similar: Large
Different: Different places	Different: Out of order

The lesson continued for a total of 25 minutes of discussing, discriminating, labeling, and verbalizing similarities and differences in four additional task cards of increasing difficulty: animals, fruit, flowers, and abstract designs. Written worksheets were discussed and corrected. Other lessons continued throughout the year and extended into similarities and differences in words, sentences, stories, and advanced designs.

Simple classification

Martin is a 7-year-old boy with difficulty in understanding sets and classification. Part of a lesson follows:

T: Martin, here is a box of different kinds of colored blocks. You place them on the table for me; thank you. Now tell me all the colors you see.

P: Red (r), green (g), blue (b), and yellow (y).

T: Right. Now watch me put a string around all of these different blocks. Now I will take another string and make a big loop—but this time I will only include some of the blocks like this:

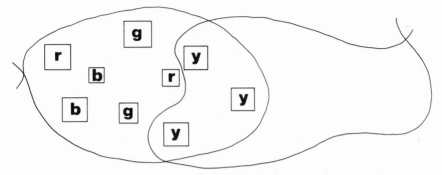

Look at all of the blocks in this small intersecting loop (pointing). What color blocks does it include?

P: Yellow—three yellow ones.

T: That is right. The first loop has all kinds of colored blocks. The second little loop has just small yellow blocks. But the small loop is also part of the larger loop that goes over here. If we add more blocks in the empty part of this loop what would they be?

P: All kinds of yellow ones.

T: Good—you take some from the box and put them in the empty loop and tell me what they are as you do so.

P: Three small yellow ones . . . two large yellow ones.

T: Fine. This time I am giving you a box of different colored triangles. Go ahead and make three loops like we did with the blocks. Tell me where and why you are placing each triangle.

Problem-solving situations

This excerpt is from a series of lessons used with a group of three junior high school boys. The lessons had all been devised to teach them these eight problem-solving steps:

1. Recognizing the problem
2. Listing possible choices and solutions
3. Analyzing the alternative solutions
4. Picking a choice
5. Planning the choice
6. Carrying out the plan
7. Evaluating the choice (how well it worked)
8. Modifying the choice (making necessary changes)

After separate lessons on each of these steps, part of a summary lesson went as follows:

T: OK boys, let's see how well we can apply all that we have learned so far. Here is the situation: You want to go to a movie but your parents tell you to be home by

10:00 P.M. and you know that the movie is not over until 10:30. The problem appears to be one of conflicting times; what do you think about it?

P: Yeah, how can you see all of the movie and still get home when your parents say?

P: I think the real problem is one of misunderstanding between the guy and his parents.

P: No—the problem is he has some dumb parents!

T: Well then, let us list some of the possible solutions that we can think of. What are the choices you can come up with? Of course, one might be to leave the movie early; what do you think of that one?

P: But that isn't right if you pay the money to go.

P: Maybe we could go earlier?

P: Parents do change their minds sometimes if you talk to them about it.

P: How about going to another show at a different time?

The lesson continued sequentially through the steps for 40 minutes, with each boy writing his own options and the group consensus. During the next 3 weeks, several other kinds of summary lessons on problem solving (homework, being late for work, losing friends, etc.) were used with the same small group.

Analogous thinking

Throughout this book we have discussed how cognitive development occurs through the interaction of appropriate experience and specific practice over time. Knowledge and understanding are slowly acquired through a long and varied process of perceptual discrimination and integration. The detection of similarities and differences between things is a fundamental skill in this educational process. Eventually, these skills and abilities are refined and extended into higher order forms of cognition such as analogous thinking and propositional logic.

To think by analogy requires the person to determine some similarity, likeness, or correspondence between things. Through such a comparison it is inferred that certain things "belong together." Once a specific likeness or similarity is perceived and clearly verbalized (overtly or covertly) this same concept can then be generalized to other objects as well. In this way, the child begins to think ever more abstractly. With continued practice in looking for and deriving analogies from actual experience, the child becomes capable of generalizing them to projected problem-solving situations.

All cognitive development programs emphasize the importance of *teaching* analogous thinking. As with other skills, we learn to think in analogies in stages that begin with concrete manipulations and comparisons of things. Then we gradually proceed to the comparison of pictures or representations of reality. Finally, we are able to do without the actual objects or their pictures as we acquire the ability to mentally visualize and compare percepts. Then, with continued practice, we begin to use concepts such as words and symbols for things that, when mentally manipulated and compared, become increasingly abstract and efficient as instruments for problem solving.

Considerable research has been done on the use and importance of analogy in higher order learning (Davidson, 1976). The sample lesson excerpts presented here are based on this research, which stresses the importance of teaching explicitly stated tasks that actually guide the child to make the desired cognitive operations.

The first lesson excerpt is on a primary level with a child who has much difficulty in understanding simple language concepts.

T: Michael, look outside at those birds on the grass. They are sparrows. Tell me what you see them doing.

P: Some are on the grass eating and some just took off and are flying away.

T: What are the birds flying through, Michael?

P: The air! They're flying up to those trees.

T: Right! Birds fly in the air. Now Michael, look at our goldfish over there in the acquarium; tell me what it is doing.

P: It's swimming around those rocks down there.

T: That's right. Birds fly in the air and fish swim around in the water. Now look at these pictures and tell me what you see.

| Bird | Air | Fish | |

P: The first picture is of a bird next to a picture of clouds and the sky. The next one is a fish.

T: Yes, and you can also see some words below the pictures. A bird goes through the air as a fish goes through the _____ ?

P: Water. A fish goes through the water.

T: Correct, Michael. Now I want you to draw in a picture of some water next to the fish and then write the word "water" in the blank space under your picture. I will help you with the spelling if you want me to.
Good. Now close your eyes and picture a bird in the air and a fish in the water. Then open your eyes and tell me why a bird is to the air as a fish is to the water.

P: I get it! A bird is to the air as a fish is to the water because they both move through them.

There are numerous simple analogies that can and should be taught in similar ways. Children should contrast, compare, and experience objects by touch, drawing, coloring, arranging, and acting out stories and charades. These objects should then be presented in simple pictorial form with appropriate labeling and extensive practice in developing mental imagery and verbalization. Some of the primary analogies that can be used in teaching 5- to 8-year-old children are listed below; as the concepts become more difficult, note that multiple choices may be provided as guides for comparative thinking:

A gun is to shoot as a knife is to _____
Snow is white; coal is _____
In is to out as up is to _____
Front is to back as top is to _____
Man is to woman as boy is to _____
An inch is short; a mile is _____
Army is to soldiers as Navy is to _____
Gloves are to hands as boots are to _____
Wood is to a table as glass is to a _____
Dark is to light as black is to _____
Long is to short as skinny is to _____
Milkman is to milk as mailman is to _____
First is to last as early is to _____
Racket is to tennis as bat is to _____
Leaves are to rake as dirt is to _____ (hammer, shovel, knife)
Chair is to sit as bed is to _____ (jump, sleep, read, sheets)
Ears are to sound as eyes are to _____ (smell, glasses, light, games)

As children mature, more difficult analogies should be taught. At this stage it is usually not necessary to begin instruction with concrete experiences. However, pictorial representations and comparisons are still essential visual mediators for learning analogies at this stage. The excerpt below illustrates how pictures can be used for refining this kind of thinking.

T: Mary, here are two pictures. Tell me what you see and what you think of when you look at them.

Shark
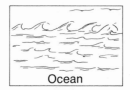
Ocean

P: The first picture is a shark and the second is an ocean. The words are below the pictures. I think that sharks swim in the ocean because they live there.

T: Right. Now look at these pictures and tell me what you think about them.

Worm

P: Well, the first picture is of some worms and the word is written under it. Then there is a house, some ground and flowers, what looks like a glass of something, and an airplane.

T: Correct. These are pictures to help you see and understand which things go together. They are called picture analogies. A shark lives, swims, and belongs in the ocean. We can say that a shark is to the ocean as a worm is to the _____.

P: Ground! Because it lives there.

T: That's right. Now you write the words beneath each of the pictures and then place a circle around the word you just told me that goes with worm. Then I want you to tell me why you did not circle any of the other words.

Some other elementary analogies that should be taught to children from 8 to 11 years of age are presented below. For this stage many commercial materials and teaching aids are available. Among the better picture analogies are those found in *The Gold Book* (Thurstone, 1967, exercises 61, 62, 77, 78, 85, 86, 93, and 94). Most children at this age are also capable of constructing their own picture books of analogies, and these are usually very valuable learning experiences. Other symbol-picture logical thinking games can also be used at this stage (Furth and Wachs, 1974). A number of more advanced body movement games have also been devised to help in the transition to more formal problem solving (Cratty, 1973):

Fingers are to hand as toes are to _____
Cat is to kitten as dog is to _____
North is to South as East is to _____
Bullets are to guns as arrows are to _____
Moon is to night as the sun is to _____
Big is to large as small is to _____
Cattle is to cows as swine is to _____
Radio is to listen as book is to _____
Smiles are to joy as frowns are to _____
Sugar is to cereal as butter is to _____
Matches are to fire as germs are to _____

Feathers are to birds as scales are to _____
Teachers are to pupils as doctors are to _____
Ring–finger : bracelet– _____
A–first : Z– _____
Authors–books : bakers– _____
Music–song : jokes– _____
Hammer–carpenter : paintbrush– _____ (mailman, farmer, artist, doctor, bus driver)

Purse–money : suitcase– _____
Fireman–fire engine : farmer _____ (rake, tractor, barn, crops, seed)
Cities–counties : states– _____
Courts–justice : studios– _____

By the time most children reach the upper elementary grades they become capable of making analogies using words alone. But even at this stage it is wise to encourage children to continue to mentally imagine or visualize what the objects, words, or concepts may look like or represent and to verbalize what meaning they have for them. It is also good to have the children continue to sketch or draw some of their visualizations and to share them with other pupils for purposes of sharpening their perceptions and verbalizations. The following are a few examples of advanced analogies that are frequently taught to children 11 years of age and older:

Rabbit–timid : lion– _____
Earth–sun : planets– _____
Strings–guitar : valves– _____
Jump–leap : stumble– _____
Debt–liability : income– _____
Pine tree–evergreen : poplar tree– _____
A–B : C– _____
Digestion–stomach : ideas– _____
Snake–reptile : horse– _____
1–4 : 5– _____
Wages–labor : profit– _____
Calm–excited : serene– _____
Reality–imagination : fact– _____ (thought, doubt, fantasy, poverty, discussion)

IMPLICATIONS

Children can be taught to think through the use of appropriate prescriptive lessons and teaching strategies. The sample lesson excerpts presented here have all emphasized the importance of directive instruction and verbalization in concept learning.

Most of the illustrations presented have been of relatively low-level cognitive thinking difficulties typical of elementary schoolchildren and those in special education programs. The same principles, however, are applicable in the instruction of secondary students and adults who may be learning higher order constructs.

In this chapter we have considered a number of different teaching strategies that can be used in most cognitive development programs. Several other strategies, such as the use of humor (humorous stories, jokes, cartoons, riddles, etc.), are also very helpful in developing divergent thought and creative expression (Phillips, 1974). The common elements in all real thinking skill strategies are those that require the pupil to observe, classify, compare, interpret, imagine, hypothesize, summarize, and critique his data and experience (Raths et al., 1967).

Good teaching strategies must be designed and executed by professionally trained and concerned teachers. They must also be modified in accord with evaluation data and results obtained. When carefully used, however, teaching strategies such as these do help in the remediation of cognitive deficits and in the development of thinking skills and abilities.

DISCUSSION QUESTIONS AND ACTIVITIES

1. Share an example of "good teaching" that you have experienced, and explain how the teacher acted.
2. Design an entry test for a specific cognitive lesson.
3. Discuss several things a teacher might do to increase pupil set and motivation for learning a given skill.
4. What are some of the distinctive characteristics of "programmed learning" kits?
5. How and when might relaxation, biofeedback, and autosuggestive training be used in cognitive therapy?
6. Create a body movement game that could be used to teach a cognitive skill.
7. What are some possible misuses of behavior modification strategies in cognitive learning programs?
8. Write a critique of current research available on IPI systems.
9. Describe the kinds of learning centers that could be established in any elementary school classroom.
10. Visit an instructional materials resource library and use some kind of programmed learning machine.
11. How did Itard know that Victor "understood" his lesson on verbs?
12. Design and teach a lesson using the prescriptive lesson plan outline of your choice. Role play your teaching procedures and demonstrate some of the actual learning tasks taught to your pupil.
13. Create a more difficult (but appropriate) similarities and differences learning task for Rosa using abstract designs.
14. Design a lesson using humorous material to help teach analogous or propositional thinking.

CHAPTER 15

The right to learn*

On July 4, 1776, our forefathers formally pledged themselves to a radical set of revolutionary values, which they printed in the Declaration of Independence. They announced their belief that men are endowed by their creator with certain inalienable rights, which include life, liberty, and the pursuit of happiness. For the support of that declaration they mutually pledged to each other their lives, their fortunes, and their sacred honor. That initial declaration of American ideals was instrumental in providing us with the basic goals and values that have given us direction for the last 200 years. And these goals and ideals remain almost as revolutionary and valid today as they were at that early stage of our history.

Let us consider a moment what happened to those early revolutionaries. Each of the 56 eventual signers of the Declaration of Independence suffered persecution of varying degrees. Most lost their homes and property and became hunted men. Nine died of wounds, five were captured and received brutal punishment, many lost family members, and one lost all 13 of his children in the war. Twelve had their houses burned to the ground. That was the cost of pledging their lives, fortunes, and sacred honor to such revolutionary values.

But of course, even that great group of men who gathered in Independence Hall, as well as those who later framed our Constitution, were products of their time and limited awareness. For instance, their concept of the "men" referred to in these great documents were of white men of some wealth and property. The concept did not include or provide for slaves, women, indentured servants, and other groups whose rights were to be established much later through cumulative constitutional amendment. Another notable lack was the failure to recognize education as a means of furthering life, liberty, and the so-called pursuit of happiness. It was assumed that each man was independently responsible for his own pursuit of happiness, and no provision for free public education was made in these documents.

---

*Much of the material in this chapter was originally presented as an invited address to a conference of the Texas Council for Exceptional Children in Houston, July 31, 1976.

EARLY EDUCATIONAL PROVISIONS

Exceptional persons such as the physically handicapped, the retarded, and the mentally ill were not really provided for outside of the family structure; as a result they were largely ill-clad, ignorant, and short lived. In 1779 Thomas Jefferson (then Governor of Virginia) wrote the Virginia Bill for the More General Diffusion of Knowledge. This radical bill proposed 3 years of free education in the basic skills for all free children (not slaves) plus a number of "promising poor boys." The Virginia legislature promptly defeated the bill, and it was not until 1834, when the Pennsylvania free school law was passed, that the poor in our country began to be educated.

Benjamin Franklin was one of our first educators to have a humanizing influence on American education. His *Poor Richard's Almanacks* were used as texts, and the sayings of poor Richard were widely used for moral and affective education. Many of his proverbs (such as "Haste makes waste" and "There are three things extremely hard: steel, a diamond and to know one's self") are still in wide use today. Unknown to most persons, Franklin also was the father of behavior modification techniques in America; in his autobiography he described in detail a self-recording system for developing desirable behaviors in one's self (such as order, temperance, and tranquility). His system worked so well it has been adapted for use in many self-control behavior modification programs now in use in special education.

However, rational provision for exceptional persons was yet to come. In the early 1800s many institutions for the deaf, blind, and retarded were constructed. But all in all, these provided a miserable form of custodial care. It was so bad, in fact, that by 1848 the famous reformer Dorothea Dix described the plight of the institutionalized person in these dramatic words:

> More than 9000 idiots, epileptics and insane in the United States, destitute of appropriate care and protection, are bound with galling chains, bowed beneath fetters and heavy, iron balls attached to drag chains, lacerated with ropes, scourged by rods and terrified beneath storms of cruel blows, now subject to jibes and scorn and torturing tricks; now abandoned to the most outrageous violations.*

Cruel and unusual treatment was not atypical for that time, and handicapped persons were not perceived as being worthy of the equal education gradually being made available to the middle class. It is interesting in this regard to note that our stated belief in the fundamental equality of men has never been taken seriously. The idealistic conception of the equality of men was most often interpreted to mean equality in the eyes of God, which may be argued to have theological validity. However, insofar as human affairs are concerned, constitutional equality refers to a proposed equality under the law, which is, of course, an ideal legal construct that is yet to be realized.

---

*From Abraham, W. The early years: Prologue to tomorrow. *Exceptional Children,* 1976, 42, 330-335.

In our early days, slaves, women, the poor, and the handicapped were not perceived as having equal rights or privileges in our society, and they were systematically relegated to subservient or menial roles and isolated from active participation in the social-political mainstream of the community. Also, there was widespread belief in various concepts of predestination in which persons were said to be born to their stage and place in this life. It was actually thought by many that Indians, blacks, the poor, the retarded, the mentally ill, and other "unfortunates" had incurred the wrath of God, who had condemned them to live accordingly. For instance, the retarded were seen as having been born with inherent natural limitations, and therefore it was thought that trying to educate them was a waste of time since they obviously could not learn; accordingly, social isolation and institutionalization became the accepted way of dealing with them.

CLINICAL TEACHING

These faulty preconceptions were slow to change, but as we know they gradually did give way to more enlightened views based on empirical work with exceptional persons of all kinds. Perhaps the two most significant and revolutionary contributions to our social-political-educational enlightenment were made by Jean Itard and Maria Montessori. In 1799 Itard began the task of teaching a 10-year-old retarded boy whose behavior was described as that of a savage. Itard was a French Idealist who was caught up in the revolutionary spirit of his time; he believed in the educability and perfectibility of man. Through careful observation of the boy whom he named Victor, Itard formulated five behavioral aims, or objectives, that became the basis for his prescriptive teaching. Two of these objectives were as follows (Itard, 1894/1962):

- To awaken Victor's nervous sensibility by the most energetic stimulation and occasionally by intense emotion
- To make Victor exercise the simplest mental operations upon the objects of his physical needs over a period of time, afterwards inducing the application of these mental processes to the objects of instruction

Itard's aspirations and objectives resulted in an intensive clinical teaching program extending over a 5-year period, which he recorded in his diary. His methods and techniques became the source of numerous special education programs to come, and they remain valid to this day. Itard demonstrated that the retarded person can learn, and he showed how it could be done through precise educational means. His work had a dramatic effect in that the new free schools began to provide for exceptional persons, and more than 100 special classes were started by the late 1800s.

Montessori was fully aware of the work of Itard and others. She adapted and extended these techniques and devised unique teaching materials for her work with retarded and disadvantaged children. Montessori (1964) was so convinced of the soundness of her approach that she wrote that her educational methods "contained educational principles more rational than those in use, so much more so, indeed, that through their means *an inferior mentality would be able to grow and develop*" (emphasis mine). This brash statement, of course, offended both the professional educators and the physicians of her time, who promptly branded her a quack and would have nothing to do with her. After all, everyone knew that one's mentality was fixed and that it was preposterous to suggest that educational methods and clinical teaching could enable it to "grow and develop."

From these brief illustrations we should be able to gain some perspective of our historical goals and the progress we have made in achieving them. The revolutionary goals for exceptional persons have been the same as for all the American people. That is, the quest for greater freedom and the pursuit of happiness through the development of our unique human capacities, which enable us to further our total self-realization. But the fulfillment of these common human aspirations has been much much slower for exceptional persons because of the prevailing ignorance and resultant inadequacy of the socio-economic and educational systems in recognizing, accepting, and providing for their distinctive needs.

Our revolutionary fathers, however, were fully aware of the need for continual change and evolution in all of our institutions, and they provided for it within our Constitution. John Adams, for instance, was among those who aspired to a more humanistic education in the years to come when he wrote, "I must study war and politics so my sons can study mathematics, commerce, and engineering, so their sons can study poetry, literature, music, and philosophy" (May, 1976). Even Thomas Jefferson prayed in 1787 that "God forbid we should ever be 20 years without a rebellion." Jefferson's words were taken seriously, as our history is one of periodic confrontation with established institutions and their prevailing beliefs and values. Later, even that most exceptional person Helen Keller wrote that "we can't have education without revolution," and the social and educational revolution certainly continues to this very day.

CURRENT GOALS

So what are some of our major aspirations and revolutionary goals today? More specifically, what are some of the priorities for exceptional persons that continue to demand revolutionary zeal and commitment if they are to be realized in the near future? First and foremost must be the continued dedication to bring free public special education to all exceptional persons regardless of their legal classification, age, race, sex, or other characteristics. With the establishment of the Council for Exceptional Children in 1922 and its legislative program, we have seen considerable progress toward this goal on both state and federal levels. But even today millions of children who have specific learning disabilities, who are slow learning, who have behavior disorders or other handicapping conditions, are receiving no special education of any kind. In some places we still see retarded and mentally ill children suffering a loss of their freedom and deprivation of proper education where they are committed to institutions without due process of law ("Court Will Weigh," 1976). In other communities, vast disparities exist between wealthy and poor districts in their support of special education, while in other districts artificial quotas, waiting lists, and scarcity of services deny persons their educational rights. This must stop, and children with specialized educational needs must be assured an appropriate education wherever they live in these United States.

A second major goal is to continue to refine our methods and to improve the quality of special education. We are slowly beginning to realize that in fact people are not created equal. Of course, we remain dedicated to the fundamental philosophical concepts of equality under God and law, but other than that we now recognize that all persons vary in both their physical and psychological makeup and that these differences are to be treasured and used accordingly. Exceptional persons differ markedly in their learning abilities and skills, in their needs and aspirations, in their cultural backgrounds, and in their rate and style of learning. They do not need equal education in the sense of being taught the same things as other people. What all persons need is equal *opportunity* to obtain appropriate education, but ideally this education should be individualized for all concerned and should allow persons to make continual progress toward their goals in accord with their unique abilities and life styles.

One of the most recent and important revolutionary concepts affecting the actual practice and quality of special education was formulated near the turn of this century by Alfred Binet. Binet proposed that the various mental abilities involved in problem solving be defined and then combined into a scale that could be used in evaluating individual performance and achievement. He was mainly concerned with four major kinds of human abilities that he thought were important in life.

- AUTOCRITICISM: The ability to evaluate one's own performance
- ADAPTATION: Being able to invent various ways or means to obtain one's goal
- DIRECTIVENESS: Purposeful, motivational, goal-seeking behavior
- COMPREHENSION: General understanding

The purpose of his mental test was to distinguish slow-learning from fast-learning children in order to establish differential and more appropriate educational programs. Contrary to popular opinion, Binet did not regard mental test scores as fixed quantities, and he actually prescribed corrective courses in "mental orthopedics" for those with low test scores (Kamin, 1976, p. 374). As we have seen, this was not exactly a new idea since both Itard and Montessori had already demonstrated the validity of teaching so-called mental orthopedics that improved children's problem-solving abilities. But we must remember that Binet's revolutionary conception was that these abilities could actually be scaled according to different maturational levels and used accordingly.

Unfortunately, these fundamental ideas were overlooked by the American psychometricians in their attempts at quantification. And for the last 70 years we have lived in the shadow of singular IQ scores, which have been misused to label and categorize people rather than to help them identify their unique abilities and to learn how to improve their skills. However, within the last few years the basic ideas of Itard, Montessori, and Binet have been rediscovered. The idea of diagnostic-prescriptive teaching has finally taken hold and we now realize that tests can be used to help us select priority teaching objectives. Many applied research studies, such as those of Bennett (1976), Whimbey (1975), and their colleagues, have shown diagnostic-prescriptive teaching does indeed produce significant gains in specific mental abilities, achievement, and in other test scores. To some educators this is still a new and revolutionary concept. And in many school districts relatively little provision has yet been made for this kind of diagnostic-prescriptive teaching in special education programs.

It might be best to reflect for a moment on how widely these concepts and programs are actually being used. How many diagnostic-prescriptive teaching programs have you actually observed being implemented within the public schools? Fortunately, the trend is clearly this way, but all too often we continue to observe a watered-down regular curriculum being superimposed on special education students—a meaningless curriculum without priorities, of poor quality and irrelevant to the child's real educational needs.

We now have the theory, the research, the instrumentation, and the educational methods and technology to make diagnostic-prescriptive teaching and individualized continuous progress instruction a reality in special education. Our goal should be to continue to improve the rational use of such instruction by thoroughly training our new professionals in these skills, by establishing diagnostic-prescriptive resource centers or rooms in all schools, and by then demanding accountability and program evaluation. To accomplish these aims we need to rededicate ourselves to our belief in the fundamental worth and educability of the person and to commit our energies to the realization of this goal.

There are numerous other revolutionary goals that we can propose for exceptional persons, but let us briefly consider just one more at this point. The goal is to achieve a meaningful place in society. Immediately, it might be said that this is what it is all about and that the other goals we have considered merely culminate in the exceptional person being educated to take his or her rightful "place in the sun." This, of course, is true but requires further elaboration as to the nature of such a monumental task.

We have already considered how during the early years of the American Revolution very few retarded or otherwise handicapped persons had any real place in our society. At that time the exceptional person was barely tolerated. This must now change to provide for such persons to become fully participating and useful members of our social order. It has long been established that many handicapped persons are superior workers and one of our immediate aims should be to extend career and prevocational education to include actual community work placement with continued on-the-job training and supervision. Like other persons, most exceptional individuals require some gainful employment to develop and maintain their self-respect and to make their own unique contribution to society, however limited that contribution may seem to be.

In this regard, full-employment legislation should be supported by all special educators and strengthened to ensure that it provides for the handicapped who are capable of gainful employment. The minimum income laws also need to be strengthened to guarantee an adequate standard of living for exceptional persons and all other Americans.

REDEDICATION

In 1976 the Saturday Review published an article on the demise of education in America; it ended with an appeal:

> In this Bicentennial year no other objective seems more urgent than helping the American people regain their faith in education. The incentive to do so is elemental: to prevent the decline and fall of American democracy.*

I would certainly agree that in recent times we may have appeared to have lost our faith in education and even in the American system itself. We might even join Tom Paine in his statement that "these are the times that try men's souls." It is good to remember, however, that all times appear to try men's souls, and we appear to have come through some of the most recent storms in rather good shape.

I believe that we have gradually accumulated both strength and wisdom from our trials and tribulations. Our fundamental ideals, aspirations, and values, together with our evolutionary constitutional system of government, have provided us with the basic support and direction needed in our quest for increased freedom and self-realization. The purpose of education has been to transmit these values, to teach oncoming generations what they might do with their lives, and to enable them to pursue a happy and meaningful existence.

It would be good to renew our faith in the importance and value of education for all and to recommit ourselves to our revolutionary ideals. For the American revolution is not yet over and the American dream is still before us. We are all a part of this ongoing dream, and our efforts will help determine to what extent the dream can become reality in our own lifetime. And in many small but important ways our contributions as educators will help to shape the future. With such rededication and continued effort, we can help take one more step forward in building the democratic society and the human community.

---

*From Hechinger, F. Murder in academe: The demise of education. *Saturday Review*, March 20, 1976, p. 76.

DISCUSSION QUESTIONS AND ACTIVITIES

1. Do you think the right to learn should be recognized constitutionally? If so, how?
2. What might be some of the reasons that our founding fathers failed to provide free public education for all?
3. Read the *Autobiography* of Benjamin Franklin and report on the behavior modification recording system he devised.
4. Discuss some of the obvious inequalities of human beings and their educational implications.
5. What are some inherent natural limitations of the mentally retarded that would affect their learning?
6. Research and critique some of the educational methods and techniques that Itard and Montessori devised for "helping inferior mentalities to grow and develop."
7. To what extent do you think that the social and educational revolution is continuing today?
8. What would be needed to offer courses in "mental orthopedics" in today's public schools?
9. Should there be any limits on the "right to learn"?

References

Chapter 1: WHY JOHNNY DOESN'T THINK

Ayres, A. J. Sensorimotor foundations of academic ability. In W. Cruickshank and D. Hallahan (Eds.), *Perceptual and learning disabilities in children* (Vol. 2). Syracuse: Syracuse University Press, 1975.

Baldwin, A., Kalhorn, J., and Breese, F. Patterns of parent behavior. *Psychological Monographs*, 1945, *58*, 1-75.

Bronfenbrenner, U. The split level American family. In S. Coopersmith and R. Feldman (Eds.), *The formative years*. San Francisco: Albion Publishing Co., 1974.

Cravioto, J. Nutrition and learning in children. In N. Springer (Ed.), *Nutrition and mental retardation*. Ann Arbor, Mich.: Institute for the Study of Mental Retardation and Related Disabilities, 1972.

Critchley, M. *Developmental dyslexia*. London: William Heinemann Medical Books, Ltd., 1964.

FDA bans two more food colors (Associated Press Release). *Fresno Bee*, Sept. 22, 1976, p. 1.

Feingold, B. *Why is your child hyperactive?* New York: Random House, Inc., 1975.

Fretz, B., Johnson, W., and Johnson, J. Intellectual and perceptual motor development as a function of therapeutic play. *Research Quarterly of the American Association for Health, Physical Education and Recreation*, 1969, *40*, 687-691.

Goldberg, H., and Schiffman, G. *Dyslexia*. New York: Grune & Stratton, Inc., 1972.

Hagen, J., and Kail, R. The role of attention in perceptual and cognitive development. In W. Cruickshank and D. Hallahan (Eds.), *Perceptual and learning disabilities in children* (Vol. 2). Syracuse: Syracuse University Press, 1975.

Hallahan, D., and Cruickshank, W. *Psychoeducational foundations of learning disabilities*. Englewood Cliffs, N.J.: Prentice-Hall, Inc., 1973.

Heston, L. The genetics of schizophrenia and schizoid disease. In D. Hawkins and L. Pauling (Eds.), *Orthomolecular Psychiatry*. San Francisco: W. H. Freeman & Co. Publishers, 1973.

Kallmann, F. The genetics of mental disease. In S. Arieti (Ed.), *American handbook of psychiatry* (Vol. 1). New York: Basic Books, Inc., 1959.

Krech, D., Rosenzweig, M., and Bennett, E. Effects of environmental complexity and training on brain chemistry. *Journal of Comparative and Physiological Psychology*, 1969, *63*, 509-519.

Jensen, A. The distribution of intelligence. In *Genetics and education*. New York: Harper & Row, Inc., 1972, pp. 89-98.

Morrison, D., and Pothier, P. Two different remedial motor training programs and the development of mentally retarded pre-schoolers. *American Journal of Mental Deficiency*, 1972, *77*, 251-258.

Myklebust, H., and Boshes, B. *Minimal brain damage in children* (Final Report, U.S. Public Health Service Contract 108-65-142, U.S. Department of Health, Education and Welfare). Evanston, Ill.: Northwestern University Press, 1969.

Ornstein, R. *The nature of human consciousness*. San Francisco: W. H. Freeman & Co. Publishers, 1973.

Ott, J. Influence of fluorescent lights on hyperactivity and learning disabilities. *Journal of Learning Disabilities*, 1976, *9*, 417-422.

Painter, G. The effect of a rhythmic and sensory motor activity program on perceptual motor spatial abilities of kindergarten children. *Exceptional Children,* 1966, *33,* 113-116.

Rennert, L. Solons charge HEW neglects children. *Fresno Bee,* Oct. 7, 1976, p. A8.

Report of the Conference on the Use of Stimulant Drugs in the Treatment of Behaviorally Disturbed Young School Children. Washington, D.C.: Office of Child Development, Department of Health Education and Welfare, 1971.

Research conference report: Problems of dyslexia and related disorders. Washington, D.C.: Office of Education, U.S. Department of Health, Education and Welfare, July 12, 1967.

Rice, B. The worry epidemic. *Psychology Today.* March 1975, pp. 74-75.

Rimland, B. An orthomolecular study of psychotic children. *Journal of Orthomolecular Psychiatry,* 1974, *3,* 371-377.

Rosenthal, R., and Jacobson, L. Teacher expectations for the disadvantaged. *Scientific American,* April 1968, *218*(4), 19-23.

Sabatino, D., and Stressguth, W. Word form configuration training of visual perceptual strengths with learning disabled children. *Journal of Learning Disabilities,* 1972, *5,* 435-441.

Trotter, R. Intensive intervention programs prevent retardation. *APA Monitor,* Sept./Oct. 1976, pp. 4-5; 19; 46.

Chapter 2: LEARNING TO THINK

Anastasi, A. *Psychological testing* (4th ed). New York: Macmillan Publishing Co., Inc., 1976.

Bennett, V. Applied research can be useful: An example. *Journal of School Psychology,* 1976, *14,* 67-73.

Block, N., and Dworkin, G. (Eds.). *The IQ Controversy.* New York: Pantheon Books, Inc., 1976.

Bloom, B. *Stability and change in human characteristics.* New York: John Wiley & Sons, Inc., 1964.

Bloom, B., Hastings, J., and Madams, G. *Handbook on formative and summative evaluation of student learning.* New York: McGraw-Hill Book Co., 1971.

Cleary, T., Humphreys, L., Kendrick, S., and Wesman, A. Educational uses of tests with disadvantaged students. *American Psychologist,* 1975, *30,* 15-41.

Covington, M. Cognitive growth, development, and a cognitive curriculum (Carnegie Corp. research project report). Berkeley: Psychology Department, University of California, 1968.

Guilford, J. P. *The nature of human intelligence.* New York: McGraw-Hill Book Co., 1967.

Inhelder, B., and Piaget, J. *The growth of logical thinking from childhood to adolescence.* New York: Basic Books, Inc., 1959.

Jensen, A. Verbal mediation and educational potential. *Psychology in the Schools,* 1966, *3,* 99-109.

Montessori, M. *Spontaneous activity in education.* Cambridge, Mass.: Robert Bentley, Inc., 1964.

Siegel, I. Contributions of piagetian theory to research on preschool environments. Paper read as part of symposium "Approaches to the Conceptualization and Measurement of Preschool Learning Environments" at annual meeting of the American Psychological Association, San Francisco, September 1968.

Stern, C. Acquisition of problem-solving strategies in young children and its relation to verbalization. *Journal of Educational Psychology,* 1967, *58,* 245-252.

Tuddenham, R. *Reflections on growing intelligence* (Instructional Monographs). Sacramento, Calif.: Sacramento County School Office, 1965.

Chapter 3: MODELS OF COGNITIVE ABILITIES

Bloom, B. S. (Ed.). *Taxonomy of educational objectives: Handbook 1, cognitive domain.* New York: Longmans, Green & Co., Inc., 1956.

Caruso, J., and Resnick, L. Task structure and transfer in children's learning of double classification skills. *Child Development,* 1972, *43,* 1297-1308.

CTBS level 1 form S examiner's manual. Monterey, Calif.: CTB/McGraw-Hill Div., 1974, p. 1.

CTBS test coordinator's handbook. Monterey, Calif.: CTB/McGraw-Hill Div., 1974, p. 93.

Engelmann, S. *Preventing failure in the primary grades.* New York: Simon & Schuster, Inc., 1969.

Ferinden, W., and Jacobson, S. *Educational interpretation of the Wechsler Intelligence Scale for Children.* Linden, N. J.: Remediation Associates, Inc., 1969.

Flavell, J. *The developmental psychology of Jean Piaget.* New York: D. Van Nostrand Co., 1966.

Glasser, A. J., and Zimmerman, I. *Clinical interpretation of the Wechsler Intelligence Scale for Children.* New York: Grune & Stratton, Inc., 1967.

Guilford, J. P. *The nature of human intelligence.* New York: McGraw-Hill Book Co., 1967.

Inhelder, B., and Piaget, J. *The growth of logical*

thinking from childhood to adolescence. New York: Basic Books, Inc., 1958.

Kingsley, R., and Hall, V. Training conservation through the use of learning sets. *Child Development,* 1967, *38,* 1111-1126.

Kirk, S., McCarthy, J., and Kirk, W. *Examiner's manual: Illinois Test of Psycholinguistic Abilities.* Urbana: University of Illinois Press, 1968.

Lavatelli, C. *Piaget's theory applied to an early childhood curriculum.* Boston: American Science & Engineering Co., 1970.

Let's look at children: A guide to understanding and fostering development in young children. Princeton, N.J.: Educational Testing Service, 1968.

Osgood, C. A behavioristic analysis. In *Contemporary approaches to cognition.* Cambridge, Mass.: Harvard University Press, 1957.

Psychoeducational interpretation of the WISC-R (2nd ed.). Belleville, N.J.: Cutronics, Inc., 1975.

Thurstone, L. Primary Mental abilities. *Psychometric Monographs,* No. 1, 1938.

Valett, R. *A psychoeducational inventory of basic learning abilities.* Belmont, Calif.: Fearon Publishers, Inc., 1968.

Valett, R. *Workbook to accompany a psychoeducational inventory of basic learning abilities.* Belmont, Calif.: Fearon Publishers, Inc., 1968.

Valett, R. *Programming learning disabilities.* Belmont, Calif.: Fearon Publishers, Inc., 1969.

Valett, R. *An inventory of basic learning skills.* Belmont, Calif.: Fearon Publishers, Inc., 1970 (Sections on class concepts, position in space concepts, descriptive concepts).

Valett, R. *The remediation of learning disabilities* (2nd ed.). Belmont, Calif.: Fearon Publishers, Inc., 1974.

Wechsler, D. *Manual for the WISC-R.* New York: The Psychological Corp., 1974.

Chapter 4: SENSORY AND PERCEPTUAL COMPONENTS OF READING

Ayres, A. J. Improving academic scores through sensory integration. *Journal of Learning Disabilities,* 1972, *5,* 24-27.

Birch, H., and Belmont, L. Auditory visual integration, intelligence and reading ability in school children. *Perceptual and Motor Skills,* 1965, *20,* 295-305.

Chall, J. *Learning to read.* New York: McGraw-Hill Book Co., 1967.

Corkin, S. Serial-ordering deficits in inferior readers. *Neuropsychologia,* 1974, *12,* 347-354.

Diamond, M., et al. Increases in cortical depth and glia numbers in rats subjected to enriched environment. *Journal of Comparative Neurology,* 1966, *1,* 117-125.

Drew, A. L. A neurological appraisal of familial congenital word blindness. *Brain,* 1956, *79,* 440-460.

Fernald, G. *Remedial techniques in basic school subjects.* New York: McGraw-Hill Book Co., 1943.

Gates, A. *Psychology of reading and spelling with special reference to disability.* Columbia University Teacher's College Contributions to Education. Monograph No. 129, 1922.

Goins, J. *Visual perception abilities and early reading progress* (Supplemental Education Monograph). Chicago: University of Chicago Press, 1958.

Goldstein, K. *Language and language disturbances.* New York: Grune & Stratton, Inc., 1948.

Gray, C. *Deficiencies in reading ability, their diagnosis and remedies.* Lexington, Mass.: D. C. Heath & Co., 1922.

Groff, P. "Sight words" and the disabled reader. *Academic Therapy,* 1974, *10,* 101-107.

Halliwell, J., and Solan, H. The effects of a supplemental perceptual training program on reading achievement. *Exceptional Children,* 1972, *38,* 613-620.

Hammill, D., and Larsen, S. The relationship of selected auditory perceptual skills and reading ability. *Journal of Learning Disabilities,* 1974, *7,* 40-45.

Hebb, D. *The organization of behavior: A neuropsychological theory.* New York: John Wiley & Sons, Inc., 1949.

Ingvar, D., and Schwartz, M. Brain blood flow and blood flow patterns induced in the dominant hemisphere by speech and reading. *Brain,* 1974, *97,* 273-288.

Itard, J. *The wild boy of Aveyron* (G. Humphrey and M. Humphrey, Trans.). New York: Appleton-Century-Crofts, 1962. (Originally published, 1894.)

Jampolsky, G. Use of hypnosis and sensory motor stimulation to aid children with learning problems. *Journal of Learning Disabilities,* 1970, *3,* 29-34.

Johnson, D. J., and Myklebust, H. *Learning Disabilities: Educational principles and practices,* New York: Grune & Stratton, Inc., 1967.

Kass, C. *Some psychological correlates of severe reading disability (dyslexia).* Doctoral Dissertation, School of Education, University of Illinois, 1962.

Katz, P., and Deutsch, M. Relation of auditory-visual shifting to reading achievement, *Perceptual and Motor Skills*, 1963, *17*, 327-332.

Krech, D. The searching mind. *Today's Education NEA Journal*, October 1970, p. 33.

Krippner, S. The use of hypnosis with elementary and secondary school children in a summer reading clinic. *American Journal of Clinical Hypnosis*, 1966, *8*, 261-266.

Luria, A. R. *Higher cortical functions in man.* New York: Basic Books, Inc., 1966.

McCormick, C., and Poetker, B. Improvement in reading achievement through perceptual-motor training. *The Research Quarterly*, 1968, *39*, 627-633.

Myklebust, H. *Learning disorders: Progress in learning disabilities.* New York: Grune & Stratton, Inc., 1968.

Orton, S. *Reading, writing, and speech problems in children.* New York: W. W. Norton & Co., Inc., 1937.

Piaget, J. *The origins of intelligence in children* (Trans., M. Cook). New York: International Universities Press, 1952.

Rosenzweig, M. Environmental complexity, cerebral change, and behavior. *American Psychologist*, 1966, *21*, 321-331.

Satz, P., and Friel, J. Some predictive antecedents of specific reading disability: A preliminary two-year follow up. *Journal of Learning Disabilities*, 1974, *7*, 48-55.

Seagoe, M. Verbal development in a mongoloid. *Exceptional Children*, 1965, *31*, 269-275.

Valett, R. *Learning disabilities: Diagnostic-prescriptive instruments.* Belmont, Calif.: Fearon Publishers, Inc., 1974.

Valett, R. *The remediation of learning disabilities* (2nd ed.). Belmont, Calif.: Fearon Publishers, Inc., 1974.

Chapter 5: A PERCEPTUAL-LINGUISTIC APPROACH TO CONCEPTUALIZATION

Gillingham, A., and Stillman, B. *Remedial training for children with specific disability in reading, spelling, and penmanship* (7th ed.). Cambridge, Mass.: Educators Publishing Service, Inc., 1965.

Halliwell, J., and Solan, H. The effects of a supplemental perceptual training program on reading achievement. *Exceptional Children*, 1972, *38*, 613-621.

Hammill, D., and Larsen, S. The effectiveness of psycholinguistic training. *Exceptional Children*, 1974, *41*, 5-14.

Health, E., Cook, P., and O'Dell, N. Eye exercises and reading efficiency. *Academic Therapy*, 1976, *11*, 435-445.

Hebb, D. *The organization of behavior: A neuropsychological theory.* New York: John Wiley & Sons, Inc., 1949.

Jensen, N., and King, E. Effects of different kinds of visual-motor discrimination on learning to read words. *Journal of Educational Psychology*, 1971, *61*, 90-96.

Johnson, D., and Myklebust, H. *Learning disabilities: Educational principles and practices.* New York: Grune & Stratton, Inc., 1967.

Keim, R. Visual-motor training, readiness and intelligence of kindergarten children. *Journal of Learning Disabilities*, 1970, *3*, 19-22.

Kephart, N. *The slow learner in the classroom.* Columbus, Ohio: Charles E. Merrill Publishing Co., 1960.

Kephart, N. Perceptual-motor aspects of learning disabilities. *Exceptional Children*, 1964, *31*, 201-206.

Krech, D., Rosenzweig, M., and Bennett, E. Environmental impoverishment, social isolation and changes in brain chemistry and anatomy. *Physiology and Behavior*, 1966, *1*, 99-104.

McCormick, C., and Schnobrich, J. Perceptual-motor training and improvement in concentration in a Montessori preschool. *Perceptual and Motor Skills*, 1971, *32*, 71-77.

McCormick, C., Schnobrich, J., and Footlik, W. The effect of perceptual-motor training on reading achievement. *Academic Therapy*, 1969, *14*, 171-175.

Minskoff, E. Research on psycholinguistic training: Critique and guidelines. *Exceptional Children*, 1975, *42*, 136-148.

Ornstein, R. (Ed.). *The nature of human consciousness.* San Francisco: W. H. Freeman & Co. Publishers, 1973.

Pearce, J. C. *The magical child: Revolution in mind-brain development.* New York: E. P. Dutton & Co., Inc., 1976.

Piaget, J. *The origins of intelligence in children* (Trans., M. Cook). New York: International Universities Press, 1952.

Rupert, H. *A sequentially compiled list of instructional materials for remediational use with the ITPA.* Greeley, Colo.: Rocky Mountain Special Education Instructional Materials Center, University of Northern Colorado, 1970.

Sartain, H. "Instruction of Disabled Learners: A Reading Perspective." *Journal of Learning Disabilities.* Vol. 9, 1976. pp. 489-497.

Strauss, A. and Kephart, N. *Psychopathology*

and education of the brain-injured child. Vol. II. New York: Grune & Stratton, 1955.

Valett, R. *The remediation of learning disabilities* (2nd ed.). Belmont, Calif.: Fearon, 1974.

Chapter 6: COGNITIVE DEVELOPMENT PROGRAMS

Binet, A., and Simon, T. *The development of intelligence in children* (E. S. Kite, Trans.). Baltimore: The Williams & Wilkins Co., 1961.

Bloom, B. (Ed.). *Taxonomy of educational objectives: Handbook 1, cognitive domain.* New York: Longmans, Green & Co., Inc.,

Guilford, J. P. Three faces of intellect. *American Psychologist,* 1959, *14,* 469-479.

Lavatelli, C. S. *Piaget's theory applied to an early childhood curriculum.* Boston, Mass.: American Science & Engineering, Inc., 1970.

Meeker, M. *The structure of intellect: Its interpretation and uses.* Columbus, Ohio: Charles E. Merrill Publishing Co., Inc., 1969.

Wilson, J., and Robeck, M. *Kindergarten evaluation of learning potential: A curricular approach to evaluation.* New York: McGraw-Hill Book Co., 1966.

Chapter 7: TASK ANALYSIS AND THE LARRY P. CASE

Executive Board Minutes. California Association of School Psychologists and Psychometrists, March 27, 1971, p. 3.

Moriarty, J. Psychologists protest testing of black children in California. *APA Monitor,* March 1972, p. 4.

Stickel, N. Larry P. *Communique* (Pub. of National Association of School Psychologists). March 1976, 4.

Valett, R. Classification of the mentally retarded: An appraisal. *Psychology In The Schools,* 1965, 2, 210-213.

Valett, R. *Programming learning disabilities.* Belmont, Calif. Fearon Publishers, Inc., 1969, pp. 66-68.

Valett, R. *A basic screening and referral form for children with suspected learning and behavioral disabilities.* Belmont, Calif.: Fearon Publishers, Inc., 1972.

Chapter 8: CRITICAL THINKING SKILLS

Buros, O. (Ed.). *The mental measurement yearbook.* Highland Park, N.J.: Gryphon Press, 1972.

Guilford, J. P. *The nature of human intelligence.* New York: McGraw-Hill Book Co., 1967.

Inhelder, B., and Piaget, J. *The growth of logical thinking from childhood to adolescence.* New York: Basic Books, Inc., 1958.

Valett, R. *The remediation of learning disabilities* (2nd ed.). Belmont, Calif.: Fearon Publishers, Inc., 1974.

Chapter 10: PRESCRIPTIVE USE OF THE STANFORD-BINET TEST

Gesell, A., and Amatruda, C. *Developmental diagnosis* (2nd ed.). New York: Harper & Row, Inc., 1967.

Terman, L., and Merrill, M. *Stanford-Binet Intelligence Scale: Manual for the third revision form L-M.* Boston: Houghton Mifflin Co., 1962.

Valett, R. A clinical profile for the Stanford-Binet L-M. *Journal of School Psychology,* 1964, 2, 49-54.

Valett, R. *A clinical profile for the Stanford-Binet L-M.* Palo Alto, Calif.: Consulting Psychologists Press, Inc., 1965.

Chapter 12: PROGRAMMING FIGURAL OPERATIONS

Engler, D. *How to raise your child's IQ.* New York: Criterion Books, 1958.

Guilford, J. P. *The nature of intelligence.* New York: McGraw-Hill Book Co., 1967.

Inhelder, B., and Piaget, J. *The growth of logical thinking from childhood to adolescence.* New York: Basic Books, Inc., 1958.

James, W. *The principles of psychology* (Vol. 2). New York: Henry Holt & Co., 1890 (Chapter 22).

Levi, A. Treatment of a disorder of perception and concept formation in a case of school failure. *Journal of Consulting Psychology,* 1965, *29,* 289-295.

Werner, H. *Comparative psychology of mental development.* New York: Science Editions, 1961.

Chapter 13: CREATIVE THINKING

Anastasi, A. *Psychological testing* (4th ed.). New York: MacMillan Publishing Co., Inc., 1976.

Assagioli, R. *Psychosynthesis.* New York: The Viking Press, 1965.

Block, N., and Dworkin, G. *The IQ controversy.* New York: Pantheon Books, Inc., 1976.

Bloomfield, H., Cain, H., Jaffe, D., and Kory, R. *TM: Discovering inner energy and overcoming stress.* New York: Dell Publishing Co., Inc., 1975.

Bogen, J. *Bulletin of the Los Angeles Neurological Societies.* 1969, *34,* 135-162.

Bucke, R. M. *Cosmic consciousness: A study in the evolution of the human mind.* New York: E. P. Dutton & Co., Inc., 1901.

Covington, M., Crutchfield, R., Davies, L., and Olton, R. *The productive thinking program.* Columbus, Ohio: Charles E. Merrill Publishing Co., Inc., 1972.

Davis, G. Research and development in training creative thinking. In J. Levin and V. Allen (Eds.), *Cognitive learning in children.* New York: Academic Press, Inc., 1976.

Davis, G., and Houtmann, S. *Thinking creatively: A guide to training imagination.* Madison, Wis.: Wisconsin Research and Development Center for Cognitive Learning, University of Wisconsin, 1968.

Deikman, A. Biomodal consciousness. *Archives of General Psychiatry,* 1971, 25, 481-489.

DiPego, G. *Imagination express.* Buffalo, N.Y.: D.O.K. Publishers, 1973.

Getzels, J., and Jackson, P. *Creativity and intelligence.* New York: John Wiley & Sons, Inc., 1962.

Greene, A., Green, E., and Wolters, E. *Psychophysiological training for creativity.* Paper presented at the meeting of the American Psychological Association, Washington, D.C., 1971.

James, W. *The principles of psychology* (Vol. 2). New York: Dover Publications, Inc., 1890/1950.

James, W. *The varieties of religious experience.* New York: New American Library, Inc., 1901-1958.

Jones, R. *Fantasy and feeling in education.* New York: Harper & Row, Publishers, Inc., 1970.

Jung, C. The structure and dynamics of the psyche. Vol. 8 of *The collected works of C. G. Jung* (Bollinger Series). Princeton, N.J.: Princeton University Press, 1960.

Jung, C. The spirit in man, art, and literature. Vol. 15 of *The collected works of C. G. Jung* (Bollingen Series). Princeton, N.J.: Princeton University Press, 1966.

Krech, D., and Crutchfield, R. Creative problem solving. In *Elements of psychology.* New York: Alfred A. Knopf, Inc., 1958.

Maslow, A. *Toward a psychology of being.* New York: D. Van Nostrand Co., 1962.

Maslow, A. *The farther reaches of human nature* (Part 2, creativeness). New York: The Viking Press, 1971.

Schopenhauer, A. *The wisdom of life.* London: M. Walter Dunne, 1901.

Sherry, M. Zapped by ZING, *Teaching Exceptional Children,* 1977, 9, 46-47.

Torrance, E., and Myers, R. *Creative learning and teaching.* New York: Dodd, Mead & Co., 1970.

Valett, R. *Self actualization.* Niles, Ill.: Argus Communications, 1974.

Valett, R. *Humanistic education.* St. Louis: The C. V. Mosby Co., 1977.

Chapter 14: TEACHING STRATEGIES

Bateman, B. A Summary of Engelmann's conceptual learning. In S. Englemann, *Conceptual learning.* San Rafael, Calif.: Dimensions Publishing Co., 1969.

Becker, W. *An empirical basis for changes in education.* Chicago: Science Research Associates, Inc., 1971.

Bloom, B. Individual differences in school achievement: A vanishing point. *Education At Chicago.* (School of Education, University of Chicago), Winter 1971, pp. 4-14.

Bloom, B. Time and learning. *American Psychologist,* 1974, 29, 682-688.

Cratty, B. *Intelligence in action.* Englewood Cliffs, N.J.: Prentice-Hall, Inc., 1973.

Davidson, R. The role of metaphor and analogy in learning. In Levin, J., and Allen, V. (Eds.), *Cognitive learning in children: Theories and strategies.* New York: Academic Press, Inc., 1976.

Engelmann, S. *Preventing failure in the primary grades.* New York: Simon & Schuster, Inc., 1969.

Esbensen, T. *The Duluth experience: Working with individualized instruction.* Belmont, Calif.: Fearon Publishers, Inc., 1968.

Furth, H., and Wachs, H. *Thinking goes to school: Piaget's theory in practice.* New York: Oxford University Press, Inc., 1974 (Chapter 12).

Gagné, R. M. *The conditions of learning.* New York: Holt, Rinehart & Winston, 1970.

Glenwick, D. Some interpersonal correlates of cognitive impulsivity in fourth graders. *Journal of School Psychology,* 1976, 14, 212-221.

Hunt, J. M. The implications of changing ideas on how children develop intellectually. *Children,* 1964, 11, 83-91.

Itard, J. *The wild boy of Aveyron* (G. Humphrey and M. Humphrey, Trans.). New York: Appleton-Century-Crofts, 1962. (Originally published, 1894.)

Lambert, N. Methodological considerations in the evaluation of differential components of supplementary education programs. *Journal of School Psychology*, 1976, *14*, 171-185.

Montessori, M. *Dr. Montessori's own handbook,* New York: Shocken Books, Inc., 1965, 124-125.

Phillips, L. Humor in the classroom: A look at Jokes. *Learning*, April 1974, pp. 75-78.

Raths, L., Jones, A., Rothstine, A., and Wasserman, S. *Teaching for thinking*. Columbus, Ohio: Charles E. Merrill Publishing Co., Inc., 1967.

Sexton, T., and Poling, D. *Can intelligence be taught?* (monograph). Phi Delta Kappa, Bloomington, Ill.: 1973.

Shannon, J., and Blaylock, L. *Parent's guide to the Bakersfield individualized reading process.* Bakersfield, Calif.: Bakersfield City School District Education Center, 1975.

Snow, R. Consequences for instruction: The state of the art of individualizing in mainstreaming: Origins and implications. *Minnesota Education* (College of Education, University of Minnesota), 1976, 2, 23-31.

Sternberg, L. Pattern recognition training: A key to mathematics and language skill development. *Teaching Exceptional Children,* Winter 1975, pp. 61-63.

Thurstone, T. *The gold book* (Learning to Think Series). Chicago: Science Research Associates, Inc., 1967.

Valett, R. *Modifying children's behavior*. Belmont, Calif.: Fearon Publishers, Inc., 1969.

Valett, R. *Effective teaching*. Belmont, Calif.: Fearon Publishers, Inc., 1970.

Valett, R. *Self actualization*. Niles, Ill.: Argus Communications, 1974.

Wittrock, M. Teaching problem solving to young children. *The Educator* (School of Education, University of California at Los Angeles), March 1966, pp. 4-6.

Chapter 15: THE RIGHT TO LEARN

Abraham, W. The early years: Prologue to tomorrow. *Exceptional Children,* March 1976, p. 331.

Bennett, V. Applied research can be useful: An example. *Journal of School Psychology*, 1976, *14*, 67-73.

Court will weigh hospitalizing of children for mental illness. *Fresno Bee,* July 4, 1976.

Hechinger, F. Murder in academe: The demise of education. *Saturday Review,* March 20, 1976, p. 76.

Itard, J. *The wild boy of Aveyron* (G. Humphrey and M. Humphrey, Trans.). New York: Appleton-Century-Crofts, 1962. (Originally published, 1894.)

Kamin, L. Heredity, intelligence, politics, and psychology: II. In N. Block and G. Dworkin (Eds.), *The IQ controversy.* New York: Pantheon Books, Inc., 1976.

May, R. Speech at the California Association of School Psychologists conference, San Francisco, April 9, 1976.

Montessori, M. The Montessori method. New York: Schocken Books, Inc., 1964.

Whimbey, A. *Intelligence can be taught.* New York: E. P. Dutton & Co., Inc., 1975.

Index

A

Abraham, W., 252, 265
Abstractions, 114, 211
Active experimentation, 33
Adams, J., 254
Adaptation, 32-33
Adaptive Behavior Scale, 109
Adult education, 25-26
Analogous thinking, 116, 124, 151-152, 244-247
Analysis, 34-35, 47, 50
Anastasi, A., 17, 260
Application, 34-35, 47, 50
Arithmetic, 44, 108
   problem solving, 116, 124, 136-137
   reasoning, 169-171
Attention, 232
Attribute Games, 92
Attribute listing, 222
Auditory association, 46
Auditory closure, 46
Auditory decoding, 69, 71-72
Auditory Discrimination in Depth, 84
Auditory processing, 58-59
Auditory reception, 46
Auditory sequential memory, 46
Auditory vocal association, 69, 74
Auditory vocal synthesis, 116, 124, 134-135
Auditory-visual integration, 60-61
Auditory-visual memory, 69, 75
Autocriticism, 32
Ayres, J., 8, 57, 259, 261

B

Baldwin, A., 5, 259
Basic Learning Abilities, 36-37
Bateman, B., 237, 264
Bayley Scales of Infant Development, 18
Becker, W., 231, 264
Behavior modification, 185-186, 231, 252
Behavioral skills, 115-116
Belmont, L., 58, 261
Bender Gestalt Test, 140, 144
Bennett, E., 8, 260
Bennett, V., 27, 65, 256, 265
Bereiter, C., 19, 237

Binet, A., 15, 31, 88, 175, 217, 255, 263
Birch, H., 58, 261
Birth defects, 4
Blank, M., 19
Block, N., 27, 218, 260, 263
Block design, 44
Bloom, B., 20, 22, 26, 27, 34, 47, 87, 229-230, 260, 263-264
Bloomfield, H., 220, 263
Boehm Test of Basic Concepts, 38-39, 161
Bogen, J., 218, 263
Boshes, B., 1, 259
Brain
   functions of, 8
   hemispheres of, 67, 218, 224
Brainstorming, 222
Breese, F., 5, 259
Broder, L., 26
Bronfenbrenner, U., 5, 259
Bucke, R., 221, 264

C

California Reading Tests, 57
Camp, H., 26
Caruso, J., 34, 260
Casey, M., 23
Cerebral development, 22-23
Chall, J., 58, 261
Classification, 33, 89, 92, 95, 201, 242-243
Cleary, T., 27, 260
Clinical teaching, 253
Coding, 44, 107
Cognitive disabilities, 11
Cognitive structure, 33-34
Cognitive taxonomy, 35
Columbia Mental Maturity Scale, 25, 142, 192
Common sense, 32
Comprehension, 32, 34-35, 44, 50, 107, 169-172
Comprehensive Test of Basic Skills (CTBS), 16, 47, 68, 71, 72, 74, 77, 132, 155, 157, 159
Concept learning, 237
Conceptual skills, 37
Concrete manipulations, 50
Concrete operations, 33
Conservation, 90

266